PRAISE

for

STEPHEN DANDO-COLLINS

"A very fine historian."

—Phillip Adams, *ABC Late Night Live*

"A gifted storyteller."

—*The Independent Weekly*

"Absorbing . . . Military history is the muscle of this book, with enough political sinews to give it coherence."

—*Washington Times*, for *Caesar's Legion*

"Unique and splendidly researched . . . Many military historians consider Caesar's legions the world's most efficient infantry before the arrival of gunpowder. This book shows why. Written in readable, popular style, *Caesar's Legion* is a must for military buffs and anyone interested in Roman history at a critical point in European civilization."

—T. R. Fehrenbach, author of *This Kind of War*, *Lone Star*, and *Commanches*, for *Caesar's Legion*

Rise of an Empire

Rise of an Empire

HOW ONE MAN UNITED GREECE

TO DEFEAT XERXES'S PERSIANS

Stephen Dando-Collins

John Wiley & Sons, Inc.

Wiley General Trade, an imprint of Turner Publishing Company
424 Church Street • Suite 2240 • Nashville, Tennessee 37219
445 Park Avenue • 9th Floor • New York, New York 10022

www.turnerpublishing.com

Rise of an Empire: How One Man United Greece to Defeat Xerxes's Persians

Book design: Michael Rutkowski
Interior design: Glen M. Edelstein
Cover Photo: © Tim Gainey (Spartan); Paul Moore (shield); North Wind Picture Archives (ship) / Alamy

Library of Congress Cataloging-in-Publication Data:
Dando-Collins, Stephen.
 Rise of an empire : how one man united Greece to defeat Xerxes's Persians / Stephen Dando-Collins.
    pages cm
  ISBN 978-1-118-45479-4 (pbk. : alkaline paper)
1. Themistocles, approximately 524 B.C.-approximately 459 B.C. 2. Greece--History--Persian Wars, 500-449 B.C. 3. Generals--Greece--Biography. I. Title.
  DF226.T45D36 2014

 938'.03--dc23
                                2013026550

Printed in the United States of America
14 15 16 17 18 19 0 1 2 3 4 5 6

For Louise, my fellow Thalamian.
And with special thanks to Stephen the captain,
and Richard the pilot.

CONTENTS

Contents

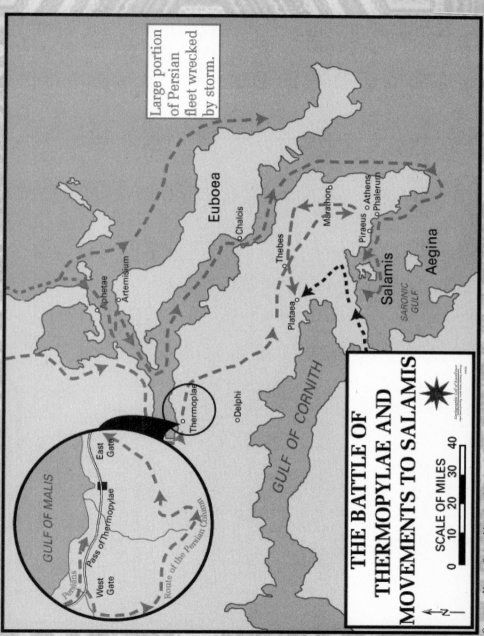

Large portion of Persian fleet wrecked by storm.

Euboea

Chalcis

Thebes

Marathon

Piraeus Athens
Phalerum

Plataea

Salamis

Aegina

SARONIC GULF

Delphi

Thermoplae

GULF OF CORNITH

Inset (circled detail)

GULF OF MALIS

East Gate

Pass of Thermopylae

Persians

West Gate

Persians

Route of the Persian Column

Artemisium

Aphetae

Legend / Title Block

THE BATTLE OF THERMOPYLAE AND MOVEMENTS TO SALAMIS

SCALE OF MILES

0   10   20   30   40

N

COURTESY UNITED STATES MILITARY ACADEMY

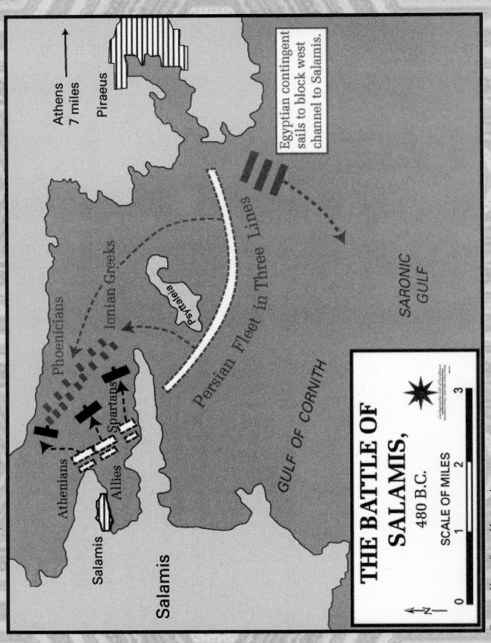

THE BATTLE OF SALAMIS,
480 B.C.

Athens
7 miles

Piraeus

Egyptian contingent sails to block west channel to Salamis.

SARONIC
GULF

Phoenicians

Ionian Greeks

Psyttaleia

Persian Fleet in Three Lines

GULF OF CORNITH

Athenians

Spartans

Allies

Salamis

Salamis

SCALE OF MILES

0   1   2   3

Rise of an Empire

1.

The Road to Marathon

In grim, disciplined silence, the Athenian army tramped along the mountain road at forced march pace. Somewhere in the forest ahead, a mounted advance party was staking out a campsite. Behind them, trailing all the way back to Athens, came wagons and slaves, bringing tents and supplies for all and furnishings for the officers. Not many miles ahead, a massive Persian army lay encamped on the Attic coast, threatening to attack Athens, just twenty-six miles to the south.

Under the blistering August sun, the men from Athens and throughout her territories in the Attica region marched in loose order, divided into ten regiments based on the voting tribe into which each man fell according to his place of birth. In the past, Athens had comprised just four tribes, but seventeen years before this the number of tribes had been enlarged to ten, all named for legendary Athenian heroes. This system had made the organization of elections for high office at Athens more manageable, and provided a structure for the city-state's citizen army when the call to arms was made—your peacetime voting tribe automatically became your regiment in time of war. Now, with roughly 900 men to a regiment, nine thousand fighters aged between eighteen and fifty followed their ten regimental commanders to war.

The general commanding the fourth regiment, the Leontis, was a solid thirty-three-year-old by the name of Themistocles. Of average height, he had a bull neck and a round, friendly face, although it was a face that did not shine with intelligence. His thick hair and beard were close-cropped, his low brow was already creased, his wide mouth

1

topped by a thick moustache. Like all Athens's tribal groupings, the ranks of the Leontis were equally divided between city dwellers, mountain men, and plainsmen. Themistocles himself had originally come from an outlying coastal district, and looked more like a dullard of a fisherman than a fighter, let alone a general of genius. A few more years were to pass before he would be in a position to display that genius.

Themistocles's recent election as military commander of his tribe was his first taste of generalship, though not of high office. Three years prior to this, once he was legally entitled to stand for election on reaching the minimum age of thirty, he had been voted into office as one of Athens's nine archons, or magistrates, for the year 493–492 BC. Ambitious Themistocles, who came from humble stock and had married into the aristocracy as soon as he turned thirty, had arrived. For, even though he was in office as archon for just one year, reaching that post automatically garnered him a lifelong seat on Athens's governing council, the council of the Areopagus. Rather like the upper house in modern parliaments, this council sat on the Areopagus, the Hill of Ares, immediately to the west of the Acropolis, the 500-foot stone mount at the center of the city that housed many of Athens's religious sanctuaries. The son of Zeus, Ares was the Greek war god—equated by the Romans with Mars. A temple dedicated to Ares sat at the foot of the Areopagus.

Themistocles the commoner, unlike his fellow regimental commanders, who all came from aristocratic families, had neither previous military experience nor a battlefield reputation. For the moment, his opinions would carry no special weight when the generals sat to discuss war strategy. With time, that would change. The generals were dressed and equipped in the same manner as their men. For, in this democratic army, generals and privates served and fought side by side. All wore red tunics, and long woollen cloaks trailed down their backs. On their left shoulders each Athenian carried a massive round shield, while long spears in their right hands rested on the opposite shoulder. Bronze helmets sat back on the crown of their heads, off their faces. Sheathed short-swords swung at each man's left side. Body armor consisted of iron and bronze corselets for the torso, and greaves to cover the shins.

In these ranks marched citizens of Athens—merchants, tradesmen, farmers, fishermen, athletes, and aristocrats. But none was a full-time soldier. Unlike the martial Greek state of Sparta, which kept a standing army and whose sons trained as soldiers full time from childhood, Athens only called its men to arms in times of emergency, such as now.

One of the soldiers in the ranks of the eighth regiment, the Hippothontis, was thirty-five-year-old Aeschylus. Son of the aristocrat Euphorion, Aeschylus came from the coastal Attic city of Eleusis, fourteen miles west of Athens and long an Athenian territory. Because his family was wealthy, Aeschylus never had to work a day in his life. Instead, he had indulged his talent as a playwright, and had become famous as a winner of Athens's annual City of Dionysia drama contest just four years before this. The writers and philosophers of Athens deliberately let their beards grow full as an advertisement of their calling, and Aeschylus's long, bushy beard made him stand out among the men around him. Close-cropped beards were more practical for those who worked with their hands rather than their minds. Yet, despite his artistic fame, Aeschylus, like his bold brother Cynaegirus, who marched at his side, would fight, and die if necessary, to help defend Athens from the Persian foe.

When he was twenty-six, Aeschylus had entered Athens's prestigious City of Dionysia contest for the first time. Held each March before a crowd of thousands in Athens's open-to-the-sky, semicircular theater, this was an exacting contest, for each entrant was required to also perform his own work. Aeschylus had multiplied the pressure on himself by going against the tradition of using just one player plus a chorus. An innovator, he had added extra parts to his plays, which would have raised eyebrows and made certain he did not win in 499 BC. But five years later, his innovation was being copied by other writers, and Aeschylus had taken away the prize and joined the list of Athens's best dramatists. Even so, despite his skill with pen and voice, he was still expected to shoulder arms when the barbarians threatened his city.

Marching at the head of the fifth regiment, the Acamantis, was the best-known and most influential commander among the Athenians. With thick grey hair and beard, this was the sixty-four-year-old Miltiades. An Athenian with Thracian ancestry, Miltiades was born to an immensely wealthy aristocratic family. When he was about thirty-eight, he had inherited family territories in the Thracian Chersonese, today's Gallipoli Peninsula in Turkey, which he had departed Athens to rule with an iron hand backed by a 500-man bodyguard. But the Persians under King Darius had subsumed Miltiades's little principality, and for a time Miltiades had served under sufferance in Darius's army.

Miltiades had turned against Darius when Greek neighbors the Ionians had rebelled against Persian rule in 499 BC. When that revolt eventually failed, Miltiades had fled to Athens in 493 BC, aboard four ships carrying his family and his treasure. Because Miltiades had fought both for and against Darius, no one in Athens was better equipped to lead her soldiers against the Persian threat. After his return to Athens, Miltiades was elected general of the Acamantis regiment for three years running.

By the time the ten regiments reached the campsite that had been laid out in a large clearing at a grove sacred to Hercules on the slopes of Mount Kotroni, after a four-hour tramp from Athens, it was the middle of the day. Once here, the Athenians set up guard outposts and raised their tents, and as night fell their campfires came to life. From the slopes, the Athenians could see, down on the plain of Marathon below, the flickering lights of thousands of campfires of the men of the massive Persian army. And, beyond that, to the east, the stern lamps of some 600 Persian warships and cargo vessels twinkled on beach and bay. That night, the military contribution of Athenian ally Plataea marched into the Athenian camp. Led by their general Arimnestos, the Plataean contingent was just six hundred strong. But their very presence bolstered the spirits of the Athenians.

The Athenian camp was well sited. From their elevated position, the Athenians could see the now-sacked town of Marathon away to their left. Directly below them ran the mountain road to Athens, cleaving between Mounts Kotroni and Agrieliki. Several miles to the east, the Persian camp spread, with marshland behind it and the coast running along its eastern edge. To the Athenians' distant right ran the coastal road to Athens. From up here on the hillside, the defenders of Athens could keep the two roads and the enemy ships under observation. One of those roads was the mountain route that the army had just negotiated. It was some miles shorter than the alternate coastal road, and less vulnerable to cavalry attack than the flat coastal way. From up here, too, the Athenians could move down to intercept the Persians if they attempted to march on Athens. Or, they could hurry back to Athens should the enemy reembark and set sail down the coast of Attica to attack the city from the south.

For the moment, the outnumbered Athenian force would sit tight and keep watch on the Persians, allowing the invader to make the first move. Every day that passed with King Darius's invasion force inactive allowed time for expected reinforcements from Athens's key ally Sparta to arrive. Even with those reinforcements, the Athenians would face daunting odds. For Themistocles, Aeschylus, Miltiades, and their comrades, their day of battle against the frightening Persian horde was on hold. But not for long.

2.

Young Themistocles

Themistocles was born in about 523 BC, in the Attic town of Phrearrhioi, some twenty miles southeast of Athens, a town covered by the Athenian deme, or political district, of the same name. His father, Neocles, was a locally born commoner. His mother, variously identified as Abrotonon and Euterpe, was a foreigner from either Thrace or Caria, and was possibly a former slave.

In the rural backwater town of Phrearrhioi, originally founded, and named, as a result of its excellent water wells, Themistocles's father dragged himself up from humble roots to succeed in commerce, and by the time that Themistocles was born he had made a moderate fortune—although, we are not told precisely from what. Neocles's somewhat meteoric economic rise made his name among his peers, and apparently prompted the naming of his son, for Themistocles means "new fame." As for siblings, Themistocles had at least one, probably a sister. Neocles's money enabled him to have his son schooled by a good tutor, and for Themistocles to move to and settle in Athens as a young man, living there without the need for employment as he set his sights on a political career.

When Themistocles began that career, he had an estimated worth of approaching 3 talents—a talent being about 57 pounds of silver and the equivalent of 6,000 drachmas in coin. By comparison, an Athenian with an inheritance of 15 talents in these times was considered affluent. As to the buying power of a talent, it helps to bear in mind that one talent would then buy a brand-new trireme warship, the then-largest form of galley commonly in use in the ancient world. Some years later, part of Themistocles's estate would be worth more than 100 talents, so, while Themistocles was reasonably comfortably off when he launched into politics, he was by no means rich at that time. Like everything else in his life, that would change with time.

A clue to his father's profession, and to Themistocles's later demonstrated passion for, and focus on, ships and the sea comes from a story in Plutarch's biography of Themistocles. One day, after the young Themistocles had been talking about his ambition to seek election to high office, his father took him down to the seaside, and to a beach quite probably on Phalerum Bay, today's Phaleron Bay, which then served as the port of Athens, to the northwest of Themistocles's hometown. There, Themistocles's father showed him the rotting hulks of Athenian war galleys lying on the shore. According to historian Thucydides, who was himself an admiral in the Athenian navy half a century after this, Athens's navy up to this time had consisted partly of some fifty-oared penteconters. The fleet, said Herodotus, also included twenty second-hand triremes purchased from neighboring city-state Corinth for the token sum of five drachmas each.

Athens had used these ships against Aegina, a rich island city-state twenty miles south of Athens with which Athens had been engaged in a running war for years. In their most recent encounters, Athens had won one sea battle and lost another. Her motley fleet had also carried Athenian arms into battle in 499–498 BC, in support of the Ionians when they rebelled against Persian hegemony in Asia Minor. According to legend, the Ionian Greeks had originally come from Athens to establish their colonies in Asia Minor. To support their Ionian cousins in their uprising, the Athenians had sent an expeditionary force of some 4,000 men to Asia Minor.

Initially, the Athenian expeditionary force fared well, capturing and burning Sardis, capital of the Persian province of Lydia, once the capital of the famously rich King Croesus, who had been defeated by Cyrus the Great during the conquests that had established the Persian Empire. But after reverses on land and sea, the Athenian contingent had withdrawn and left the Ionians to ultimate defeat at Persian hands.

Four of the twenty former Corinthian triremes had been lost to the Aeginetans, and since then the remaining secondhand ships had been abandoned and left to rot away, after the governing council at Athens terminated payment for their crews and their maintenance. The Ionian expedition had been a costly and embarrassing failure, while the Aegina operation had only resulted in 800 Athenian citizen-sailors becoming prisoners of the Aeginetans. The voters of Athens expressed the belief that continued expenditure on an Athenian navy was a waste of government money. Athenians, they said, were soldiers, not sailors.

"Forsaken and cast about on the seashore," said Neocles bitterly to his son Themistocles, pointing to the abandoned warships. "See how the commoners behave toward their leaders when they no longer have use for them."

This, Neocles was saying, would be how the voters would treat Themistocles if he entered politics. They would abandon him, too, when they no longer had use for him. Neocles's bitter attitude was in all likelihood shaped by personal experience—not as a politician, but as a shipbuilder. Prior to 499 BC, Athens had no navy and no ambitions as a naval power. Her military focus was always on foot soldiers and cavalry. It is highly likely that Neocles was a builder of fishing boats and cargo vessels, and saw the potential for a powerful Athenian navy—for shipwrights like himself as well as for Athens. Yet, here was Athens turning its back on the sea and laying up its triremes, sending Neocles's aspirations tumbling.

It is easy to imagine Themistocles as a child, roving about a small shipyard on the Saronic Gulf coast, watching his father's craftsmen at work with wood and plane and chisel, asking his father how and why a ship was built the way it was. It is equally easy to picture the boy with the wind in his hair and spray lashing his face as he sailed with his father on the maiden voyage of one craft and another that had slid from Neocles's stocks.

Most sons grow with the dreams and disappointments of their fathers locked in their memories. Some quite deliberately disavow both the father and the memories. Others become imbued with a passion to impress by succeeding where their parent failed, or to take up where their father left off. It is conceivable that Themistocles grew to manhood indoctrinated by his father into a belief that Athens's future lay with the sea. For, that is the course that Themistocles would advocate in years to come, to the mystification of historians and scholars down through the ages, who have scratched their heads to find a source for Themistocles's policy, which went against Athens's landlocked history to that time.

They had only to look at the age-old proverb—like father, like son. Neocles, it is likely, desired to see Athens a sea power so that he could profit from it commercially. Themistocles would promote the same policy, but to make Athens great, and himself along with it. His profit would initially be tallied in glory, not silver. Achieve the former, he would have said, and the latter would follow. But such a future could only be dreamed of when Themistocles was a provincial student.

Until the age of seven, Themistocles would have been tutored at home, by his mother or a servant. He thereafter attended an Athenian all-male day school in his hometown. Such schools were small private affairs, open only to those families with money to pay the tutors' fees. Classes were generally held in the tutors' houses, with the student body of each relatively small. Various educated men throughout Greece set up schools and advertised themselves as professors of this or that. As well as teaching their students reading and writing, mathematics and the liberal arts, these professors led their charges in the study of philosophy, and rhetoric, or public speaking.

Themistocles's master was, some say, Mnesiphilus, a native of his seaside deme of Phrearrhioi. Mnesiphilus was described by Plutarch as neither a rhetorician nor a philosopher, but rather a professor of wisdom, combining political awareness and pragmatic sagacity in his teachings. The school of thought to which Mnesiphilus belonged came to be called sophism, with the sophists accused by their critics of delivering pretty-sounding arguments that were based on misleading premises.

In both their written and oral exercises, the Greek student was expected to offer a balanced argument, but Themistocles was in trouble early with his professor when his essays too earnestly put a case for one side or another. Eventually, his master taught him to curb his natural enthusiasm and approach an argument from all sides. Themistocles himself was later to say, "The wildest colts make the best horses, as long as they are properly trained and broken in."

All the school's students shared the same classroom, despite the fact that their ages varied, and when Themistocles was still an infant he first encountered a classmate by the name Aristides, who was several years his senior. This Athenian boy came from the deme of Alopece, which, in Athens, was renowned for being the home of the most aristocratic of families. Yet Aristides's aristocratic family had fallen on hard times, and even in adulthood he would be rated financially hard off to the end of his days. So it was that Aristides was sent to the same school in rural Phrearrhioi as Themistocles, where the fees would have been lower.

The boys soon became rivals, despite their age difference. Themistocles, in both schoolwork and play, was eager and adventurous. Yet, he could be subtle when the occasion required. And he would try his hand at anything. Conversely, Aristides was staid, aloof, and intent on seeing justice done. Even in their play, when Themistocles showed a natural cheek, and charm, playing tricks on his classmates, the serious-minded Aristides could not be induced to resort to any pretence or to deviate from the straight and narrow. It would always be Themistocles and Aristides who would be at variance when the students put arguments in quest of the prize for eloquence.

Unlike Aristides, Themistocles was not much interested in lessons on the manners and behavior expected of a gentleman, and even less interested in poetry, singing, and dance lessons. He skipped music classes altogether. But he showed an interest and confidence beyond his years in those lessons that would improve his knowledge and wisdom when it came to public affairs. During holidays and other school breaks, when his fellow students were lazing or playing, he would continue his studies, on his own. During these school breaks he particularly liked to deliver speeches to an empty room, sometimes in defense of school-mates, sometimes putting a case accusing them of a fictitious crime.

"You, my boy," said his schoolmaster, on overhearing several of these youthful speeches, "will not end up anything small in life. You will be great in one way or another—for good, or else for bad."

By the time Themistocles was in his mid-twenties, he was lead-ing the typical life of the modern college student, mixing studies with an exhausting social life. His father, Neocles, despite initially trying to dissuade Themistocles from pursuing a political career, was talked around by his persuasive son. Perhaps the idea of the son of a trades-man climbing to the top of Athenian society finally swayed him. To further Themistocles's ambitions, Neocles now set the young man up in Athens with a house and servants. That house was in one of the less salubrious parts of the city, the Ceramicus, or "place of potter's clay," northwest of the Acropolis, and covered by the deme of Melite. Potters clustered here because it was rich in river clay.

This potters' quarter, as the Ceramicus became, was an industrial area, home to the workshops of craftsmen, smiths, carpenters, and tanners, and full of the noise, smoke and stench produced by their trades. What was worse, the house where Themistocles lived was near the road that passed out through Athens's Demian or Hangman's Gate. Beyond that gate lay the Barathrum, the detestable place where the naked bodies and clothes of executed criminals and suicides were dumped to rot. But at least the house was affordable. And it was spacious enough to provide the facilities that a young gentleman required, including a field and stabling for his horses and chariot.

While never losing sight of his ambition to make a name for himself as a political leader, attending the lectures of the great Athenian thinkers of his day to improve both his mind and the circle he mixed in, Themistocles threw himself into extracurricular activities. He liked nothing more than to entertain friends and strangers alike at his city home, where he was a convivial host. It was the Greek custom, after dining, to drink toasts of diluted wine to the gods, and then to resort to entertainment, be it party games, recitations, or music. At one such dinner party at Themistocles's house, guests, knowing full well that, unlike themselves, their host had developed no musical skills, teased him by offering him a lyre and urging him to give them a song.

"I certainly cannot make use of any stringed instrument," Themistocles retorted, no doubt with a grin, as his companions laughed. "But, I can, if a small and obscure city were put into my hands, make it great and glorious."

This probably produced even more laughter. But, amid the fun of the dinner party, Themistocles was in deadly earnest. Just the same, conscious of a need to improve his musical credentials, he invited the popular lute player Episcles of Hermione to practice regularly at his house. As the musician's beautiful music wafted from his host's open windows, the word soon spread that Themistocles from Phrearrhioi was the patron of the most sought-after musician in Athens. Another talented man added by Themistocles to his circle was the celebrated poet Simonides, a native of the Aegean island of Ceos, today's Kea, in the Cyclades archipelago. Approaching fifty years of age at this time, Simonides, himself from a poor family, survived via the support of wealthy patrons. Not only did Themistocles support him financially— Simonides may have even lived under his roof—the pair also became firm friends.

That friendship survived Themistocles's habit of good-naturedly poking fun at his friends. On one occasion, when Simonides spoke disparagingly of the vanity of the people of Corinth, Themistocles responded, "Simonides, you're a man of little judgment to speak against the Corinthians, inhabitants of a great city, while so frequently having your own portrait drawn—possessing such an ugly face as you do!"

Young Themistocles was friendly with, and popular with, men from all walks of life, and had a phenomenal memory for names, impressing all by hailing every Athenian citizen he met in the street by name. But he particularly went out of his way to court the friendship of the sons of the aristocracy. With his sights set on a political career, he knew that it was *who* he knew as much as *what* he knew that would make or break his future career. Like other male Athenian citizens, Themistocles trained every day, naked, at a gymnasium. It would have stung him to the quick that, not himself being the son of an aristocrat, he was barred from training at the Academy and the Lyceum, city gymnasia reserved for the "pure-bloods," the elite.

Because his mother did not hold Athenian citizenship, Themistocles was forced to train at the Cynosarges gymnasium, outside the city to the southeast, on the far bank of the River Ilissus. The Cynosarges was dedicated to the legendary hero Hercules. Because Hercules was said to be a son of both a god and a mortal, and technically was not of "pure" blood, the gymnasium welcomed the likes of Themistocles, who could boast only one parent with Athenian citizenship. There was no law preventing blue bloods from training at the Cynosarges, only the class system. To buck that system and batter down the class barrier instead

13

of attempting to gain entry to the Academy or Lyceum, Themistocles cunningly approached the situation from the opposite direction. He convinced his blue-blood friends to desert the Academy and Lyceum on the other side of town and come and train at Cynosarges with him. It was a step toward social equality for which citizens of "mixed blood" would applaud Themistocles.

During these youthful years, Themistocles was also renowned for cavorting with prostitutes. Far from being exceptional, this was the norm for youths in Themistocles's day. Greek men could not legally marry until they reached the age of thirty. And their brides-to-be were expected to be virgins. In the meantime, young men had to sow their wild oats somewhere. As a result, many Greek men would father illegitimate children with prostitutes and slaves during these years leading up to marriage. It became so prevalent that cities such as Athens and Sparta framed their laws so that only married men, or widowers, with *legitimate* children could hold important posts. So, until Athens's young men reached the legal marrying age, prostitutes were kept busy satisfying their needs. These prostitutes were seen as a necessary evil by Athenian families, as long as their sons didn't make a show of it.

Themistocles caused a sensation when several of the city's most infamous prostitutes hitched themselves up to his chariot and drew it into Athens's main market one morning at the height of the trading day, with a laughing Themistocles riding in the car, reins in hand. Plutarch repeated one report that Themistocles's mother was so scandalized by this affair she committed suicide. Although it is possible that she did pass away around this time, historians then and now have dismissed the suicide story as a fiction. Certainly, the story of the prostitutes and the chariot would have been told throughout Athens, and only increased Themistocles's popularity with the average voter of Athens, even if it did embarrass his family.

Another sexual diversion for Greek men was homosexuality. It was common for Greeks to be openly gay, or bisexual, with no stigma attached to it. Gay men served openly in the Greek military. In fact, such was the reputation of gay Greeks as warriors, a century after Themistocles the Greek city of Thebes would raise an elite and feared fighting unit whose members had all to be pairs of gay lovers. That unit, the Sacred Band, would, for four decades, lead the Theban army to victory after victory over every other Greek state including Sparta and Athens, and make Thebes the greatest military power in Greece.

In Themistocles's day, it was common for older aristocrats to have gay lovers in their teens and twenties. It was equally common for young men like Themistocles to have homosexual affairs with pretty youths. A story, doubted by some historians, would be told by Plutarch that Themistocles and his old school rival Aristides vied for the affection of a youth called Stesilaus. It was probably at the Cynosarges gymnasium that Themistocles first saw the youth. Stesilaus, it was said, was a beautiful boy from Ceos, the same island from which Simonides the poet hailed, and he caught the eye of both Themistocles and Aristides. The pair went overboard in their attempts to outdo each other for Stesilaus's attention. It seems that Aristides won this contest, and apparently in a manner that Themistocles considered underhanded and unfair.

Even when Stesilaus departed the picture, the enmity caused by the contest for his affections lived on, and was so great that it made Themistocles and Aristides fierce enemies in public life. Or so the story went. It was true that by the time Themistocles and Aristides entered politics they were bitter rivals. Staid Aristides would oppose everything that Themistocles proposed, supporting the entrenched aristocratic faction in opposition to Themistocles's fresh, bold initiatives, which were frequently without precedent. As for Themistocles's homosexual inclinations, we hear nothing about them from any other classical source. We do know that he would marry as soon as he was legally able, and would father ten children by two wives.

It was at the Olympic Games that Themistocles first came to the attention of the leading men of the other states of the Greek world. Greek colonizing had seen that world expand to 1,500 Greek cities all around the Mediterranean and Black Seas. All those cities were entitled to send athletes to compete when the games were held at Olympia every four years, when, traditionally, all wars between Greek states ceased, and an Olympic truce prevailed. In addition to the athletes, leading men from each city traveled to Olympia to watch the games and support their countrymen. Themistocles turned up at one such Olympiad as a spectator. These were almost certainly the games of 394

15

BC. For, that was just a year before the elections in which he would be entitled to stand for archon of Athens, and his appearance at Olympia was clearly a calculated publicity stunt designed to have him talked about back home in Athens.

For, Themistocles arrived at Olympia with the finest tents and most luxurious trappings that anyone had seen from an Athenian. He then proceeded to throw lavish dinners for competitors and spectators. Leading men from both Athens and other cities were affronted by the showiness of this twenty-nine-year-old Athenian, a young man of humble birth who had yet to serve in any public office or accomplish any achievement to boast of, asking who he thought he was. But Themistocles wasn't trying to impress Greek aristocrats. He was only trying to impress the voters of Athens.

Themistocles was a master of self-promotion. That year, too, he had agreed to sponsor the play of established playwright Phrynicus in Athens's annual drama competition of 393 BC. Phrynicus, who had been competing for a decade and a half, would go on to win that year's City of Dionysia prize, the win handily occurring for Themistocles just prior to the elections. In the stone tablet Themistocles erected at the theater to record Phrynicus's win, Themistocles listed his own name first, as the sponsor who paid for it, advertising both his altruism and his ability to pick winners. Just as his successful venture into arts sponsorship was designed to put his name before his fellow Athenians, his ostentatious capture of the limelight at the Olympic Games was meant to make Athenian tongues wag. Which they did. Word flew back home, and his name was on everyone's lips. Athenian aristocrats were appalled. But Themistocles's gall, and panache, clearly delighted the Athenian man in the street, for Themistocles was elected archon the following year, at his first attempt.

According to historian Herodotus, even now that Themistocles had come to political prominence he was more commonly referred to as the son of Neocles than by his own name. This was a putdown from the aristocrats, for whom the noble family line was everything. The aristocrats were snobbishly emphasizing the fact that Themistocles was "not one of us." But this condescending attitude only backfired, for it made Themistocles a hero of the common people, who had never seen one of their own sitting as a powerful city archon prior to this.

Athens's nine archons had a dual role. First, they were the city's chief magistrates. In addition to hearing and deciding legal cases, the archons were the city-state's elected government ministers. While answerable to the Assembly, each archon had a specific government responsibility during his unpaid one-year tenure. One archon, for example was the Polemarch, the war archon, or secretary for war. Another was responsible for administering the city treasury. And so on. Candidates stood for specific archonships. Aristides, for example, was elected treasury archon on several occasions. We know for a fact that Themistocles at one time held the post of Athens's superintendent of public waterways, the *Epistates Hydaton,* and it is highly likely that this formed part of his portfolio as archon in 393–392 BC—perhaps a broad public works portfolio. The primary role of the waterways superintendent was to keep Athens's water supply in good shape. In addition to ensuring that the river Cephisus and other waterways serving Athens flowed free and pure, the superintendant also had to ensure that members of the public observed the water supply regulations.

Attacking his new job with an enthusiasm that had not been displayed by his predecessors, Themistocles soon found that numerous citizens were illegally tapping into the water supply's pipes, siphoning off water without paying for it. Most of these wrongdoers would have been aristocrats. Ordinary citizens did not have the wherewithal to pay for private water pipes, and had to use buckets to obtain their needs from wells and public water cisterns. Past superintendents of the waterways would have been aristocrats, who winked at their fellow nobles' offenses, and their own. But Themistocles, a commoner, had no such allegiances. Sealing off illegal water pipes, Themistocles imposed hefty fines on lawbreakers. Those fines funded the casting of a bronze statue, of a virgin water carrier more than three feet in height, that Themistocles had set up in an Athenian temple; the inscription indicates that it was Themistocles who dedicated it. Little could Themistocles have known that in decades to come he would encounter this same statue in very different circumstances.

Plutarch suggested that, when sitting as a magistrate, Themistocles was not always strictly impartial—certainly compared to Aristides, who earned himself the nickname Aristides the Just. According to Plutarch, when someone said to Themistocles that he would make a good magistrate if he were impartial, Themistocles replied, "I will never sit on a tribunal where my friends cannot plead a greater privilege than strangers."

Yet, Plutarch also related that when Themistocles's good friend the poet Simonides asked him to decide a legal case a particular way, as a favor to him, Themistocles answered, "Simonides, you would not be a good poet if you wrote with false measure. Neither would I be a good magistrate if, for favor, I made false law."

This, combined with the fact that there is no recorded instance of Themistocles's favoring anyone while a magistrate, indicates that Themistocles, who was demonstrably fond of joking at others' expense, was speaking tongue-in-cheek when he said his friends could expect a better hearing than strangers when he was sitting in judgment.

It was Athens's waterways that most interested the young archon in 493 BC. He had probably stood for this archonship with a precise agenda in mind. For, apparently taking "waterways" to mean that his authority as *Epistates Hydaton* also covered Athens's port, he set about changing the entire way that Athenians looked at the sea. Up to this time, Athens's port had been the relatively exposed Bay of Phalerum. Themistocles had been born and grown up close by the township of Piraeus, southwest of Athens. And, as his father is likely to have pointed out to him, the three linked coves of Piraeus could offer a much more sheltered set of harbors. The most northerly of these, the Cantharos, which was shaped like an inverted cup, offered particularly good protection against both the weather and attack from the sea by Athens's enemies. So, during his year as archon, Themistocles had the harbors of Piraeus surveyed, as he laid out a grand plan for Piraeus to become both the civil and naval port of Athens.

He also planned protective walls to surround Piraeus, and mapped out a pair of parallel Long Walls that ran inland from Piraeus all the way to Athens, five miles away, creating a secure highway between the walls. In one fell swoop, Themistocles's brilliant and inspired blueprint created a set of excellent defended harbors and linked Athens to the sea.

Athens had many enemies among its fellow Greek city-states, but the economic and military superpower of this era was Persia. And it was expanding, threatening all the Greek city-states. Persia's King Darius was a warrior king who in 521 BC had staged a military coup to seize his throne and the Persian Empire founded by Cyrus the Great three decades earlier. Darius and able subordinates had then led his massive and vaunted army in putting down numerous internal revolts before swallowing up one neighboring city-state after another. Athens had incurred the wrath of Darius by supporting the Ionian Revolt. While, later in his rule, Darius devoted much of his energy to efficiently reorganizing his empire into twenty provinces and building massive edifices at his several capitals, Themistocles was convinced that it would not be long before the Persian king turned his eyes Athens's way. Themistocles was equally convinced that his blueprint for Piraeus was a vital imperative for the defense of Athens.

It is unlikely that much physical work was done that year to turn this Piraeus blueprint into reality, because Themistocles had neither the funds nor the authority to do it. It would take a vote of the full Assembly to muster sufficient political will and funds to make it happen. And most of his fellow councillors, men such as Aristides, only saw his scheme as a colossally expensive departure from all they were accustomed to. Like all brilliant new ideas, Themistocles's plan needed open minds to appreciate its worth. And most aristocrats of Athens were of a fixed mindset.

Still, Themistocles had laid the groundwork, and had won enough of his colleagues to his way of thinking to head up a minority faction within the council. In the elections of the next two years, Themistocles failed again to win office as an archon, no doubt with Aristides and other vocal detractors deriding his Piraeus blueprint as madness. So, he was not in a position to push his pet Piraeus scheme with any author-ity. But now being a permanent member of the Areopagus, he was at least able to speak to matters of defense in council. Now, too, he regu-larly visited his old professor, Mnesiphilus, and took his counsel. The professor would have advised him to keep ringing alarm bells about the expansionist intentions of King Darius of Persia, which was at odds with the leading aristocrats' desire to appease Darius.

The fleeing Miltiades had arrived back in his birthplace with four ships laden with family members and his personal treasure. A fifth ship, carrying his eldest son, had been captured by pursuing Persians. Miltiades's son became a prisoner of the Persian monarch, and would remain so for the rest of his days. Miltiades's personal loss resonated with many Athenians, of all classes. This was why he'd been elected one of the city's generals every year since 392 BC—the year that news reached Athens that a Persian fleet of 300 warships commanded by King Darius's young son-in-law Mardonius had foundered in a storm while sailing south to invade Attica and take Athens. By the spring of 490 BC, the warnings of Miltiades, Themistocles, and other leading Athenians that Darius would make a fresh attempt to invade their homeland sooner or later had been proven correct.

The Persian flood had crept closer and closer to Athens, and now another vast Persian fleet was known to be heading for Attica, carrying a large Persian army—estimated by modern historians to number 20,000 infantry and 5,000 cavalry. The sixty-year-old Darius's orders to his generals Datis, a Median, and Artaphernes, the king's nephew, were to take the city of Eretria on Euboea, Greece's largest island, just to the north of Attica, and then take Athens, bringing all their residents back to him as slaves.

Eretria and Athens had both aided the Ionians in their failed revolt against Darius's rule, and Artaphernes's father had been governor of Sardis when it was destroyed by the Athenians and Eritreans. Datis would prove to be the chief commander on this campaign, with Artaphernes serving as his protégé and symbolic representative of the Persian royal house. Although Artaphernes Senior had ultimately put down the Ionian Revolt, the appointment of his son as co-commander of this expeditionary force gave the young man a debt of honor to expunge on behalf of both his father and his uncle. For, Darius was determined to make both Athens and Eretria pay for opposing him. Especially, he said, because the two cities had taken up arms against him unprovoked by any direct action or threat by Persia.

Chief among King Darius's advisors for this campaign was Hippias, a noble native of Athens. Hippias had been the last of a long line of tyrants who had ruled Athens. After Hippias's brother had been assassinated and he himself was driven out of Athens in 510 BC, when the

Athenians turned to democracy, Hippias had lived in exile in Persian territory. Despite the fact that he was now in his eighties, Hippias had not lost the lust for power. With a promise from Darius that he would reinstate him as ruler of Athens—albeit a ruler who paid allegiance and taxes to Darius—Hippias was accompanying Datis and Artaphernes to guide the Persians in their assault on the city of his birth.

The first stage of the Persian campaign had been successful. In July, Eretria, on the island of Euboea, had been taken with relative ease. Its residents were now being held prisoner on another island, and the city of Eretria itself was a smoking ruin. Now, it was Athens's turn to face the might of the Persian war machine. On Hippias's advice, Datis landed his army early in August on the northeast coast of Attica, near the town of Marathon. Hippias knew this area well from personal experience. His father Pisistratus had landed an army in this same place sixty years earlier, from where he had proceeded to capture Athens and make himself its ruler.

As Hippias told Datis and Artaphernes, the plain of Marathon was flat, and ideal for cavalry, in which the Persians specialized. Not only did Hippias influence the location of the Persian landing in 490 BC, but he also is likely to have influenced the timing of the previous attempt to invade Attica, two years earlier, reminding King Darius that in August of 492 BC all the Greek city-states would have been preoccupied with the upcoming Olympic Games and unprepared for war. Some of their best fighters would have already gone to Olympia to complete their training there prior to taking part in the games. The weather gods had saved Athens in 492 BC by wrecking the Persian invasion fleet, but this time the landing, at Marathon, went ahead unimpeded by bad weather.

A massive Persian camp of thousands of tents blossomed beside the landing beach near Marathon, and the Persian cavalry quickly spread throughout the district, foraging for food, livestock, and firewood, pillaging then burning the town of Marathon and outlying villages and farms, laying waste to the region before returning to the camp. As thousands of terrified Greek refugees flooded from northeast Attica along the two roads to Athens, Datis and Artaphernes decided to wait to see what the reaction of the Athenians would be. Knowing that Hippias had relatives and sympathizers among the aristocrats of Athens, and that other nobles were in favor of appeasing the Persians rather than take on his army, Datis and Artaphernes were fully expecting the Athenians to follow the example of other Greek cities and send envoys to negotiate Athens's surrender.

In times of war, it was Athens's ten generals, sitting in a council of war, who decided the city's fate. In a vote that was led by Miltiades, a majority of these commanders had quickly decided to resist the Persian invasion. They did not want to pay allegiance and tribute to the Persian king, or to see Hippias again rule over Athens, when he could be expected to avenge himself on the Athenians who had turned against him. As a first step, it had been agreed by the war council that help should be summoned from Athens's allies. One of those allies was the small city of Plataea, in Boeotia, to the west of Athens. Boeotia was traditionally dominated by the city of Thebes, long ago the seat of famed King Oedipus. But in 519 BC Plataea had surrendered itself to Athenian overlordship in return for protection against Thebes. The Plataeans believed that subservience to the liberal Athenians would be less onerous than subservience to aggressive Thebes. The price for Athenian protection was payment of tax money annually to Athens, and the provision of troops to fight under Athenian command when called to do so.

The other Athenian ally whose help was sought was Sparta, famously the most martial of the Greek states and Athens's equal in economic and military power. Because slaves and subject workers did all the work in the Spartan state, all Spartan boys were taken from their parents at the age of seven and sent to military school. There they lived and trained as soldiers until the age of thirty. Spartan men were then permitted to leave the school and marry, but they still had to dine every night with the men of their military company. This martial upbringing made the Spartans the most militarily successful and most feared fighters among all the Greeks.

The Athenians chosen as envoy to the Spartans the renowned athlete Philippides. He would run the entire 140-mile distance south to Sparta in the Peloponnese, over a route that included several steep mountain passes. The use of a runner was by far the most viable way to speedily transmit a message long distance in Greece at this time. A horseman or charioteer would have had to regularly change his steeds, and this required an established system of horse-changing stations en route. Just such a system existed in the Persian Empire, where official messages were transmitted by the *Angarum*, the royal courier service that involved mounted couriers who rode for a day until the next courier took charge of the message bag. The Romans, hundreds of years later, would emulate the Persians by operating a similar public courier service, the *Cursus Publicus Velox*, initially with runners, later using mounted couriers and coaches with horse-changing stations every ten to twelve miles throughout the Roman Empire. In the event, Philippides would cover the run south in two days.

But, while the Athenian leaders had chosen to resist the Persian invasion, they were divided over what tactics to use. The more conservative leaders were all in favor of preparing to defend Athens from within against a Persian siege. But the world had seen how the Persians prosecuted sieges against cities that held out against them. Four years before this, the Greek city of Miletus in Ionia had attempted to withstand a siege by Darius's army, in the last great contest of the Ionian Revolt. After the city had been starved into submission, Darius had executed all male inhabitants and dragged the Miletian women and children off into slavery.

Athens's second option was to march out and go against the vast Persian army in the open. Led by Miltiades, who had seen the Persian army at work from both sides and who argued for a proactive answer to the invasion, the majority of generals voted in favor of fighting the Persians in the open. As Miltiades told his colleagues, the standard, lightly armored Persian infantryman was no match for the heavily armored hoplite, as Greek infantrymen were called. Fighting from behind city walls, the hoplite gave up that advantage. But in the open, in close battle order, a phalanx of disciplined Greek hoplites was a fearsome weapon. Their armor, their training and courage, argued Miltiades, would make up for inferior numbers against an army principally made up of poorly equipped rural conscripts. Besides, an army on the attack seized the tactical momentum.

And so it was agreed to march to Marathon. No doubt Themistocles, who, throughout his career was always in favor of taking the initiative, voted with Miltiades. Early in the first week of August 490 BC, the call to arms went out to all Athenian fighting men, to don their equipment, gather their weapons and a few days' rations, and assemble in their regiments to march to Marathon.

3.

To Fight, or Not to Fight

By August 10, 490 BC, the Athenian army had been sitting tight at the Agrielci, its Pentele mountain camp, for six days, watching the Persians encamped on the plain below. Throughout this period, overall command of the Athenian army changed daily; it was the custom of the Athenian military for each of the regimental commanders to take a turn as commander in chief for twenty-four hours. Yet, four of Miltiades's fellow commanders felt that he was the most qualified to lead the army, and each surrendered their day's command to him. Themistocles's rival Aristides had command of the tenth regiment, the Antiochis, and, even though he had always opposed Miltiades in council, he was one of those generals who voluntarily gave up the command to Miltiades. It seems that Themistocles was another.

The runner Philippides now arrived at the Athenian camp after completing his epic courier mission on foot to Sparta and back. The news he brought to the war archon, Callimachus of Aphidnai, and to Themistocles and the nine other unit commanders, was both good and bad. The Spartans had agreed to the Athenian request for military assistance against the Persian invaders. But their contingent would not set off to join the Athenians for another week. The Spartans were scrupulous in their religious observance, and their beliefs prevented them from marching for war until the moon was full, another six days away.

This was deeply troubling to the Athenian commanders. The delay of a week in the dispatch of the promised Spartan army could be disastrous. The Athenian army could have been defeated and their city taken in that time. Some historians have suggested this delay by the Spartans was deliberate, and was intended to buy them time in which they expected the Persians to overwhelm the Athenians. After all, the Persians were not the declared enemies of Sparta, and the intent of the Persian campaign was only to punish the Eritreans and Athenians. But the Spartans knew there was no good reason that Datis and Artaphernes would stop at Athens, particularly if the defeat of Athens proved as easy as the defeat of Eretria. As it turned out, the Spartans would be true to their treaty, and true to their word to aid the Athenians.

In the middle of the night of August 10–11, Callimachus the Athenian war archon was awakened in camp with the news that defectors from the Persian army had turned up at an outpost, bringing word of activity in the enemy camp. Those defectors were from the large Ionian contingent that had been conscripted into military service by their Persian overlords. Callimachus immediately called a meeting of the war council. In the light of campfire and burning torches, Callimachus, his ten regimental commanders, and Arimnestos, commander of the Plataean contingent, listened as the Ionian defectors delivered startling news. The Persians, said the defectors, were busy loading many of their troops onto their fleet. Their cavalry had already been embarked.

The Persian plan was to catch the Athenians napping by putting to sea at night, sailing down the coast, around Cape Sunium, today's Cape Sounis, and into Phalerum Bay, the port of Athens. Landing there, the Persians would march unopposed up to Athens from the south and surround the city while the Athenian army was still sitting in its mountain camp looking down at Marathon, where a large Persian infantry rear guard would do its best to make it look as if the entire invading army was still encamped there. It was a brilliant plan, and it would probably have succeeded had it not been for the Ionian defectors' giving it away to the Athenians.

Callimachus, as war minister, would not express a view about battle tactics in the war council. Withdrawing to his tent, Callimachus left the Athenian generals to discuss what course of action the army should take. As the generals took turns expressing their views, several spoke of hurrying back to Athens and preparing to face a siege by the Persians once they landed at Phalerum Bay. After the mature, vastly experienced

Miltiades, Aristides's was the most valued opinion in the generals' war council. Up until now, Aristides had always opposed Miltiades, just as he always opposed Themistocles. Aristides had voted against marching from Athens to Marathon, a course advocated by Miltiades. But now he listened intently as Miltiades proposed a far bolder strategy in the wake of the news from the defectors.

Miltiades urged his fellow commanders to agree to march their troops down to the enemy camp at first light and attack the rearguard while the rest of the enemy army were aboard ship or in the process of being embarked. This way, the Athenians would seize the initiative, and would catch the enemy divided. Most important, if the defectors were right and the Persian cavalry, the most feared and effective part of the enemy army, were aboard ship and unable to participate, the Athenian hoplites would have their best opportunity of securing victory, even if outnumbered by the infantry of the Persian rear guard.

A vote was taken among the Athenian commanders. The Plataean commander, leading a force from a subservient ally, would not have been entitled to participate. The vote came down evenly divided, with five regimental commanders in favor of withdrawing to Athens, and five, including Miltiades, in favor of attacking at Marathon. Without doubt, Themistocles was a member of the group that supported Miltiades's proactive course. Aristides, meanwhile, surprised his colleagues by joining Miltiades in voting for going onto the offensive. But his vote was not enough to carry the decision for Miltiades. The vote was deadlocked.

Only now, with a majority decision out of the question, did Athenian law allow the war archon to become involved. To break a tie, he could cast the deciding vote. Gray-bearded Miltiades, holding command for the day in the stead of one of his colleagues, went to Callimachus's tent with the news that the generals were evenly divided over what to do. The decision on Athens's fate now rested with the war archon.

Miltiades did not refrain from letting Callimachus know which course he advocated. Never before, declared the general, had the Athenian people been in such danger of losing their freedom. He made it clear that his greatest fear was not of a fight, but of not fighting. For, in the latter event he could foresee agitation at Athens that would shake the resolve of the people and convince them to surrender the city to the

Persians. He was talking about those at Athens who either supported deposed ruler Hippias or advocated giving in to the Persians without a fight in the hope of getting favorable surrender terms, including positions of power under Persian overlordship. If the Athenian army retreated, Miltiades could see those two negative groups holding sway in a citywide vote on Athens's fate.

Miltiades, a man of action, wanted to fight the Persians before any lack of confidence could be capitalized on by the pro-Persian lobby. If the gods were with them, he argued, the Athenian hoplites were perfectly capable of defeating the enemy in a fair fight. If Callimachus were to vote with him, Miltiades declared, Athens would not only ensure its freedom by defeating the Persians, but it would also rank as the first state in Greece, above Sparta, above Thebes, above Argos, above Corinth. But if the war archon voted with the five commanders who were against fighting, Athens would become a Persian slave state, devoid of freedom or rank.

Miltiades's argument won over the war archon. Returning to the waiting regimental commanders with Miltiades, Callimachus cast his vote with Miltiades, Themistocles, Aristides, and the two other commanders who favored combat over retreat. With the decision to go to war made, Miltiades announced that he would wait until his legitimate day of command came around before ordering the army to prepare for battle. That day would begin at dawn the following morning. The Greek commanders went to their beds knowing that next day Athens's fate would be decided, on the battlefield.

4.

The Battle of Marathon

At sunrise on August 11, which came at around 6:30 A.M. that day, the Athenian and Plataean commanders joined Miltiades at the command tent on the mountain slope. Now that his day of command had officially come, Miltiades issued an order. The long, slender trumpets of each regiment came up to the lips of their trumpeters. A preserved Greek military trumpet of the fifth century BC, the *salpinx*, has been found to consist of an ivory tube and a bronze bell. With this elegant instrument, the Athenian trumpeters blasted out the command: "To Arms," followed by "Form battle order."

Word would have spread through the camp the previous night that the war council had voted six to five to give battle on the Plain of Marathon this morning. So, the dawn trumpet calls would have been no surprise. A good many men, through excitement or apprehension, would have slept little as they awaited the dawn, knowing that some of them would not live to see another sunset. The men of the army would have risen well before the first hints of the new day's sun clawed above the mountaintops to the east. Some would have breakfasted, but many would have been unable to eat.

A story was soon spreading through the ranks that the courier Philippides, on his return run from Sparta, had been passing over a mountain pass between the cities of Sparta and Tegea when the rural god Pan, who, according to mythology, resided in the hills and mountains, had appeared to him on the road. According to Philippides, Pan demanded to know why Athenians neglected to worship him. His displeasure was exacerbated by the fact that he had frequently helped Athens in the past, he said, and would again in the future—if only the Athenians would honor him.

This story has been explained away by some modern writers as the sort of hallucination that long-distance runners sometimes experience when the physical and mental strains of their exertions combine. But to many an Athenian in the military camp that morning, it was a sign that Pan would be on the side of his Athenian flock on the plain of Marathon in the coming battle, as long as they paid due homage to him. As a consequence, it was to Pan that many Athenians would direct their prayers this day. And when they marched to battle, it would be with confidence that the god would give them victory.

They would also march with a self-confidence that could only be matched by the Spartans among the Greeks at that time. Athenians firmly believed that Athens had been the first city established in Greece, a millennia before this, and that, with the help of the agricultural gods including Pan, they had introduced the art of agriculture to all the Greeks. Archaeologists today would argue with that view, considering Thebes to have been the oldest city in Greece. But the Athenians' self-view gave them a sense of superiority that would be backed by their intellectual rigor during this fifth century, a period when Athens would give the world great thinkers and writers of the ilk of Socrates, Plato, Sophocles, Euripides, Thucydides, Aristophanes, and Aeschylus, and attract and foster the likes of Aristotle.

In the Athenian camp, amid urgent activity and hubbub, 9,600 Athenians and Plataeans were now preparing for battle and donning their panoply, their combat equipment. That equipment was basically the same for officers as for the rank and file, although aristocrats were able to afford better and more richly decorated equipment. One modern historian has estimated that the cost of that panoply to its Greek owners was similar to the cost of a family car today. That panoply was considered essential to every householder in those times, just as a car is today.

As with a family car, the better your means, or the grander your aspirations, the more luxurious the panoply you purchased. Among the Athenian commanders, Miltiades and Themistocles would have spent heavily on their equipment. Miltiades could more than afford it, while

Themistocles was intent on keeping up appearances. Meanwhile, their fellow regimental commander Aristides, who always struggled to find money, would have only possessed the most basic panoply.

With the help of their armor-bearers, Aeschylus and his brother Cynaegirus were strapping corselet armor around their torsos, over the top of tunics that fell to just above their bare knees. The brothers could afford the more expensive bronze muscled cuirass, a style that would still be worn by senior officers in the imperial Roman army centuries later. The most common form of Greek hoplite corselet of this era was made from layers of linen or canvas glued together to form a thick shirt, and reinforced by small metal plates or scales sown to the shirt. The corselet's two ends were laced together down the wearer's left side, the side protected in battle by his shield. This lacing up was only something that could be efficiently accomplished by a hoplite's assistant, be it a servant or a fellow infantryman. To complete the outfit, yokes of similar material were tied in place over each shoulder.

Next, a pair or bronze greaves were fitted over the hoplite's knees and shins. These curved plates were modeled on the individual's legs, and were flexible enough to be sprung snugly onto the leg. The sword baldric could now be slung over the shoulder, and helmets donned. The Athenians' helmets were of the Corinthian style. Made from a single piece of bronze and frequently topped by a neatly trimmed, dyed horsehair plume in a removable metal plume holder, these handsome helmets covered the head to the nape of the neck. Covering nose and ears, the helmets left just slits for the eyes and mouth. While providing good head protection, this wraparound design limited the wearer's peripheral vision. And, because these helmets covered the ears, hearing ability was significantly reduced once the helmet was in place. As a consequence, hoplites marching to battle did so with helmets sitting on the back of their heads and off their faces, a pose seen in Greek busts and vase portraits of the period.

One famous vase illustration by ancient Greek artist Exekias shows two Greek fighting men sitting in their armor as they played a board game in camp, with one typically wearing his crested Corinthian helmet on the back of his head. The other player wears a round skullcap, and it is believed that, for comfort's sake, felt skullcaps were worn beneath all Greek helmets. Only just prior to battle would the hoplite pull his helmet down over his face.

Aeschylus's skullcap and helmet hid the fact that he had lost much of his hair. Before many years had passed he would be entirely bald, and his cranium would shine like a polished rock. Thirty years later, Aeschylus would pass away, and a legend would grow that he died when an eagle, mistaking that shining head for a rock, would drop a tortoise onto it, killing him—eagles were known to seize tortoises, then drop them from a great height onto rocks, to break open their shells. Had there been modern tabloid-style newspapers around then, a typical headline might have been: "Award-winning dramatist killed by flying tortoise."

As the regiments were called to form up in their prearranged battle order, each hoplite took up his shield, the *hoplon*. This gave the hoplites their name; they were literally shield men. Athenians had universally adopted the Argive shield, named for the Greek city of Argos in the Peloponnese, where it had originated. The Argive shield was round, with its outer side convex in shape. The other popular shield design of the time was the Boeotian style. Used by the city of Thebes and other city-states of central Greece, this was lighter than the Argive shield and based on the earlier Mycenaean shield of Siege of Troy period, a shield that was shaped like the figure eight. Oval, and with a semicircular gap on each side, the Boeotian shield allowed a fighter to lock his shield with men either side of him to form a wall of shields, yet jab a javelin out through one of the gaps in the shield's side to strike at his opponents. But the Boeotian shield did not have the inherent strength of the circular Argive model, and so did not offer as much protection against missile strike, spear thrust, or sword blow.

Three feet across, the round Argive shield was formed from layers of wood topped by either a bronze covering or bronze fittings. Athenian citizens of military age, eighteen to fifty, purchased shields from professional shield makers, and hung them up at home until called to arms. The face of the shield was painted in a design chosen by the buyer, but tended to relate to his home city's emblem or emblems. The Gorgon's face was a common design on Athenian shields. Pegasus the flying horse appeared on shields carried by men from Corinth. When Aeschylus, not many years after this, wrote his classic war play *Seven Against Thebes*, he described in detail the different shield designs of the seven Greek heroes who went against Thebes in the time of King Oedipus, and they similarly related to the heroes' home districts.

A shield was always carried on the left arm, and the spear and sword in the right. Natural lefthanders had to learn to become right-handers to do this. The Argive shield weighed something like eighteen pounds. To support it there was a metal armband at the central rear of the shield, through which the bearer slipped his left arm up to the elbow, allowing the left hand to grasp a handgrip on the right extremity of the rim. Because the shield was concave on the inside, the bearer could rest the upper rim on his shoulder, supporting some of the weight.

When Greek soldiers fled a battlefield after, or during, a defeat, the first thing they discarded was the heavy shield, so that they could run faster. A century and a half later, Athenian leader Demosthenes would talk the Thebans into going to war against the Macedonian army of the future Alexander the Great and his father King Philip of Macedon, only to personally discard his shield on the battlefield and flee when the going got tough. Another Greek soldier fleeing a battlefield during this era would hide his shield under a bush, hoping to return later for it and save himself the cost of buying a new one— and to avoid the disgrace of going home without his shield. It is part of legend that when any Spartan warrior set off for war, his wife, or his mother if he was single or a widower, would hand him his shield, with the words, "Come back with this, or on it." In other words, don't bother coming home without it.

A sheathed iron short-sword with a cutting blade roughly two feet long formed the Greek soldier's secondary armament. It was draped from a leather baldric that hung over the hoplite's right shoulder and crossed the body so that the sheath hung on the left side. The sheath was made from wood, covered in leather, with bronze fittings. The hoplite could also carry light throwing spears, or bolts, which would be loosed off at the enemy as he advanced for the attack. But once the hoplite closed with the other side and it was time for hand-to-hand combat, the thrusting spear, seven to ten feet long and used both underhand

and overhand—so that it could be thrust over the top of shields—was his chief weapon.

Vase portraits depicting two champions for opposing Greek cities fighting in single combat, which happened from time to time, show those fighters stalking each other with shields raised and thrusting spears at the ready. Swords were very much weapons to be used as a last resort, and to cut away the equipment of a downed opponent. The thrusting spear, commonly made from cornel wood, had a leather grip two-thirds of the way from the metal point, and a bronze butt spike; if the spear was broken in battle, the hoplite could reverse it and use the spiked end offensively.

According to Herodotus, who was born several years after the Battle of Marathon, the Athenian regiments formed up at the grove of Hercules that morning in number order—that is, from the first to the tenth. And in that battle order they marched from their camp as the noncombatant servants being left behind cheered their departure. Down from the mountainside the army came, led by Callimachus the war archon and the first regiment. The Plataeans brought up the rear. Themistocles, leading the sixth regiment, marched in the middle of the column. Along the narrow Valley of Avlona the hoplites tramped, until they reached the Athens road. Joining this, they swung hard right, and, following the road, came out onto the plain of Marathon.

By the time that the Greek army was on the march, a number of Persian ships had left the bay during the night, heading to sea with the outgoing tide. The Persian rear guard, thought to be made up of a good part of Datis and Artaphernes's infantry, with between 12,000 and 15,000 men, had formed up in a long line covering the Persian camp and the cove. On the beach, a number of Persian ships were drawn up with their sterns on the sand and their prows in the water, ready to be heaved out through the waves. Other ships were moored in the bay. The identity of the Persian commander of the rear guard is unknown; the expedition's commanders in chief, Datis and Artaphernes, had sailed with the cavalry, their most valued troops, accompanied by the Athenian turncoat Hippias.

Miltiades, in overall command of the Athenian army, ordered his force to halt a little under a mile from the Persian line, and form into a battle line on the plain, in what was known as "open formation." This his troops did, efficiently forming up from right to left in silent, well-practiced style, with the first regiment on the extreme right, and the tenth on the extreme left. Miltiades had Arimnestos and his Plataeans occupy the outer left wing, beside the last regiment. This additional force was allocated to the left wing quite deliberately. The right wing of a classical army was the most vulnerable part of the battle line, because, with their shields on their left arms, the men of the extreme right were exposed on their right sides.

In the Greek and Roman military, it was considered the greatest honor, and the greatest responsibility, for a unit to be assigned to the extreme right of a battle line. With the Athenians, it was the rule that the war archon joined the men on the right wing, in a symbolic nod to its importance. So it was that Callimachus took his station with the troops on the Athenian right, from where he would command that wing in battle. Conversely, the left wing was the attacking wing, because it faced the enemy's right. The more weight that could be placed on the left, the better. This was why Miltiades had added the Plataeans to his left wing.

In the well-practiced Greek open formation, the hoplites formed up in eight lines, or ranks, one behind the other, with about six feet between each man in a line, creating a gap, or file, and with the next line some eight feet back. Overall, this created the phalanx, the Greek fighting formation. Every man knew his exact place in the phalanx. As battle was joined, the command "close order" would be trumpeted, and ranks and files would close up until just three feet remained between each man, with the shield of the man on the right overlapping with that of the man on his left. When a hoplite fell in battle, the man in the rank immediately behind him was expected to step up and take his place. As for the regimental commanders, they joined the front lines of their regiments, which were filled with the more mature men, to fight alongside their countrymen.

Once the Greek battle lines had been formed, and Miltiades's men stood with the butt end of their spears jabbed into the earth and their shields resting on the ground and against their legs, the Athenian commander could see that the distant Persian lines had extended a lot farther than his. This meant that once the two armies came together the Persian wings could wrap around the sides of the Greek phalanx, outflank it, and, pressing in, envelop and pulverize it. To prevent being outflanked, Miltiades had to extend his own front line to equal the Persians. To do this, he ordered Aristides to relocate his tenth regiment, the Antiochis, to the center, beside Themistocles's fourth regiment, the Leontis. This left the first, second, and third regiments on the right, the tenth, fourth, fifth, and sixth in the center, and the seventh, eighth, ninth, and the Plataeans on the right.

This relocation of the Antiochis regiment alone did not achieve the required result, that of equaling the length of the Persian front. Miltiades then ordered all four regiments now occupying the center to thin out, bringing men from the rear to the front to further extend the line. The entire Greek line shuffled left and right to make room for the additional men coming up through the ranks from the rear of the four central regiments. In this way, the Greek front line was made to match the Persian front line in length, but at the expense of halving the depth of the regiments occupying the center.

While all this was taking place, Greek priests behind the lines were carrying out animal sacrifices to the gods and inspecting the entrails of the victims. If those entrails were clear of imperfection, it meant that the auspices were good, that the gods were smiling on Athens. If they were not, it meant the opposite. The ancients believed that if a general led his army into battle with bad auspices he was courting the wrath of the gods, and courting disaster for his army. Word would quickly spread through the ranks if the omens were bad, with a resultant deleterious effect on morale.

Four hundred and fifty years after this, Roman dictator Julius Caesar would famously ignore the ill omens of two sacrifices on the Ides of March, 44 BC, and go to the sitting of the Senate at the Theater of Pompey, where he was assassinated. There were some generals in classical times who had the auspices taken until they got the omens they wanted, and it is tempting to wonder if Miltiades would have done that—with the Persian cavalry apparently at sea and unable to play any part in the battle, this was the best chance of victory the Athenians were going to get. As it happened, word was delivered to Miltiades that the omens were good: the gods were with Athens. Now, Miltiades made a surprising decision. Instead of marching to the attack, which was the normal tactic of the day, the Athenians and Plataeans would run all the way, a distance of close to a mile.

As Miltiades's herald passed along the lines loudly informing the troops and the regimental trumpeters of the tactic they would shortly be expected to employ—running to the attack when "Quick march" was sounded by the trumpeters—the men in the ranks would have looked at each other with surprise, before smiles appeared on their faces. The idea of crossing no man's land in as short a time as possible would have been an appealing one, for it reduced each man's risk of being hit by a flying enemy javelin or arrow before they closed with the opposing front line. The Athenians and Plataeans would also have keenly appreciated how this previously unheard of deviation from the normal battle tactic would have surprised and unsettled the Persians. Historian Herodotus believed that the Athenians' running to the attack at Marathon was the first example of Greeks charging the enemy at the run. The Persians had certainly not been on the receiving end of such a tactic prior to this.

A number of modern historians have questioned whether the Athenians did run the full distance wearing their armor and carrying their shields and weapons. Some suggest that Miltiades and his army only ran the last hundred yards or so. Yet, to the Greeks, such a lengthy dash in full equipment would not have seemed so completely unusual. Around 520 BC, a new running event was added to the Olympic Games program. Called the *Hoplitdromos*, or the hoplite endurance race, its competitors had to wear full hoplite panoply and carry a shield as they ran a long distance in the heat of Olympia in summer. Some competitors who strove too hard to win are known to have died from exhaustion following these races.

Miltiades is likely to have attended several Olympic Games as a spectator, watching his father Cimon, who won the chariot race at three Olympics. And Miltiades may have been so impressed by the Hoplitdromos event that he filed memories of it away with a view to employing it on the battlefield. In addition, just as athletes trained for this grueling Olympic event, so it is possible that Greek citizens, as part of their hoplite training, likewise trained to run in full panoply as a fitness measure, just as Roman legionaries would be required to do under the military reforms of the consul Marius early in the first century BC. If the Greeks did indeed run all the way to reach the Persians at Marathon, sixty-four-year-old Miltiades, in the front rank of the Acamantis regiment, at the center of the charging line, clearly considered himself fit enough to keep up with his younger comrades.

Now Miltiades gave another order. A trumpet call was repeated throughout the Greek phalanx, and each of the 9,600 men pulled his helmet down over his face, raised up his shield and lifted it onto his left shoulder, then took his spear in the right hand and slanted it so that it rested beneath the right arm, with the point reaching for the sky. A forest of spearheads now formed above the heads of the hoplites. It was normal for the Greeks, as they attacked, to chant the *paean*, a form of battle hymn. Perhaps they recited the paean before they moved off. And then, "Quick march" was sounded.

Herodotus was unequivocal in his belief that the Greeks ran to the attack from the moment the command was given. That they leaped forward like this also indicates how pent up for action they were, and that they sprang from the proverbial blocks. Perhaps, they jogged the first part of the way, then, with a roar, charged at full pace as they covered the last part of the distance. The men of the Persian force had watched with amusement as the men of the outnumbered Greek line had shuffled around, thinned out and extended to match the length of their own. Now, they were surprised by the sight of the Athenians and Plataeans running toward them. The shield-bearers of the waiting army's front line planted their feet and raised their shields to receive the Greek rush. A rush, unsupported by cavalry or archers, which seemed to the Persians to be madness, Herodotus wrote in his *History*.

The wings of the Persian army were occupied by men from Persia's many provinces. The center was the domain of swarthy native Persian troops from today's Iran, who were among King Darius's best. Alongside them stood the Sacae, Scythians from the Middle East whose territory was now part of King Darius's Persian Empire and who were famed for their skill as archers. A conquered people whose country now formed one of the twenty provinces of the Persian Empire, the Sacae were required to send Darius a tax contribution of 250 talents a year and a number of troops for his army.

The Greeks called all Persians Medes, the name of the people of Media, the first state to become a Persian province when Cyrus the Great began his historic expansion by conquest. The Medes were a people with much in common with the Persians. Both lived in the same area, and both shared the same language and the habit of wearing their hair long, as opposed to most Greeks' custom of cutting their hair short. Herodotus described the long-haired native Persian troops of this time as being clad in their typical battledress—tunics with long, multicolored sleeves and small fish-scale iron armor fastened to the cloth around the torso, plus long trousers. Many also wore rich gold jewelry. On their heads, the Persians wore soft turbans called tiaras, the origin of the term for the bejewelled headdress familiar to us today.

Persian frontline infantrymen carried large but light rectangular shields made from woven wicker. These men were armed with short jabbing spears. In the ranks behind them stood bowmen, each with a large leather quiver on his back, packed with dozens of arrows. The Sacae were easily identified by their tall stiff felt hats, which rose to a point. These men wore no armor, and their weapons were the bow and arrow, a battleaxe called the *sagaris*, and a dagger sheathed at their waist. Compared to Greek hoplites, Persian foot soldiers could be classified as "light infantry."

As the Greeks troops came at them at speed across the plain of Marathon, the Persians and Sacae standing in good order in their battle lines behind the initial shield line filled their bows with arrows, then raised them toward the heavens. The running charge of the Greeks had caught them off guard, as Miltiades had hoped and expected. Bowmen in these times didn't shoot their arrows flat and level at their target like modern competitive archers. Once their opponents were about 150 yards away, they fired into the air, so that the arrows rained down like hail onto the heads of the approaching troops. The Persian and Sacae archers were expert at calculating where a marching enemy army would be between the time they loosed off their arrows and when those arrows rained to earth. The only problem today was that the Greeks were crossing the open ground much more quickly than the Persians and Sacae expected.

Quite probably, it was the task of master bowmen in the Persian and Sacae ranks to call out the range for each volley fired. But now those range-callers were suddenly trumped by Miltiades's tactic. Perhaps there was only time for one or two volleys to be sent into the air before the charging Greeks collided with the Persian front line. By that stage, the running Greeks had lifted their shields above their heads to protect heads and shoulders from falling arrows. Only at the last moment would the men at the front of their charge bring their shields down in front of them.

With a *thwack* of bronze shield meeting wicker shield, the two frontlines joined. Now, while some men would fall in both frontlines, claimed by the thrust of spear and the blow of ax from opponents immediately in front of them, the battle came down to a giant pushing match, as each bunched army attempted to push the other back while thousands of voices yelled in numerous tongues. Here and there a man would scream as a spear point punctured his face, took out an eye, or plunged into his throat.

In the center of the battle, the weight of numbers soon told. The thinned Athenian lines began to give ground against superior opposition numbers. Before long, the Athenian center gave way altogether, and Persians and Sacae pressed the slowly backpedaling Athenians across the plain, step by battling step. In the thick of the fight, an Athenian named Epizelus stood his ground and valiantly fought off the enemy. Suddenly, he was struck partially blind, without being hit by either sword or spear. Through the mist that now cloaked his eyes, Epizelus saw a huge enemy warrior with a massive beard appear in front of him. For a moment, Epizelus was certain that he was about to die at the hands of the giant. But the Persian ignored him, and with a mighty sword blow cut down the Athenian fighting at Epizelus's side, then moved on. Epizelus would survive the battle, although he never regained his sight. In later life he would tell the tale of his miraculous survival on the field of Marathon to all who would listen. It would come to the ears of the historian Herodotus, perhaps from Epizelus himself, when Herodotus visited Athens some decades after the battle.

The Athenian center drew back into the plain like an outgoing tide, and the Persians and Sacae followed. But, at the same time, the Athenians and Plataeans on the two wings gained the advantage over the troops opposing them, and were pushing them back toward the sea. While the Persians and Sacae pursued the Greek center, the Greeks on the wings outflanked their opposite numbers. The Greeks believed that in times of war their war god Ares came to the battlefield accompanied by his sister Strife (Eris) and his sons Panic and Rout (Phobos and Deimos). On this day, while Strife had affected the Athenian center, Panic and Rout took hold on the Persian wings.

On both wings, the Persian allied troops broke, and fled toward the water and the ships still drawn up on the beach, hoping for refuge and escape. Led by Callimachus the war archon, Greeks and Plataeans of the two wings linked up and chased the enemy all the way. They cut many down before they could reach the ships, especially once the terrified men already aboard the ships drew up their boarding ladders. Other vessels pulled frantically away from the shore and out onto the bay. In this way several thousand Persian troops were able to escape, but thousands more were stranded onshore. With their backs to the bay and nowhere left to flee, they had to fight, and die, at the water's edge.

"Fire!" yelled Athenian commanders, who wanted to set alight the Persian ships still beached and with several thousand men aboard flinging spears and firing arrows at the Athenians. "Bring fire!"

But even as messengers set off to find their way through the chaos that was the battlefield to collect burning torches from the Athenian camp in the hills, where the noncombatants anxiously awaited news of the battle's outcome, it was realized that this would take too long. If any of these Persian ships were to be prevented from departing, it would only be by boarding and seizing them. Many Athenians cast their spears at the enemy then began climbing up beached sterns to board and capture the ships.

One of the Greeks to attempt this was Cynaegirus, brother of Aeschylus. In the combined Athenian-Plataean force on the Greek left wing, both brothers had joined the surge after the fleeing enemy that ended on the beach. Cynaegirus succeeded in climbing up high enough to gain a grip on the elegant, curved stern ornament of one ship. It may have been an Egyptian ship, which carried marines equipped with pole-axes. For, out of the blue, an enemy ax came crashing down and severed Cynaegirus's right hand at the wrist as it gripped the stern ornament.

Cynaegirus fell back, crashing onto Greeks behind and below him. We don't know whether he died as a result of this fall, or from loss of blood flowing from his savage wound, but perish there on the Marathon shore he did. His brother Aeschylus now performed a deed of great valor. We know this from Aeschylus's later tombstone, but the precise nature of that deed is not recorded. Aeschylus may have stood over his brother's body and defended him as he died, or fought his way onto the Persian ship. Or both.

The Greeks went to enormous lengths to recover the bodies of their fallen so that they could be given a proper funeral. They believed that the souls of men who failed to receive funeral rites were doomed to wander the earth forever. This was why, at the Battle of Thermopylae, ten years later, Spartan troops would four times attempt to recover the body of their king, Leonidas. It is likely that Aeschylus succeeded in boarding the Persian ship where his brother had failed and played a leading role in its capture.

Seven Persian ships were boarded and captured in this way, and their occupants slaughtered. Meanwhile, Miltiades, Themistocles, and Aristides had succeeded in regrouping their regiments and leading them back into the battle. Their Persian and Sacae pursuers had turned around and were fleeing back toward the shore. The Greek troops on the beach now stood between these Persian troops and escape. Caught between the two Greek forces, the fleeing enemy were cut down in their thousands. The rout became a massacre.

Modern historians estimate that the Battle of Marathon lasted little more than two hours. When the last of the Persian ships to clear the beach pulled out into the bay, the last surviving men on shore had surrendered and the killing had ended. Miltiades found to his regret that Callimachus the war archon had been killed while leading from the front. One of the Athenian regimental commanders, Stesilaus, had also fallen. But, to the astonishment of the Greeks, just one hundred and ninety-two of their number, including Callimachus and Stesilaus, had been killed in the battle.

The Persian death toll ran into the thousands. A precise body count would be made, for, prior to departing Athens, the regimental commanders had vowed to sacrifice one goat to the hunting goddess Artemis for every invader they killed. That body count would total 6,400 dead Persians troops. Such numbers had seemed impossible to the Athenians when they had embarked on this campaign. They would meet their vow, but neither religion nor the purse would be benefit from the mass slaughter of 6,400 goats. The Athenians would find a pragmatic solution, sacrificing 500 goats a year for the next thirteen years.

The battle had ended in a comprehensive Athenian victory. But the danger had not passed. The last of the escaping Persian ships were seen to turn south after leaving the bay, following the course that the bulk of the fleet had taken when departing in the night. It was obvious to Miltiades that Datis and Artaphernes were intent on landing south of Athens and striking at the city while the Athenian army was still at Marathon. Miltiades promptly instructed Aristides to remain behind with the men of his Antiochis regiment to bury the Greek dead with full funeral rites. Persian dead would be left to rot on the battlefield, with their bones much later collected and heaped up to form a victory monument. Aristides's men would also have the pleasure of counting the enemy corpses and stripping them of their equipment, valuables, and clothing, and looting the enemy camp.

Miltiades ordered the remainder of the army to march at once back to Athens, to counter the continuing Persian threat. They would have to march at forced pace if they were to reach their capital before the enemy did. As Miltiades led nine regiments and the Plataeans briskly away, Aristides and the men of his regiment reverently collected the Greek dead and gave them the required rites. They buried their bodies in a mass grave at the site of the first encounter on the plain, where most Athenians and Plataeans had fallen. Over the top of the grave they heaped a tall conical-shaped earth mound that became known as the Soros. A small hill on the plain of Marathon, that bare burial mound still stands today.

Aristides's men then moved through the Persian bodies and camp like a swarm of locusts, picking them bare. The intent was to collect the loot for the good of Athens, but few men couldn't resist the temptation to purloin something of value for himself when Aristides wasn't looking. Upright Aristides himself had no interest in profiting in the slightest from the victory, but behind his back some men displayed considerable greed. One such man was Aristides's own cousin, Callias, who was a young officer of the Antiochis regiment who was also a torch-bearer in the cult of the Eleusinian Demeter. Callias had distinguished himself in the battle, and was celebrated as the winner of both the horse race and the four-horse chariot race at the Olympic Games, apparently in 392 BC, having previously won similar victories at the biennial Pythian Games at Delphi.

Callias wore his hair longer than other Athenians, having it drawn back and tied with a band. Perhaps this was a prerogative and distinguishing mark of Olympic champions, or otherwise it was connected with his torch-bearer rank at religious ceremonies involving the Eleusinian Mysteries. Either way, because Callias's hairstyle differentiated him from the other Greek soldiers at Marathon, a senior Persian captive took him for a king. Thinking this king would spare his life if he enriched him, the Persian took Callias by the hand and led him to where a vast quantity of gold lay hidden in a ditch. Callias was well known for his avarice, and his expenditures, and when Aristides was not looking Callias killed the Persian and kept the gold. But the story would leak out, so that comic poets of Athens nicknamed Callias's family *Laccopluti*, or Enriched by the Ditch.

Another story would come down to modern times that, following the Battle of Marathon, an Athenian athlete would run the twenty-six miles over the mountains from the Marathon battlefield to Athens, to announce that the Greeks had won a great victory against the Persian invaders, before falling down dead from exhaustion. Some accounts named this athlete as Philippides, the man who had made the run to and from Sparta only days before. Based on this story, Frenchman Baron Pierre de Coubertin, founder of the modern Olympic Games, would introduce the long distance marathon run to the program of the modern Olympics, an event emulated in the streets of numerous great cities around the world since.

Because the first accounts of this Marathon run by Philippides were not published until the Roman era, by the likes of Plutarch, who had a habit of including some dubious stories in his histories and biographies, many modern scholars have dismissed the Marathon run of Philippides as nothing more than a colorful invention. They believe that Plutarch and other Roman writers were confusing this run with Philippides's earlier and much more epic run to and from Sparta. Plutarch, however, did say that his original source for this story was the fourth-century BC Greek author Heraclides Ponticos. Our only detailed source for details of the Battle of Marathon is Herodotus, who is likely to have spoken personally with Athenian veterans of the battle in later years. He never mentions Philippides again after his Spartan run, and makes no mention of the run to Athens from the Marathon battlefield.

Still, that does not preclude Philippides from having made a run from Marathon with the news of the victory. It is easy to believe that the combined strains of the Spartan run, the battle, and then a run to Athens would have killed even the fittest of runners. And it is logical to suspect that Miltiades, as he ordered nine of his regiments to accompany him back to Athens at forced march pace, would have sent a runner on ahead to pass on news of the Athenian victory to the tens of thousands of waiting Athenians.

Miltiades would have worried that the peace party at Athens—those who had always been in favor of submitting to the Persians—on receiving reports that the Persian fleet was approaching or had anchored in Phalerum Bay, and assuming that the Athenian army at Marathon had been destroyed, might send envoys to Datis and Artaphernes to negotiate the city's surrender. To prevent such a surrender, it was vital that a runner reach the archons at Athens with the news that the Athenian army had been victorious. So, an athlete quite possibly did make a run from Marathon to Athens. And who better to entrust with this mission than Philippides, the man who had successfully undertaken the much longer run to and from Sparta?

Meanwhile, Miltiades and his troops were marching as fast as they could back to Athens. There has been some disagreement among scholars as to which route, mountain or coastal, the Athenians and Plataeans took on this forced march, although it has been suggested that the army may have split in two and used both routes. Whichever route or routes they used, by the early afternoon Miltiades and his army were outside Athens, despite having just run a mile, fought a battle, and marched at speed for a minimum of four hours. They made camp at another grove of Hercules, this one at Cynosarges. On a riverbank on the southwest outskirts of Athens, this was the site of the gymnasium of Hercules where Themistocles daily trained. Most important, the site overlooked Phalerum Bay. And as the hoplites wearily laid out their camp and the lookouts took up the watch, there was no sign of Persian ships on the waters of the bay. The Greeks had won the race to Phalerum Bay.

About an hour later, Datis and Artaphernes arrived with the lead elements of the Persian fleet to find, to their astonishment, that the Athenian army was encamped close by, intact and ready to oppose any attempt by his troops to land. The Persian oarsmen were exhausted after rowing all the way down the coast at speed, so Datis and Artaphernes now allowed their men to rest at their oars as he surveyed the scene on shore.

The Persian commanders' elderly chief advisor Hippias, the aristocratic Athenian defector, is likely to have advised them to abort the mission and go home. Little more than a week before this, Hippias had returned to Attica full of hopes of regaining his Athenian throne. The night before he had landed at Marathon with the Persian invasion force, he had dreamed that he was lying in his late mother's arms. Highly superstitious, he took this to mean he would soon be reclaimed by mother Athens, city of his birth. But the next day, while he was on the beach marshaling the landing Persian army, he sneezed, with such force that he lost a loose tooth, which fell somewhere on the sand. When his attendants could not find the tooth, the old man took this as an ill omen, and lost heart in the entire enterprise. Overcome by depression, he declared that the land did not belong to the invaders, and never would. His only share of this land, he lamented, would be that infinitesimal piece covered by his lost tooth.

Perhaps Datis and Artaphernes were influenced by Hippias's negativity. But they had lost their best Persian and Sacae troops at Marathon, and were sensibly wary of landing with their reduced force in the face of the waiting Athenian army, an army buoyed by that morning's victory. Attempting a landing in the prevailing circumstances risked being overwhelmed as the Persian force straggled ashore. Datis and Artaphernes decided to withdraw. A signal was passed among the ships, and, once the rowers had rested, the invasion fleet put to sea and headed back to Asia Minor. There, Datis and Artaphernes would courageously report to King Darius, and admit that they had failed him, and that the Persian army had suffered a great defeat at the hands of the Greeks. We never again hear of Datis. At best, Darius permitted him to go into retirement. Artaphernes would reemerge as a Persian military leader a decade after this failed campaign.

Just days after the Athenian victory at Marathon, and in the wake of the full moon, an army of 2,000 Spartans marched up to the gates of Athens. Sparta was keeping her word to support the Athenians against the Persians. After digesting the amazing news of the Athenian success, the Spartans, most of whom had never laid their eyes on a Persian in their lives, asked to see the site of the battle and the sight of the Persian dead. Athenian leaders proudly conducted the Spartans to Marathon. There the visitors paid their respects to the Athenian and Plataean dead at the Soros, and surveyed the plain and beach littered with the naked bodies of thousands of bloating Persians and their allies. After giving the Athenians fulsome praise for their victory, the Spartans marched back the way they had come and returned home again.

The Athenians had not only won a battle, they had also won a war, and saved Athens. Miltiades had led the outnumbered Athenians and Plataeans in an astonishing campaign, becoming the first Greeks to defeat the Persians. Some scholars would declare that Greek independence was founded on the field of Marathon. Some would even consider this a turning point in history. As comprehensive and surprising as the victory at Marathon was, that description, of a turning point in history, should probably more rightly be reserved for a battle a decade later, when Themistocles would be the hero of Athens.

But at this moment, it was Miltiades who rightfully won the praise, and the glory, for masterminding and leading the victory at Marathon. A monument would be erected to him at Marathon, another at Delphi—probably in or near the Doric temple erected by Athens at

Delphi following the Battle of Marathon. Within the mountainside sanctuary of the Oracle of Delphi and called the Treasury of Athens, this temple contained thanks offerings to Apollo and was built specifically by the Athenians to commemorate their victory at Marathon. That temple stands today at the Delphi sanctuary after being rebuilt early in the twentieth century, beside the Sacred Way and just below the temple terrace.

Miltiades himself probably dedicated his shield to the goddess Artemis, hanging it in her temple at Athens, as many other heroes of Marathon would do. And he definitely sent or took his helmet to Olympia, where he dedicated it to Zeus, king of the gods, at the Temple of Zeus. We know this because, in modern times that helmet, with its dedicatory inscription, was found at Olympia. And when Miltiades's term as regimental commander ended, he stood for reelection, and the grateful people of Athens voted him back into the generalship for a fourth consecutive term.

Themistocles had survived the battle, and joined in all the thanksgiving and celebrations at Athens following the retreat of the Persians. He had fought honorably and well, but the fact that his regiment had buckled during the initial stages of the battle meant that he was not going to be hailed a hero the way that Miltiades was. As the deeds of Miltiades occupied the lips of all in Athens, Themistocles, who hungered for glory, was quiet and reserved, and kept away from the gymnasium and his other usual haunts. At night, he tossed in his bed for days after the battle. Finally, a friend asked what was troubling him.

"The trophy of Miltiades will not let me sleep," Themistocles replied. That trophy was the glory of victory at Marathon.

Themistocles was not the only great general in history to lament, in his thirties and prior to obtaining his greatest victories, that others had achieved what he sorely wanted for himself. Four hundred and twenty-nine years after this, Julius Caesar was aged thirty-eight when he received his first appointment of note, that of governor of the Roman province of Baetia in western Spain. On a visit to the Spanish city of Cadiz shortly after he took up his appointment, Caesar came upon a statue of Alexander the Great, and, to the astonishment of his staff, burst into tears. When asked what was wrong, Caesar replied that, before Alexander had reached Caesar's age, he had conquered much of the known world, and here he, Caesar, was, in a backwater with no great achievements to boast of.

Just as Caesar's glorious military career then lay several years ahead of him, so too would Themistocles have to wait for his chance at glory. If Themistocles had known that an even greater trophy than victory at Marathon awaited him, albeit after a lengthy delay, he might have slept a little better in 490 BC.

5.

Turning to the Sea

The joy at Athens following the Battle at Marathon was unbounded. Not only had Athens won a great victory, but most Athenians were also convinced that this had put an end to the war with the Persians. Themistocles, however, counseled caution. As he was to demonstrate in the coming years, he had great insight into human nature. And he could not see the king of Persia, with all his ambition and resources, accepting the defeat at Marathon as anything more than the loss of round one in a longer contest.

"This is only the beginning of far greater conflicts," he warned.

But Themistocles's critics would only dismiss him as a spoilsport trying to lessen Miltiades's glory, while his friends could see no downside to victory. Miltiades was the darling of Athens. His renown was so great, the gratitude of the Athenian people so effusive, and their confidence in him so complete, that he could do no wrong in his countrymen's eyes. So when, on the heels of the Battle of Marathon, Miltiades asked the council to provide him with seventy trireme warships and thousands of men to man them, for a secret mission of conquest, the council eagerly granted his request despite not knowing what that mission was to be. That council was led by the newly elected chief archon for the year, none other than Aristides the Just. The Athenians were, said Herodotus, quite carried away with enthusiasm for the project, particularly when Miltiades promised that every man who took part in the mission would come away from it with more plundered gold than he could carry.

According to Thucydides, who was born several decades later, the permanent Athenian navy at this point consisted merely of a few pente-conters, slow old fifty-oared ships. Athens could now add the seven triremes captured from the Persians at Marathon to her small fleet. So, it seems that, over the winter of 490–489 BC, to give Miltiades the total of seventy triremes he'd requested, sixty-three brand-new triremes were constructed, ready for launching in the spring. It is possible that Themistocles's father may have been one of the contractors used for this shipbuilding task.

Once all seventy ships were equipped and manned, Miltiades sailed them away, on his secret mission. Buoyed by his stunning military success at Marathon, Miltiades had decided to conquer the island of Paros in the Cyclades group. His excuse for attacking Paros was that it had aided the Persians in their invasion of Attica. In fact, the Parians had sent just a single warship to sail with Datis's fleet. The real reason for Miltiades's campaign against the island, apart from the expectation of easy plunder, was supposedly the fact that he had a grudge against a Parian leader who had spoken ill of him to the Persians in the past.

The Athenian expeditionary force landed on the island unopposed. But, despite taking some prisoners and laying waste to the island's farms, the Athenians were unable to prevent most of the population from holing up behind the walls of the city of Paros and closing their gates. After surrounding the city, Miltiades demanded 100 talents in gold. But the Parians refused point-blank to pay up, or to even negotiate. Instead, each night, they industriously beavered away unseen, adding to the walls, until they had doubled their former height. For more than three weeks, Miltiades lay siege to the Parians, hoping to starve them out. Then, one of the Parian prisoners, a woman named Timo, asked for an audience with him, saying that she was an underpriestess at the island's Temple of Ceres and had vital information for him.

When Timo came to Miltiades, she told him that, if he was seri-ous about capturing Paros, he should follow a suggestion from her. After Timo had whispered her advice to him, Miltiades took himself to a hill in front of the city of Paros, where there was a sanctuary and temple dedicated to Ceres, an earth goddess. The door in the wall surrounding the sanctuary was locked, so Miltiades athletically scaled the wall, then made his way to the temple entrance. But, according to the Parians, as he was about to go inside, a feeling of horror overcame him, and he retraced his steps to the wall. It's possible that Miltiades simply failed to find whatever Timo had told him he would find there. He probably expected to locate a secret tunnel connecting the temple with the city—in Athens, just such a secret entrance provided access to the top of the Acropolis via a temple below the outcrop.

After clambering up the wall, Miltiades jumped down to the ground outside. But he landed badly, cracking his knee on the rocky ground. He limped back to his headquarters without accomplishing his mission. Later, Timo would be charged by her people with giving information to the enemy. But she would be exonerated after claiming she had deliberately lured Miltiades to the Temple of Ceres, knowing that the goddess she served would punish Miltiades there.

Miltiades's damaged knee would trouble him greatly. Bereft of modern medical knowledge, he could do nothing to treat it, and eventually gangrene would set in. His injury ended a twenty-six-day siege that had accomplished little and cost a great deal. Miltiades called off the little invasion and sailed the fleet back to Athens. His inglorious return, without a military victory and minus the horde of gold he had guaranteed, surprised his fans and armed his critics. Led by his political rival Xanthippus, those critics called for Miltiades's impeachment for his Parian failure, and he was ordered to face a hearing before the governing council and the people of Athens. The charge was of having dealt deceitfully with the Athenians. It carried a death sentence.

Miltiades was now so debilitated as a result of the spreading gangrene he had to be carried into the council chamber for his trial. He lay on a couch throughout, in great pain, and was so unwell that he was unable to conduct his own defense; several friends acted as his advocates. They spoke of the great things Miltiades had done for Athens, of his brilliant generalship and personal courage at Marathon. They also reminded their listeners that, some years before, Miltiades had led an independent force that had captured the island of Lemnos, which he had then handed over to Athenian control. The council still found Miltiades guilty as charged, especially as his ill-advised Parian venture had cost the Athenian treasury a small fortune. But in recognition of the service he had done the city in the past, the council commuted his death sentence to a fine, of fifty talents, in an attempt to recoup the cost of the Parian campaign.

Miltiades, it turned out, was close to broke. It was clear now that he had hoped to rebuild his personal fortune with the Paros venture. Unable to pay his fine, he was locked away in prison. It now fell to his son, the eighteen-year-old Cimon, to find the money. But while Cimon was trying to raise the vast sum, his father died an agonizing death in prison. That was not the end to the matter. The father's debt now fell on the son's shoulders. Miltiades's children were just as impoverished as their father. There was not even enough money for Cimon's unmarried sister Elpinice to have a home of her own, and she lived under Cimon's roof. This caused a scandal, with gossips accusing Cimon and his sister of sleeping together.

It now looked as if Cimon, unable to find the fifty talents to pay his late father's fine, would also end up in prison. But now he came up with a solution. He offered Elpinice's hand in marriage to a rich suitor—none other than Aristides's cousin Callias, he who had been enriched by the ditch. Callias, a widower, agreed, paid off the fifty-talent debt, and took Elpinice as his wife. Elpinice married Callias without complaint and would be a loyal supporter of her brother Cimon for the rest of her days.

The conviction of Miltiades was a graphic example of how a powerful and famous Athenian could be pulled down by a vote of his peers, and it encouraged some of the city's more venal politicians to turn to a previously unused mechanism to remove their leading opponents from power. Back in 508–507 BC, when Hippias had been driven out of Athens and democracy instituted, one of the new laws enacted at that time had been a provision that allowed for a wrongdoer to be exiled from Athens for ten years on the majority vote of his fellow citizens. This was called "ostracism," after the ostraca, a shell on which, initially, each man wrote his vote.

Ostracism had lain dormant on the statute books for two decades until, in the spring of 488 BC, the year after the demise of Miltiades and about two years after the Battle of Marathon, it was employed for the first time. Ostracism would become an established part of Athenian political life for several decades to come, and would have a major influence on the life of Themistocles. Some historians have suggested that he was actually behind its implementation, giving him a tool for the removal of aristocratic opponents. Conversely, others have suggested that it was the aristocrats who first promoted ostracism, in an attempt to rid themselves of opponents like Themistocles.

Under the law of ostracism, the names of several leading Athenian politicians were put forward, and the tribes voted. Classical writers make clear that the number 6,000 was central to the ostracism vote, but scholars have been divided as to whether this meant that a minimum of 6,000 votes needed to be cast in the plebiscite for the ostracism to be enacted, or whether it was necessary for a nominee to receive at least 6,000 votes to be sent into exile. Recent archaeological finds suggest it was the former.

The voting was supervised by the archons who had been appointed for the year and the entire Council of 500, which had voted in January to implement an ostracism vote in the spring. In March, citizens were required to go to Athens's agora, the market place, which had been fenced off with high wooden palings for the vote. Ten entrances had been left in this wooden wall, one for the exclusive use of each tribe. Citizens filed into the market place and cast their votes by depositing an ostraca bearing the name of a candidate they wished to see exiled. This was of course a vote that a candidate did not want to win.

Although the original plan had been for votes to be written on seashells, by the time that ostracism was first implemented a potsherd, a broken piece of pottery, was used. These were deposited face down by the voters. In addition to the name of the man they wished to see ostracized, many voters also wrote a curse or negative comment about the candidate, or even included rough caricatures of them in Persian dress. These ostraca were subsequently divided by the magistrates into piles of 100 for each candidate as the count proceeded, with the result subsequently announced to the gathered citizenry.

In this first ostracism vote in 488 BC, Hipparchus, brother-in-law of the old tyrant Hippias, was voted into exile. An archon in 496–495, Hipparchus was accused of having been the leader of the friends of the tyrants in Athens. The exile of an ostracised man did not involve any financial penalty—he could retain all his property—and he could choose where outside Athens he removed himself to for the next decade. Six or seven years later the law would be tightened by the addition of geographical boundaries that kept the victim well away from Athens.

With this precedent established, the ostracism vote became an annual event at Athens, with any politician who flew too high liable to have his wings clipped. The year after Hipparchus was exiled, Themistocles found himself one of those nominated for ostracism. Themistocles had not been elected to any public office since the Battle of Marathon, but he had been vocal in the Areopagus council about the ongoing threat posed by the Persian Empire. According to Plutarch, Themistocles kept himself and men of the city—almost certainly the lower classes—in constant and proper training for the battles against the Persians that he was convinced lay ahead. His aristocratic enemies labeled him a friend of the tyrants and probably insinuated that he was leading this military training with a view to himself becoming a tyrant of Athens. Another of the candidates for ostracism that year of 487 BC was a noble by the name of Megacles, a longtime supporter of the Alcmaeonids, the family of the former tyrants.

In recent times, in 1938, and again in 1965 and 1966, archaeologists unearthed thousands of buried potsherds in Athens bearing the names of Themistocles and other leading politicians of his day. The more recent finds were at the agora of ancient Athens and in a cemetery in the old potters' quarter. These potsherds all date back to the fifth century BC, and the agora and potters' quarter ostraca clearly had been used in the ostracism election of 487 BC, for they bore the names of Megacles, Themistocles, and other political leaders.

A fierce war of words would have been waged between the supporters of the candidates before polling day came around. In the end, Themistocles's supporters held sway. Megacles was voted into exile and sent away for ten years. In the agora and potters quarter potsherd finds, a total of approximately 4,650 votes were cast for Megacles and 1,696 for Themistocles. Another candidate was Callias. He had previously been married to a daughter of Megacles. Although that wife had apparently died, most likely in childbirth, as so many women unfortunately did in classical times, Callias seems to have been painted with the same brush as his former father-in-law. He received 790 votes. Callias's new brother-in-law, young Cimon, was also a candidate this year, apparently for his connection to Callias, but only a small number of ostraca were cast bearing his name.

During that same year of 486 BC, several key events occurred. First, the way that Athens's nine archons were annually appointed changed. Now, a panel of citizens was elected, and this panel chose nine of its members by lot to fill the archonships. No longer could a candidate stand for election to a particular portfolio. This lessened the power of the archons and the attraction of standing for election to the archonship. From now on, the ten elected regimental commanders had much more influence, particularly with, in the wake of Marathon, Athens seeing itself as a formidable military power. In 486 BC, too, Persia's King Darius died after a reign of sixty-three years. He was succeeded by Xerxes, his thirty-three-year-old son and eldest boy by influential second wife, Atossa, who was a daughter of Cyrus the Great, founder of the Persian Empire.

Word reached Athens that the new Persian king, Xerxes, was not warm to the idea of going to war against the Greeks to avenge the loss at Marathon, even when it was advocated by members of his court. This only encouraged the Athenian critics of Themistocles, who would cite this as proof that Themistocles didn't know what he was talking about. For, Themistocles didn't cease to warn his fellow Athenians that Persia was still a threat, despite the death of Darius. Themistocles was well aware that there were a number of Greeks at Xerxes's court, including a former king of Sparta who had influenced Darius's selection of Xerxes as his successor. Themistocles, that excellent judge of human nature, knew that such men wouldn't relent in their advocacy of a Persian invasion of Greece, for they were intent on reclaiming their own lost power. As a result of the change at the top in Persia, most Athenians dismissed the Persians from their thoughts and fears. But not Themistocles.

Meanwhile, the political jostling, and the annual ostracisms, continued in Athens. The results of Athens's ostracism vote of the year following Megacles's banishment are unknown, but in the next electoral year, that of 485–484 BC, the politician to be exiled was Xanthippus, another whose family connections put him at the head of supporters of past Athenian tyrants—he was related by marriage to the previously ostracized Megacles. It would not have escaped many voters, either, that Xanthippus had led the prosecution of Miltiades, hero of Marathon, four years before.

Year after year, Themistocles had been able to muster sufficient support among the working classes to defeat every attempt by the aristocrats to have him exiled. The nobles simply could not muster the numbers to have this annoying commoner removed. Meanwhile, ostracism votes had seen several of Themistocles's leading opponents literally sent packing. In his personal life, Thermistocles had also prospered. His wife Archippe, daughter of wealthy Athenian nobleman Lysandros of the Alopece deme, had brought him a certain respectability among the elite and had borne him five sons, although the eldest had been killed when kicked by a horse. Themistocles's finances had also improved significantly; his wife would have brought him a large dowry, and he had received many gifts from admirers. Made parsimonious by years of scrimping when younger, when these gifts involved foodstuffs he would sell them. Yet he was clearly and unquestioningly the voice of Athens's commoners and had a large following with the ordinary people.

By 483 BC, Themistocles was feeling politically impregnable and able to push forward with his pet policy, that of turning Athens into a sea power. With the threat from Persia seemingly removed with the death of Darius—although Themistocles himself was still wary of Persian expansionism—Themistocles focused Athenian attention on an old enemy, the island of Aegina in the Saronic Gulf. On Athens's doorstep, this irritating and undemocratic adversary was located just twenty miles to the south. The island could actually be seen from Athens's Acropolis.

Despite a population of just forty thousand, 25 percent of that in Athens, Aegina had grown extremely wealthy on maritime trade, helped in no small part by the fact that it had been granted exclusive rights to a trading post on the River Nile in Egypt. As a result of its trade, Aegina had standardized the Greek system of weights and measures. Money poured into the island. So much money, in fact, that one of Aegina's leading merchants was considered the richest man in all Greece, and other merchants on the island were similarly wealthy. To protect its trade, its wealth, and itself, Aegina had become a sea power with an effective war fleet of dozens of triremes. Aegina had been in conflict with Athens for two decades. To rub salt into the festering wound, in the lead-up to the Battle of Marathon, the Aeginetans had expressed submission to Persia.

To become a sea power that could contend with rich Aegina, Athens needed a navy, with a large number of fighting ships and trained crews. The means to finance that navy now materialized. For many years, silver had been mined at Laurium, near where Themistocles had been born and raised, with the profits coming to Athens. Prisoners, such as those taken at the Battle of Marathon, worked these mines. In 483 BC, a large new silver strike was made at Laurium, in hills just to the south of Themistocles's hometown. Although privately operated, the rich new underground mines yielded a royalty of one hundred talents in silver annually to the city of Athens. A proposal was brought into the Athenian assembly that every Athenian citizen receive a payment of ten drachmas a year from these mining profits. Ten drachmas was not a vast sum; enough to purchase an ox, for example. Who tabled this proposal for universal distribution of the silver bounty is unknown, but it may have been Aristides.

Alternatively, this windfall of one hundred talents offered the source of funding that Thermistocles's naval plan required. So, Themistocles made a counterproposal to the assembly, that the one hundred talents from the mines not be distributed among the citizenry, but be used to pay for the construction of one hundred triremes for a powerful navy for Athens, a navy to be used against old enemy Aegina, which had several times humiliated Athens in the past with her maritime superiority. To make it clear that he was not trying to siphon off the money for himself, Themistocles proposed that the hundred talents be distributed among one hundred leading citizens, and that each be held responsible for the construction of one new trireme.

The idea was imaginative, it would give Athens a powerful weapon against Aegina and other foes, and it contained a wise safeguard via the use of the one hundred leading citizens as administrators of the project.

Despite all these attributes, Aristides led vehement opposition to the whole idea, and time and again he and Themistocles clashed in council meetings, as they always had in the past. Aristides had a reputation as a man who always followed the straight and narrow course; yet to beat Themistocles he had others advocate initiatives in council that were in fact his own, believing that Thermistocles would oppose any idea of his on principle, just as he himself always opposed the initiatives of Themistocles. Aristides's purpose, said Plutarch, was to ensure that Themistocles did not increase his influence, and he didn't hesitate to interfere whenever he saw Themistocles urging all kinds of enterprises and innovations on the people of Athens. To Aristides, the old ways had served Athens well in the past, and he simply could not see why Athenians should change and build a navy.

Neither was Aristides's opposition to Themistocles's naval plan motivated by a desire to pocket the additional money from the silver mines himself, even though he clearly could have benefited from a cash injection. When, one cold winter's day, he was seen to be going about the city in a woollen cloak that was threadbare, his friends became so angry with his rich cousin Callias that they called Callias before the council and publicly admonished him for not helping out his relative. Callias replied that he had many times offered Aristides money, and, every time, Aristides had rejected his help. Aristides himself had risen to confirm his cousin's claim.

Aristides opposed Themistocles's naval proposal because he genuinely believed the worst of Themistocles, genuinely believed that any attempt to turn Athenians into seamen would rob Athens of her army and make her defenseless. After one bruising council meeting in which the pair had clashed, Aristides said to a colleague, "Unless they send both Themistocles and myself to the Barathrum (the repository for the bodies of criminals not far from Themistocles's house), there can be no safety for Athens."

Cimon, the son of Miltiades, also opposed Thermistocles's naval plan. One of Athens's elite, he had no interest in the sea and was for a strong Athenian land army. He was no doubt influenced in this view by his late father's great land victory at Marathon, a battle Cimon had missed because he'd been a year short of military age at the time.

Now aged twenty-five, Cimon was still five years short of being able to stand for election to office or sit on either of the city's councils. Nonetheless, he allied himself to Aristides in this bitter policy contest with Themistocles, publicly advocating Aristides's view and pouring scorn on Themistocles's naval proposal.

When nominations for ostracism were called this January, not surprisingly both Aristides's and Themistocles's names were put forward by those who opposed each of them. If Themistocles was to see his naval plan and vision for a mighty Athens approved, he had to avoid ostracism and ensure that Aristides was sent into exile. To achieve that, Themistocles had a story spread among all the propaganda by both sides in the lead-up to the March vote. According to this story, when Aristides was an archon he had held court sittings in his own home, away from public scrutiny, and was secretly making way for a monarchy where he would rule Athens as king. Some historians have been critical of Themistocles for this, although none have denied that Aristides may well have flouted convention by holding private court sessions and denying litigants full transparency. As shown by one ostraca that survives from this vote, Aristides was also accused of being a "Mede," a supporter of the Persians. A groundless smear by his opponents, it would appear.

That the opponents of Themistocles also played dirty in this vote became clear only in recent times. In the 1930s, a collection of 191 ostraca was found in an ancient well on the north side of the Acropolis. All these ostraca bear the name of Themistocles. A close study by experts has shown that these ostraca had been inscribed by only fourteen hands, not 191. This led archaeologists to conclude that the ostraca had either been prepared by fourteen men who supported the aristocratic party opposed to Themistocles, to be handed to voters on their way to cast their vote, or were intended to be used to "stuff the ballot box" with false votes. As these ostraca were found a considerable distance from the polling area of the agora, the consensus among archaeologists is that the latter was the intent, and that the plan went awry or someone had cold feet, and the ostraca were hastily dumped into the then-working well and never used.

A story would be told by Plutarch in his *Aristides* that on voting day Aristides was approached by an illiterate man who, not recognizing him, asked him to write on his ostraca for him.

When Aristides asked the man what name he wanted him to write, the fellow replied, "Aristides."

"Oh?" said Aristides. "Has Aristides ever done you any harm?"

"None at all," came the reply. "I don't know the man, but I'm tired of hearing him all over the place being called "the Just"!"

Aristides duly wrote his own name on the ostraca as requested, and handed it back to the man, who cast his vote.

The result of this vote was resounding. Aristides the Just received by far the most votes, and was sent into exile for ten years. As he departed Athens, Aristides reportedly raised his hands to heaven and prayed that the Athenians would not forget him. He chose as his place of exile the nearby island of Aegina, enemy of Athens and the very place that Themistocles wanted to arm Athens against. Because Aristides had opposed Themistocles's naval plans, which were publicly directed at Aegina, the islanders welcomed the exiled Athenian as a friend and ally. Exiles did generally take refuge in cities that were on unfriendly terms with their home cities, but it is striking that Aristides chose as his place of exile a place that was then in an ongoing state of war with Athens. Some would have deemed it a treasonous act.

As Aristides sailed away to Aegina, Themistocles's naval proposal aimed against Aegina was approved by the assembly at Athens. A decree was issued announcing that one hundred talents would be directed from the city's silver mine income for the construction of one hundred triremes. And all Athenians of military age were required henceforth to train to man those ships. Not only did Themistocles see his measure approved, he also personally dictated the design and construction of the new warships, doing so with particular care, according to Plutarch.

Above all, Themistocles wanted these ships to be the fastest triremes on the seas. This would enable them to respond quickly to enemy threats by covering distances in record time, and in battle would ensure they could attack at high speed and maneuver and wheel about with ease. To create the fastest, most maneuverable triremes afloat, Themistocles specified that the ships of Athens's new fleet be especially narrow and sleek, and that instead of being decked over for their full length, as was the custom, they were only to have small decks fore and aft, making them lighter than the usual warship of their size. Where Themistocles came by his knowledge of warship construction can only be guessed at. Once again, it might be speculated that his chief influencer was his father, who was still alive at this time and would in fact live for some years yet.

After advocating a focus on the sea for a decade or more, Themistocles was seeing his dream realized. Athens's navy was under construction. And just in time.

6.

The Persians are Coming

When the year 482 BC arrived, thirty-eight-year-old Xerxes, son of the late King Darius and ruler of the Persian Empire for almost two years, controlled a domain that stretched from the Nile to the Danube, the Oxus to the Indus. His twenty subservient provinces delivered him a massive annual "tribute," or taxation, and provided him with an almost unlimited source of manpower for his army. Xerxes had never forgotten his father's humiliation as a result of the defeat at Marathon at the hands of the Athenians. And once Xerxes had put down a revolt in Egypt that had broken out even while his father was still alive, Xerxes finally bowed to pressure from members of his court and turned his attention to avenging the Persian loss at Marathon and to bringing all Greece under his power.

Xerxes had plenty of foreign advisors who would urge him to proceed with this Greek campaign. Old Hippias, former tyrant of Athens, had died since Marathon. But his sons were at the Persian court, and, with an eye on the Athenian throne their father had hankered after reclaiming, they would have urged the Persian monarch to invade Attica. Then there was Demaratus, former king of Sparta, who had influenced Darius's choice of Xerxes as his successor. Demaratus wanted his Spartan throne back, and the best way to achieve that would be by convincing Xerxes to invade all of Greece. All these Greek advisors would have reminded Xerxes that the next quadrennial Olympic Games were coming up at Olympia in August, 480 BC, and that would be an ideal time to invade Greece, when the Greeks were preoccupied with preparations for the games.

Now, once Xerxes had made up his mind to go forward with the Greek campaign, he summoned all the rulers of his various dominions to his summer capital, Susa. Those rulers came from as far away as India and North Africa, and included a solitary female, the enigmatic Queen Artemisia of Halicarnassus, today's city of Bodrom in western Turkey. Queen Artemisia was unique in those times, and rare in history. She had inherited her little kingdom when her husband died. In addition to the port city of Halicarnassus, which had been founded long before by Greek settlers, that kingdom included the nearby islands of Cos and Nisyrus (modern Nisiri), and the mainland city of Calydna in Caria.

Queen Artemisia, who was named after the Greek goddess Artemis, had a son and heir, Pisindelis, who was now about twenty and had probably accompanied her to Susa from Halicarnassus for the grand council of Persian leaders with Xerxes. As women in classical times often had children when they were as young as thirteen, and frequently when in their teens, it is likely that Artemisia was only in her thirties at this time. We do not know what Artemisia looked like, but events were to show that she had a powerful personality and a wise head on her shoulders. King Xerxes was, we are told by Herodotus, impressed by the queen and had considerable time for her, and her views, which was unusual in a time when women were generally neither seen nor heard in the corridors of power.

Xerxes himself is shown on statues, engravings, and coins as tall and slim, with an intricate bob of a hairdo topped by a large crown. He had a long nose and face, his beard was long and shaped, and he wore richly embroidered robes that fell to the floor. Typically, he is shown with a scepter in one hand and a bow in the other. Once his vassals had gathered in his audience hall at Susa, Xerxes, seated on a golden throne topped by a canopy, delivered a long address. Speaking in Persian, he began by saying that ever since he had taken his throne he had mused on what deed he could perform that would enable him to equal his illustrious forebears. He then announced that he intended to throw a bridge across the Hellespont, and then march an army across that bridge and lead it against Greece.

This announcement would have brought gasps from his royal audience. The Hellespont, or the Sea of Helles, known today as the Dardanelles, is that channel that separates Asia Minor from Europe and links the Aegean and Black seas. On the European side stood the Greek-settled city of Byzantium—later Constantinople, and later still Istanbul. While it's likely that the kings and queen suspected, or had been alerted by friends at court that Xerxes was planning to launch the military campaign against Athens that Darius had planned, they would have expected another amphibious operation such as those of 392 and 390 BC, the latter culminating in the disaster at Marathon. This audacious plan to throw a bridge across the broad Hellespont would have taken them all by surprise.

Xerxes reminded his subject princes that they had witnessed Darius's preparations for just such a campaign with their own eyes. That campaign had been delayed by Darius's death, but not terminated, said Xerxes. On Darius's behalf, and on behalf of all Persians, Xerxes would prosecute this war, and he vowed that he would never rest until he'd taken and burned Athens, a state that, he said, had dared to injure both him and his father without provocation. But Xerxes's ambitions did not end with the burning of Athens. He told his listeners that he would go on to lead his army on the conquest of the Peloponnese, with its seven rich Greek city-states that included Sparta, Corinth, and Argos. But neither would he stop there. Xerxes intended to conquer all of Europe, and make it one vast country under Persian rule.

Some modern writers such as Gore Vidal—in his novel *Creation*, which has a Persian hero—have suggested that this may not have been such a bad thing, unifying Europe under the Persian banner. Certainly it would have brought excellent Persian administrative skills to the West, and prosperity as trade flourished. And wars between neighbor states within the newly expanded empire would have been eliminated. Later, under Rome, Europe would benefit in terms of administrative organization, defense, economic stability, and engineering developments as a result just such a unified rule. But at a cost of a loss of independence and ethnicity. As it became under Rome, Persian Europe would have been an ancient European Union. It would, however, have been a union ruled by one man, Xerxes. And he was no benign ruler, as those in the grand audience chamber of one hundred pillars at Susa knew all too well.

Xerxes told the listening satraps that if they wished to please him, they would assemble with their troops where and when he commanded, to accompany him on this massive undertaking, no less than the conquest of all of Europe. In return, they could expect great rewards from him. But, he said, he did not want to be seen as entirely self-willed in this exercise, so he laid the planned campaign open to discussion. There was a nervous pause before Xerxes's brother-in-law Mardonius spoke up.

Xerxes liked and trusted Mardonius. The two men were of a similar age and of the same blood—not only was Mardonius married to Xerxes's sister Artozostra, he was his cousin. Eight years before, when he was only relatively young, Mardonius had been entrusted by Xerxes's father Darius with the Persian fleet that had foundered in a storm in 392 BC on its way to invade Euboea and Attica. Mardonius had only survived because he was fighting a land battle in Macedonia at the time. Wounded in that battle, and deprived of the fleet, Mardonius had taken the remainder of the Persian expeditionary force home, where Darius had relieved him of command.

Although Xerxes respected his late father's decisions and appointments, he had been quick to welcome Mardonius into his own circle of senior advisors. Mardonius favored Xerxes's projected Greek invasion, and now he expressed the opinion that when faced by the might of Persia, the Greeks would run from a fight. But if they didn't run, he said, he would relish doing battle with them. Even so, he cautioned that the Persians should make painstaking preparations for such a far-reaching campaign before they embarked on it.

Most of the others present were far too wary of sparking Xerxes's famous short temper to comment one way or another on the king's plan, a plan that would involve massive expenditure for them. It would also mean enormous social upheaval for the empire, with farmers taken away from their fields to serve in the Persian army, and fishermen from their nets to serve in the fleets of the Persian allies, perhaps for several years to come.

One man not afraid to speak out was Artabanus, uncle of the young king. In days past, Artabanus had taken part in his brother King Darius's Scythian campaign north of the River Danube, a campaign that had been a failure tactically and strategically, and that had only just skirted disaster. With that venture in the West in mind, Artabanus declared that he could only see disaster ahead for Xerxes's broader European campaign. Just as a bridge thrown across the Danube on Darius's Scythian campaign had almost been destroyed behind Darius's back, Artabanus feared that the Greeks would send a naval expedition to destroy the Hellespont bridge behind Xerxes's back once he'd crossed it, leaving the king and his army stranded in Europe.

Artabanus also angrily admonished Mardonius for taking the Greeks so lightly. He even proposed that if Xerxes was determined to launch his campaign, the king remain at home while Mardonius and Artabanus led the army. Should the campaign end in the disaster he predicted, Artabanus suggested, Mardonius should be prepared to offer his children and himself up for execution. On the other hand, should Artabanus be proven wrong and the campaign was a success, Artabanus would offer his own children and himself for execution by Xerxes.

Xerxes exploded with rage on hearing this. Only the fact that Artabanus was the brother of Xerxes's late father's saved him from an appointment with the executioner. Artabanus's punishment, said Xerxes, would be banishment from Xerxes's entourage for the campaign. Instead, Artabanus would be shamefully left behind with the women. There Xerxes let the matter rest, welcoming further discussion over the next few days. But it was clear that what he was looking for was acquiescence, not opposition.

That night, Artabanus's words began to play on Xerxes's mind, and he lost confidence in his grand scheme of conquest. So, next day, he surprised his subordinates by announcing that the grand campaign was off. His listeners tried hard not to let their relief show as they fell at the king's feet and paid him obeisance. Then, the next night, the king had a dream in which he was instructed to proceed with the campaign. Convinced this was a message from his god, Ahura Mazda, Xerxes sent for Artabanus, apologized to him for his earlier angry reaction to his advice, and told him of his dream.

When Artabanus still stood by his original advice not to proceed with the campaign, Xerxes commanded him to put on his clothes and sleep in his bed, to see if he had the same dream as Xerxes. Autosuggestion seems to have come into play here, for, sure enough, Artabanus dreamed the same dream as Xerxes, and when he awoke he was terrified. Now he altered his advice to the king, urging Xerxes to proceed with the campaign without delay. Come the morning, Xerxes again called together the kings, the queen, his sons, his brothers, his brothers-in-law, his cousins, and his forthright uncle, and announced that the campaign was going ahead after all. He then introduced Artabanus, who spoke of the dream that he and the king had shared in the night and advocated adoption of the war plan.

After this, no one voiced any opposition to the scheme, especially when, the night before the vassal rulers were due to depart for their own domains, Xerxes had another dream, one that was interpreted by the court magi, the Persian priests, that their god ordained that all mankind would become subservient to Xerxes. Away went the king's minions to prepare their forces and resources for the grand campaign with orders to meet Xerxes at the Hellespont the following year with their armies and fleets. The invasion of Greece was now inevitable, and unstoppable.

7.

Preparing to Face Xerxes

Via traders and travelers, word of massive Persian invasion preparations in the East soon reached Greece. Themistocles had been proved correct all along. His critics were silenced by the grim news from Susa. But there was no joy among his supporters. The future and the very lives of all Athenians was now at grave risk.

To counter the Persian threat, the assembly met and decided that it must appoint a war archon with extraordinary powers, one who would act as single commander in chief to marshal and command the forces of Athens. A number of names were put forward, but most of those named withdrew from contention, being terrified by the task, according to Plutarch. Just two candidates for the post remained: Themistocles and Epicydes. This Epicydes was a wealthy aristocrat well known as a speaker with a velvet tongue.

Themistocles also knew that Epicydes was a fainthearted man who would make a poor military leader. He was convinced that, if the command should fall into Epicydes's hands, all would be lost for Athens. It became clear to Themistocles that Epicydes's blue blood would secure him the votes of the aristocrats, and his tongue the votes of many commoners. He also knew that Epicydes was a greedy and pretentious man who was only interested in what he could get out of the post. So, Themistocles secretly approached his opponent, offered him a large sum of money, and bought him off. Epicydes withdrew his candidature, and Themistocles was elected Athens's commander in chief, a first for a commoner.

Meanwhile, in the hope of receiving a morale-boosting forecast, the city sent representatives to consult the Oracle of Delphi, history's most famous fortune-teller. Located at the sanctuary of Apollo on the slopes of Mount Parnassus, west of Athens in Boetia and near the city of Delphi, which administered the sanctuary, the Oracle had been dispensing cryptic rhyming predictions to Greeks since the eighth century BC. That Oracle took the form of a priestess, called the Pythia, or Pythoness. The role of Pythia was shared by three women on rotation, chosen and trained for this vaunted post based on their special "gifts." When one Pythia died or became incapacitated, another young woman was recruited to add to the trio. The temple and visits to the Oracle were supervised by two honorary part-time priests, usually leading members of the community at Delphi. This was a highly prestigious appointment. Five hundred years later, biographer Plutarch would serve a term as one of these priests. The priests of Delphic Apollo also oversaw the Pythian Games, an event similar to the Olympic Games and one of three major recurring Panhellenic games, but that ran over three months every two years at Delphi.

Between spring and autumn each year, a Pythia would occupy a cavern beneath the Temple of Apollo, where a "sacred vapor" rose from a fissure in the rocks. Modern-day scientists believe this vapor to have been a naturally occurring, mildly hallucinatory gas. After paying tribute to Apollo and sacrificing an animal in the temple, applicants were led down the steps into the cavern, where the Pythia sat on a three-legged chair above the gas fissure. The applicant posed a question to the Pythia, who seemed to go into a trance before giving an often obscure response in verse that was noted down by an assistant.

The Athenian representatives came to Mount Parnassus, walked up the sloping, zigzag Sacred Way, passing the Athenian Treasury erected a decade before to celebrate the Battle of Marathon and no doubt reflecting on that famous victory and wondering whether Athens was fated to again defeat the Persians. In the Temple of Apollo the members of the party performed the obligatory animal sacrifice before being conducted down into the cavern beneath. Here, in the yellow light of spluttering torches, a Pythia sat, dressed all in white. The chief of the Athenian party then asked the Pythia whether Athens would prevail against the Persians, and she gave a reply that shook the Athenians. She told them to hurry away and evacuate their city. Many cities would fall to the invader, she said, and many temples would be burned.

After leaving cavern, the Athenian representatives were fearful of returning to Athens with such a prediction, one that was sure to cause panic and political division. Seeing their dismay, a leading man of Delphi named Timon, perhaps one of the priests of Apollo, advised the Athenians to pay the Pythia a second visit and beg on bended knees for a better prophesy. This they did, and received in return a prophesy that said that a wooden wall would keep Athens safe, but not before the Athenians evacuated their city. The day would come when the Athenians would meet the enemy in battle, the Pythia went on, and there holy Salamis would destroy the offspring of women.

Armed with this more encouraging although essentially baffling prophesy, the Athenian representatives hurried home. All the way, they puzzled about the reference to a wooden wall, and to Salamis, an island off Piraeus that was part of Athens's territory. Some took the reference to a wooden wall to be a wooden palisade that had once circled the Acropolis. But when the representatives repeated the Pythia's words to the priests of Athens whose job it was to interpret omens, most interpreted "wooden wall" to mean the ships of Athens's new navy, especially as the prophesy also involved Salamis, an island. But the interpreters also took the reference to defeated "offspring of women" to mean the Athenians.

When these views were aired in the assembly, war archon Themistocles came to his feet. He disagreed with the interpreters of the Oracle, he said. Yes, the wooden wall clearly referred to Athens's new navy. But if it were the Athenians who were fated to be defeated at Salamis, the Pythia's phrase would have been something like "luckless Salamis," not "holy Salamis," he said, reminding his listeners that the island of Salamis was not holy to the Persians, nor could it ever be. The Pythia, said Themistocles, had predicted an Athenian victory at Salamis.

This argument was almost universally accepted by Thermistocles's colleagues, and they thanked him for clearing up the matter. As a result, all Athenians grew confident that, in the end, they would be victorious at Salamis. In the debate that followed the agreement on the interpretation of the Oracle, the assembly agreed that, with Themistocles at their head, the Athenians would embark their forces on their ships, and, supported by those other Greek city-states that would agree to join them, give battle to the barbarians.

Through 482–481 BC, Thermistocles oversaw the construction of the one hundred triremes and the conversion of Athenian hoplites into rowers. The new triremes were built precisely as Themistocles specified. Once the woodsmen of Attica had leveled entire forests, and the trees had been carted down from the hills by wagon and stripped and shaped, each ship began with a single piece of oak at least seventy feet long used to form the keel. This keel was laid on wooden stocks, themselves hammered into the ground at the water's edge to create a solid construction platform. To the keel were added the graceful, curving sternpost, and the shaped piece of wood that formed the bow post.

Part of the keel projected forward of the bow; to this would later be attached the ship's "beak," its primary offensive weapon. Ramming was a principal attacking tactic of classical warships. The objective was to ram the bronze beak, which usually had several prongs projecting forward, below the surface of the water, into an opposition vessel. The attacking warship would charge across the water to make the connection, preferably into the side of the opposition vessel. The oarsmen of the attacking vessel would then reverse away, leaving a gaping hole in the victim's hull, with much of that hole below the waterline. Water would rush in though the hole, and, if the mortally damaged ship didn't go under, it would invariably capsize, toppling over toward the damaged side. Ships' rams became war trophies in classical times, and for centuries, the rostra, the public speaking platform in Rome's main forum, was decorated with the bronze beaks of Carthaginian warships destroyed by the Roman navy.

To create the hull of a trireme, pine planks were attached to a temporary scaffold set up for the purpose. They were laid edge to edge, in the carvel form of construction, as opposed to overlapping in the clinker-built style of boatbuilding. Being green, the pine planks could be bent to the vessel's required curved shape. Wooden dowels and fine cords made from flax held the planks together. A pair of tensing rope cables ran around the hull, and these were kept taut by winches. This method of boat construction would also be used in the Viking long ships almost two thousand years later. As the Vikings found, a ship built in this way actually flexed as waves hit it. As a result, the craft was light and fast, yet possessed remarkably good seagoing qualities.

A wooden rowing frame was added to the interior of the vessel. This would accommodate the ship's 170 seated rowers, each manning a single oar, on three levels—hence the "tri" in the trireme's name. Most triremes were built with outriggers. Not the sort of outrigger hulls that are common on small boats in the Pacific today; these outriggers extended the rowers' position out over the sides of the hull, well above the water. But Themistocles didn't include outriggers in his warships. He wanted the new Athenian triremes to be narrow, sleek, and light. Most of these Athenian triremes built between 482 and 480 BC would still be in service a decade and a half later, when Cimon, the son of Miltiades, by that time commander of the Athenian navy, would have outriggers added so the ships could carry many more marines.

Themistocles, to further reduce the weight of his triremes, deviated from the normal design in another way. Usually, triremes had a solid planked deck that ran from bow to stern and roofed over the rowing compartments on either side of the vessel. Themistocles's triremes had just short planked decks fore and aft, with a walkway or "bridge" running down the center of the ship and linking fore and aft desks. The reduced deck area would lessen the number of archers and marines that his ships could carry, but this too further lightened each vessel.

Over the heads of his rowers, and in the outer openings flanking the two upper tiers, Themistocles had screens of thick canvas fitted. These provided shade and protection from enemy spears and arrows. The reduced number of fighting men aboard would put Themistocles's vessels at a disadvantage when in close contact with enemy ships that carried many more archers and marines, but this did not bother Themistocles. His plan was for his fast ships to concentrate on outmaneuvering their opponents, nipping in and ramming them rather than boarding them or staging running battles between archers and spearmen.

It seems that the single silver talent allocated from the city treasury for the construction of a trireme only got the completed hull into the water. The cost of fitting it out with oars, masts, sails, rigging, anchors, ropes, and so on was apparently additional, and half a century later Athenian playwright Aristophanes would say that in these earlier times the custom was for some wealthy Athenian aristocrats to pay the cost of outfitting warships from their own purse. It is on record that Callias paid for the outfitting of one of Themistocles's new ships, a trireme of which Callias became captain, or *trierarch*—literally, a trireme archon.

Some modern writers have suggested that all 100 Athenian triremes were fitted out in the same way, by rich aristocrats who became the ships' captains. But there is no evidence that this was universal, and perhaps these writers have confused the fitting out with the original naval law's requirement that 100 citizens each administer one talent of the 100 allocated by the council to the construction of the first batch of vessels. If the Themistocles Decree of Troizen is to believed (see Chapter 9), the aristocratic captains of Athens's triremes were in fact only appointed to each ship the day before the navy was mobilized for action against the approaching Persians, which was still two years away when construction began in 382 BC.

In a trireme's final stages of construction, oars made from lengths of fir were added. A mainmast was fashioned from a single tree, and a smaller foremast made. The latter, when fitted, angled a little forward. Each mast would be equipped with a single square linen sail. Sails would be used when the ship was at sea, but before battle was joined they were stowed away. In battle, the oarsmen would provide the sole means of propulsion.

Before the trireme hit the water, its hull was coated with black pitch, primarily to protect the timbers against wood borer attack. This meant that every trireme had a black hull, as had been the case for centuries past. In *The Iliad*, Homer referred to the "dark fleet," which carried the Greek heroes to and from Troy during the Trojan War. Likewise, Aeschylus, who was a participant in the sea battles of 480 BC, described the "black ships" of the Greeks. On a triremes' stern post, which curved as elegantly as a swan's neck, an ornament such as a mythological figure was added. And, each side of the prow, a large eye was painted. These symbolic eyes were designed as a protection, to see the way ahead for the seafarers through every kind of sea, weather, and trial. To this day, wooden boats in Greece carry the all-seeing pair of eyes painted on their prows.

Every ship had its own name. Those names frequently referred to the pantheon of Greek gods, characters from Greek mythology, and places sacred to the Greeks. Following a long-observed tradition, all ships' names were female, but we don't know for sure the names of any of the ships in Themistocles's navy. We know more about the ship names of Roman times; some 800 names of Roman ships are recorded. Probably the most famous warship of Roman times was the *Antonia*, flagship of Queen Cleopatra's Egyptian navy. It was named after Cleopatra's last love, Mark Antony (actual name Marcus Antonius).

The ships of Themistocles's Athenian navy would have carried names such as the *Olympias*. In modern times, in the 1980s, inspired by three Britons—an academic historian, a naval architect, and a writer—the Greek navy would reconstruct a full scale trireme, naming it the *Olympias*. With no design drawings extant, they had to go by illustrations on ancient vases, descriptions by Herodotus and other historians of yore, and findings at ancient ship sheds where triremes were built and housed. Hull construction was aided by study of wrecks of ancient Greek ships such as one discovered off Cyprus and today housed in a museum on the island.

The *Olympias* replica was launched in 1987, after which its volunteer crew had to master the operation of the trireme from scratch. Most important, the *Olympias* project was able to disprove critics who held that rowing a vessel using a three-tier system of rowers was impractical, if not impossible. After training, the replica's oarsmen were able to row in unison over long distances and work the ship up to a speed approaching ten miles an hour. The modern *Olympias* conveyed the Olympic flame to Piraeus as part of the lead-up to the 2004 Olympic Games at Athens. (See Appendix B for more details of the *Olympias* Project.)

There can be no doubt that Themistocles was constantly active during the construction of his triremes. One day he might appear at the Piraeus and Phalerum Bay shipyards to inspect progress on the stocks. The next, he could unexpectedly turn up at rope-makers' yards to test the strength of the ropes of papyrus and flax that were churned out by the mile for the girding hawsers, the rigging, the mooring ropes, and the anchor chains. Women in Athens working at their looms to produce the expensive linen sails for the ships would have found Themistocles looking over their shoulders. Blacksmiths pounding out the pair of iron anchors for each trireme would have received visits of inspection from the commander in chief, as would have the foundry men casting the all-important bronze rams.

Apart from the urgency of the threat from Xerxes, Themistocles was also driven by personal factors now—the need to prove himself and his naval plan, and the loss of his wife, Archippe. The exact date of Archippe's death is unknown, but it seems to have come, through illness or complications during pregnancy, around this time, the most hectic and demanding period in Themistocles's life. He and Archippe adored their eldest boy; the child knew it, and was able to wrap his parents around his little finger, as the saying goes. Plutarch records an occasion, now that Themistocles was Athens's commander in chief and while his beloved first wife was still alive, when Themistocles, exasperated by his precocious son, had declared the child the most powerful individual in all of Greece. He had explained to the boy, with a laugh, "Athens commands all of Greece, I command Athens, your mother commands me, and *you* command your mother!"

To help Themistocles at this traumatic time following the death of his wife, Themistocles's father-in-law Lysandros took his now eldest son Diocles off his hands, adopting him as his own. Later, following the Persian War, Themistocles would remarry. Although the name of his second wife does not come down to us, she is likely to have come from one of the Greek cities in southern Italy, quite possibly Siris, which, when the fate of Athenians seemed grim, Themistocles would suggest as a place to which to retreat. Some scholars have suggested that this second wife's Italian background was confirmed by the names of several of the five daughters she would bear Thermistocles—Italia, Sybaris, Nicomanche, Mnesiptolema, and Asia. The last, the youngest, was most likely born in Asia later in Themistocles's career. For now, Themistocles hid his grief at the loss of Archippe by burying himself in his important, all-consuming work.

With his focus on training for years past, Themistocles would have also personally supervised the training of ships' crews. Before the ships were launched, exercises for rowers would have taken place on land, as it did in Roman times. This involved crews in mock ships using oars to pull through imaginary seas in unison with their comrades and becoming accustomed to the calls of the twin-piped instrument of each ship's musician, whose shrill notes pierced the noise of wind, sea, and rolling oars to pass on changes in rowing rate called by the ship's rowing master.

A total of two hundred men were allocated to each trireme. One hundred and seventy were oarsmen. In addition, ten fully armed hoplites were selected to serve as marines. They are likely to have been primarily from aristocratic families, but would certainly have been the most outstanding infantrymen from their regiments, men who had shown particular skill as spear-throwers. And, according to the Themistocles Decree, men chosen as marines for Themistocles's navy were limited to those aged between twenty and thirty.

Four archers were also assigned to each ship. Some modern historians have suggested that these men were Scythian mercenaries employed by Athens. There is no historical evidence of this, but, according to the Troizen Decree, "aliens" who were resident at Athens—foreigners, such as Scythians, who did not have citizen status—were among those drafted into Themistocles's navy. Some fifteen seamen were also used on each ship. These were deckhands to handle the sails, anchors and mooring ropes, and to make running repairs. Fishermen, men with seagoing experience, are likely to have been allocated to these duties. Themistocles probably reduced the number of seamen on each trireme to a minimum before battle, sending them ashore once the sails were removed, to further lighten the ship.

The rowing master was one of the most important crew members, a petty officer who issued rowing commands to the crew, via the pipe player. He could speed up or slow the ship, reverse it, and turn it almost in its own length as oarsmen on one side rowed in one direction and those on the other side did the opposite. The penultimate member of the crew and senior petty officer was the steersman, or pilot. Triremes did not posses rudders as such. They were steered by a pair of connected oars that hung over each side of the vessel at the stern. The pilot stood on the stern deck to man the crossbar mechanism that changed the direction of the steering oars. He was the true final decider of a ship's course, and fate.

Finally there was the captain, an aristocrat with little or no naval experience. According to the Themistocles Decree, the triremes' captains were appointed by the city's ten regimental commanders and had to be men with a house and land at Athens, no older than fifty, and had to possess legitimate children. Often, at sea, an inexperienced captain would defer to his experienced steersman on literally what course to take, making the pilot the most influential man aboard.

As for the oarsmen, they were broken up into three groups in each ship, sitting one above the other in three staggered tiers. The most senior men among them were allocated to the top tier of 62 rowers, called the *thranites*. Below them sat the middle tier of 54 *zygians*, and below them, 54 *thalamians*, who sat deep within the hull in the *thalamos*, the hold. The latter was the stuffiest, most claustrophobic and least pleasant of the rowing positions. Unlike the men above them, who could at least look out to the water beside the ship, thalamians could see nothing but the men above and in front of them. It was like rowing in a box. These bottom tier positions went to the lowest-ranking citizen members of the crew and noncitizen aliens.

Aristophanes, born some thirty-five years after this, would apparently serve as a rower aboard an Athenian trireme in his youth. He was to point out one of the pitfalls of being an oarsman on the bottom tier. He described crewmen on a trireme relieving themselves over the ship's stern, and, with a following wind to fill the sails, a man's urine blowing back into the eyes of thalamians seated on the bottom tier, for all trireme oarsmen sat facing the stern. In addition to the hazards of ablutions in high winds, the rear-facing rowers could not see what dangers lay in their ship's path. Only the captain, pilot, and other men on deck could see ahead. At sea, it was the custom for ships of classical times to "coast" from point A to point B, rarely letting the coastline from their sight. This way, if a storm sprang up, they could duck into a harbor or cove to shelter. In the same way, where possible, ships beached for the night, with their sterns drawn up on a beach, their prows in the water, their two anchors stretching out from the bow, and most crewmen sleeping ashore.

Despite this concentration on matters maritime, hoplite training for land battles was not neglected ashore by Themistocles, as would be demonstrated before long. It seems that Themistocles also did something else, something quite unusual but eminently practical. According to Herodotus, by the time that Themistocles's new navy went into action in 480 BC, most of the men aboard his ships could swim. This sounds incredible. Athens was an inland city, one without a maritime tradition. Like the Romans, whose only contact with water was at the bathhouse, apart from its fishermen Athens's citizens had little contact with and even less interest in the sea. There was absolutely no reason for Athenians to learn to swim prior to this.

We know from several ancient sources that Themistocles kept the people of Athens focused on training for war in the decade between the Battle of Marathon and the coming of Xerxes's invasion force. We also know that he was obsessed with turning Athens into a naval power. If Herodotus is to be believed and all or most of the men aboard Athens's war fleet in 480 BC—some 40,000 of them—could swim by that time, Themistocles must have implemented a massive learn-to-swim campaign among Athenian men.

By the summer of 481 BC, numerous new triremes had been launched and could be daily seen out on Phalerum Bay and pushing around the island of Salamis as pilots and rowing masters put Athenian crews through their paces and broke in these new war machines. If the Themistocles Decree is accurate, at this point crewmen were not yet permanently assigned to individual ships. Those postings would only be decided by Athens's ten regimental commanders when full mobilization was ordered in 480 BC. So, in their regimental groups, men trained on whichever vessel in the growing fleet was available.

By the summer of 481 BC, too, Themistocles had summoned a meeting of the assembly where it was agreed that a decree of total mobilization would be issued, calling on all Athenians to face Xerxes on land and sea together with all other Greeks who would stand with them—once Persian forces entered Greece. To muster the support of other Greek city-states, a summit conference was needed. Themistocles would have been in contact with Athens's chief ally Sparta in this regard, and either Themistocles or the Spartans seem to have suggested that, to ensure that those cities who had differences with Athens turned up, the summit should take place on neutral ground. Spartan ally Corinth emerged as acceptable neutral ground for such a meeting.

Heralds went around all the nations of Greece inviting their leaders to a war conference at the city of Corinth, at the Isthmus of Corinth, fifty miles to the west of Athens. Here, representatives from some thirty city-states gathered late in 481 BC. Significantly, Argos, long one of the great powers of the Peloponnese, did not send delegates. Sparta did, and this explains the absence of the Argives. Argos and Sparta were bitter enemies. Argos had suffered a terrible military defeat at the hands of the Spartans at Sepeia thirteen years prior to this, losing 6,000 men, and wounded Argive pride had never healed.

Similarly, some of the city-states, such as Aegina and Thebes, were old enemies of Athens, and their leaders eyed Themistocles and the other members of the Athenian delegation with great suspicion. Many of them blamed Athens for their current predicament. After all, it was Athens that had bloodied Persia's nose at Marathon nine years before, and it was Athens that Xerxes had singled out by name for his revenge. Yet, they all knew that Xerxes had announced that he intended conquering all of Greece on his way to bringing every part of Europe into his empire. All the Greek city-states were now under equal threat. But would they all fight the Persians?

Sitting in the same council were traditional enemies; apart from Athens and Aegina, there were the likes of Thebes and Plataea. Just getting all these old foes into the one room was a feat in itself. Getting them to cooperate was another thing. Themistocles addressed the gathering and urged each of the cities to bury old enmities and work together for the good of all Greece. They could settle old differences later, he said, once the Persian threat had been dealt with. Themistocles's conciliatory stance, strongly supported by Arcadian delegate Chileus, won over the other delegates. Thermistocles then informed the other leaders that Athens was building a fleet of many triremes and proposed taking on the Persian fleet before it reached southern Greece. Most of the city-states at the meeting possessed navies, some considered the best in the region, and they agreed with Themistocles's strategy of meeting the Persians at sea and taking them on before they could make landfall in southern Greece.

After much discussion, all the nations present agreed to join a coalition against the Persians, with Corinth to act as the center of operations. Although, some cities imposed conditions on their involvement, including a determination not to allow Athens to lead. Sparta was to emerge as the nation preferred by most city-states to take command, and Themistocles wisely did not oppose this. Sparta was, after all, an ally of Athens, and one with excellent military credentials. As the meeting continued, word arrived that Xerxes had landed at Sardis in Lydia with the Persian and Median contingents of his army, and that other contingents were streaming toward the meeting place at the Hellespont that Xerxes had specified. Xerxes's choice of Sardis as a stopping place on his route west was deliberate and symbolic; this was the city, now rebuilt, burned by Athenian troops close to two decades earlier.

This news spurred the Greeks to terminate the Corinth meeting and hurry back to their respective cities. As their last act, they agreed to send spies into Asia Minor to gain information about Persian preparations and movements, and to send envoys off to Argos, Crete, Corcyra (today's island of Corfu), and Sicily urging the Greeks there to join their coalition. In the end, only Corcyra agreed to join, promising to send sixty triremes. They would fail to keep their promise. The thirty cities were on their own.

Once Themistocles arrived back at Athens, he called for a meeting of the assembly. There he reported on the successful conference at Corinth then urged the assembly to repeal the ostracism of the leading men exiled from Athens since 488 BC, so that they could return and play a part in the defense of Athens. This idea would have met with widespread opposition, especially as most of the ostracized men had been sent into exile because they were considered either friends of the tyrants or friends of the Persians, or both. Yet, Themistocles would win the day, and a decree would be issued by the assembly terminating the ostracism of Xanthippus, Megacles, Aristides, and the other victims of the ostraca, and recalling them to Athens.

Was this a magnanimous act by Themistocles, bringing his most bitter rivals back to Athens at such a crucial time? It was more likely a mixture of pragmatism and politics. It was probable that Aegina, as a price for signing up to the anti-Persian coalition, required Athens to recall Aristides, who had been living in exile with the Aeginetans for the past several years. The crafty Aeginetans probably thought this would set the cat among the pigeons at Athens, by restoring Themistocles's most ardent rival to the Athenian political stage—with the result that Themistocles's power would be challenged, if not immediately, then after the Persian threat had been dealt with.

Themistocles may well have agreed to recall Aristides to cement Aegina into the coalition. But Themistocles, like the Aeginetans, thinking about the post-Persian future, did not want Aristides to be seen as singly vital to Athens's war effort. So, he proposed that *all* the ostracized men be returned, an act that incidentally made him look good in the eyes of Athenians. Plutarch was to speculate that Themistocles had the recall extended to all Athenian exiles to prevent them from going over to the Persians. But it's unlikely the outcome of the war would have been the slightest bit different had all the exiles defected to Persia, and Themistocles knew it.

Some modern scholars suggest that Themistocles may have delayed implementation of the recall decree, at least in the case of Aristides, for Aristides did not return to Athens until late in the summer of 480 BC, even though he was living just twenty miles away on Aegina when the decree was issued. But did Themistocles's post of war archon give him the power to delay a decree of the council? It's unlikely. We know that at least one of the other ostracized men, Xanthippus, returned to Athens some time before Aristides did. It is likely that Aristides's delayed return was his own choice because he was distrustful of Themistocles's motives, or his friends, and fearful for his life if and when he returned to Athens.

During the winter of 481–480 BC, from Sardis, Xerxes sent out envoys to all the city-states of Greece, except for two. Those Persian envoys demanded earth and water from each city, a symbolic gesture of submission to King Xerxes. The exceptions were Athens and Sparta, which Xerxes had no desire conciliate. He planned to destroy both. When his father Darius had sent heralds to Greece on a similar mission years before, the Athenians had thrown the Persian heralds into a pit, while the Spartans threw those that came to them into a well, telling them to gather earth and water there.

Many cities would subsequently comply with the earth and water demand, even powerful Thebes in Boeotia, although Thebans were conflicted over this matter. The Thebans wanted to see their old enemy Athens destroyed by the Persians. But did it have to be at the price of surrendering their sovereignty to those same Persians? In the end, the procoalition party prevailed at Thebes, and the city agreed to contribute troops to the Greek coalition in defiance of Xerxes, despite initially sending the Persian king earth and water.

As the spring of 480 BC approached, preparations continued at frantic pace both east and west of the Aegean, one to launch a great war of conquest, the other to defend homeland and independence.

8.

The Greatest Army and Navy on Earth

From the Mysian port town of Abydos at the Hellespont, following the plan of King Xerxes, Egyptian and Phoenician engineers built a double floating bridge kept in place by cables of papyrus and flax. That bridge stretched across the strait between Asia Minor and Europe, connecting the two. Even at this, the narrowest part of the Dardanelles, the beavering engineers had to cover almost a mile of open water from today's Nara Burnu, or Nagara Point, to the western side.

The bridge project, always tricky, struck trouble almost as soon as it was completed. Xerxes, wintering at Sardis, received news that a storm had sprung up and swept the waterway, destroying his bridges. Xerxes flew into a rage. He issued orders that the waters of the Hellespont receive 300 lashes and be branded with hot irons as punishment for defying him, after which a pair of leg-fetters be cast into the water to show that these waters were now the prisoner of Xerxes. The Egyptian and Phoenician overseers responsible for the bridge's construction were not spared the king's wrath, either. Xerxes ordered them beheaded for faulty workmanship.

As heads rolled, a new design team was given the task by the Persian king of creating a bridge that would withstand wind and wave. Knowing that their lives depended on the outcome, these engineers came up with a scheme for two parallel but separate bridges of boats, a plan that Xerxes approved. According to Herodotus, a total of 674 ships were lined up, side by side, across the Hellespont from one coast to the other, to create these two bridges. Egyptian and Phoenician construction crews then laid planks across the ships' decks and from hull to hull, and raised wooden walls on each edge of the wooden roadway so that cavalry and supply animals crossing the bridge could not be unsettled by the sight of the water over which they were passing. Breakwaters were also built to calm the waters during high winds and so protect the bridges from damage or destruction. It was a mammoth undertaking, but by the time that Xerxes departed Sardis in the spring of 480 BC and headed for the Hellespont, the twin bridges were ready and waiting for him and his huge army.

Before Xerxes left Sardis, three spies sent by the Greek coalition were discovered in the Persian camp. Xerxes's subordinates were in the process of executing the trio when Xerxes heard of it. He sent for the spies and ordered them taken on a guided tour of the massive military encampment, with nothing hidden from them. He then sent the spies on their way, to report back to the Greeks all they had seen. Xerxes hoped they would terrify the Athenians, Spartans, and others who opposed him, with their report of an enormous army that would stretch from horizon to horizon on the march. As the spies scurried away, marveling at their survival, Xerxes gave the order for his army to prepare to leave.

The same day that Xerxes set off from Sardis there was a total eclipse of the sun that briefly turned day into night, alarming the marching Persians and their allies. Xerxes quickly consulted his court magi, who reassured him that this was not a bad omen for him. It was a portent of the destruction of the cities of Greece, they said, for, the fortunes of the Greeks were ruled by the sun, while Persia's fortunes were ruled by the moon. But Pythius, King of Lydia, was not so sure about that. Marching with Xerxes, and bringing his army and all five of his sons on the campaign, Pythius began to dread disaster once they reached Greece, foreseeing his own death and that of all his sons. Just a few days into the march, he approached Xerxes and begged him to allow his eldest son to stay behind, so that he could rule over his father's domain should Pythius and his brothers fall during the campaign ahead.

Xerxes burst into a rage. This was defeatist talk, and Xerxes would have none of it. He ordered his guards to arrest Pythius's eldest son, then execute him by cutting his body in half, after which the halves was to be placed either side of the road along which the army passed. So it was that Pythius lost his son and heir. And the soldiers and generals of Xerxes gained a lesson, learning to refrain from defeatist talk, as they marched by the divided corpse of the luckless Lydian prince.

On the march, a vast baggage train preceded the army. The forces of many allied nations, infantry and cavalry, followed. A gap was then left in the column ahead of Xerxes and his entourage. A thousand chosen Persian cavalrymen of Xerxes's bodyguard came along the road at the head of the royal procession, followed by a thousand elite Persian infantrymen of the bodyguard, also especially selected to protect their king with their lives. Those infantrymen of the bodyguard could be easily identified, for they, of all the men in Xerxes's army, marched with the points of their spears pointing to the ground.

Ten sacred Nisaean horses from the Median plain were led along next. Huge animals, they were covered in golden ornaments. An empty ceremonial chariot sacred to the Persian god followed, drawn by eight milk-white horses who were led by their handlers; no man was permitted to ride in the sacred chariot. Xerxes followed, riding in a chariot drawn by massive Nisaean horses and driven by the king's personal charioteer, Patiramphes. Occasionally, Xerxes would tire of riding or standing in the chariot and would transfer to a closed litter carried on the shoulders of slaves, where he could travel sitting or lying down separated from his subjects by a crimson curtain.

Immediately behind the king came another 1,000 spearmen, then a thousand mounted lancers. A force of 10,000 spearmen, known as the Immortals, followed. This was Xerxes's crack unit. The name Immortals came from the fact that if ever a vacancy arose in their ranks through illness or death, a replacement would be immediately promoted into the unit from the rest of the Persian army, so that the Immortals' number never fell below 10,000, and the unit seemingly lived forever. Ten thousand Persian cavalry followed the Immortals, after which there was a gap of a quarter of a mile before the remainder of the army came tramping along. A chaos of camp followers brought up the rear, including the wives, concubines, and children of Persian and allied officers, as well as prostitutes, tradesmen, merchants, and general hangers-on.

One day in May 480 BC, after many weeks en route and with a stop at the site of ancient Troy, where Xerxes had a thousand oxen slain as an offering in remembrance of the heroes who had fallen in the Trojan War a thousand years before, the Persian army reached Abydos. The town offered the best harbor on the Asiatic side of the Hellespont, and here the armies of countless subject nations were encamped in waiting for the king of Persia, their lord and master. At the same time, many of the ships of his navy lined the shore. On a hill overlooking Abydos, a throne of white marble had been prepared for Xerxes. After ordering his army and navy to form up for his review, the king took a seat on his throne, and surveyed his massive force.

Herodotus, writing just several decades after this campaign, would calculate the eventual size of Xerxes's army, giving the numbers for each national contingent. That army would grow even larger than that gathered at Abydos. Once Xerxes crossed the Hellespont, it would be reinforced by tens of thousands more allied troops and ships from Thrace, Macedonia, and Thessaly, on Xerxes's route down to southern Greece. Herodotus's grand total came to more than 2.6 million men, to which he added as many camp followers again, making a total of more than 5 million men, women, and children. Modern scholars consider this number much exaggerated. Even so, Herodotus's numbers for Xerxes's navy in this campaign, that of 1,200 warships and 3,000 support and cargo vessels, most of the latter sail-powered, ring true in relation to what we know of this campaign, and these would have required at least 350,000 crewmen. As for land troops, figures of 300,000 to 500,000 has been suggested as more realistic than Herodotus's close to 3 million. Combined, then, as many as 850,000 men would march and sail for Xerxes. And some 80 percent of them were assembled here at the Hellespont in front of proud King Xerxes, along with countless camp followers.

For his generals on this campaign, Xerxes had chosen six relatives, including brother-in-law Mardonius and a son of his outspoken uncle Artabanus. While Xerxes had brought Artabanus himself along as an advisor, he had not given him a command. In addition to the six generals, the Immortals also had their own separate commander, who answered directly to Xerxes. The Persian army and allied armies were organized into divisions of 10,000 and regiments of 1,000, each with their own dedicated commanders chosen by Xerxes and answerable to his generals. Each regiment was broken down into subunits of 100, and these into basic units of 10. The junior officers in charge of these lesser units were chosen by their regimental commanders. This was a marvel of organization of which the Greeks and Romans would have been proud.

Xerxes's navy was provided entirely by his allies. The Persians and Medes, coming essentially from landlocked areas, were not sailors. Many of the seamen in Xerxes's fleet were of Greek extraction and spoke Greek as their native language. Xerxes's best ships, in terms of the vessels themselves and the skill and experience of their crews, came from Phoenicia and Egypt. Throughout classical times, the Egyptians were considered the Mediterranean's finest shipbuilders. The Phoenicians, meanwhile, had been adventurous seamen since truly ancient times and had established colonies such as Carthage around the Mediterranean. In Xerxes's navy, the Phoenician squadron from Sidon in what is today's Lebanon was rated the best of the best.

The overall command of his war fleet Xerxes entrusted to four relatives, including two of his brothers, serving as admirals in chief. To prevent defection, flight, or surrender of his vessels, Xerxes frequently had Persian captains allocated to allied ships, even though these men knew nothing about naval matters. And marine contingents on all ships included Persian, Mede, and Sacae soldiers, Xerxes's most loyal men. National naval contingents had as their admirals their individual sovereigns. The five triremes supplied by Halicarnassus were not conspicuous by their number, but they were among the most famous ships in Xerxes's massive fleet. This was for two reasons. First, the ships had an enviable record. More important, they had as their admiral Queen Artemisia, who would lead them into battle.

Xerxes, from his hillside throne at Abydos, viewed hundreds of thousands of troops conducting drills on the plain below for as far as the eye could see, then watched as selected triremes raced on the Hellespont expressly for his entertainment. His uncle Artabanus was in the royal entourage around the throne, and he was told that Xerxes was crying. Going to the king, Artabanus asked why he was in tears.

Xerxes replied that he'd been so moved by the majestic scenes playing out before him that he had reflected on how short life was, and that within a hundred years these fine soldiers would all be dead and gone, and with them the grandeur that was his reign.

When Artabanus said there were sadder things in life, Xerxes changed the subject and asked his uncle if he was still in favor of the campaign ahead. Artabanus replied that he was, but he was still afraid, especially when two things were opposed to their success. When Xerxes asked him what those two things were, Artabanus replied that they were the land and the sea. He worried that the Persian fleet was simply too large, and that no harbor could provide enough shelter for them, and many ships and crews would be lost to storms. As for the land, the farther Xerxes advanced, the more hostile the land would become to him, and the less food it would provide for his massive army until famine prevailed and the army starved.

Xerxes countered that success came to the bold, not to those who held back to consider every potential pitfall. To which Artabanus replied that if Xerxes was determined to proceed with this campaign, he should leave the Ionian contingents behind. These were the same Ionian Greeks who had risen in revolt against Xerxes's father, the same Ionian Greeks who claimed a shared ancestry with the Athenians and whom Athens had helped in their revolt, burning Sardis. But Xerxes answered that the Ionians had proven their loyalty during his father's campaign north of the River Danube—approached by the Scythian enemy to cut Darius's Danube bridge behind his back, a bridge that the Ionians were guarding, the Ionians had remained loyal to their Persian overlords. Besides, had Xerxes left the Ionian squadrons behind, he would have lost two hundred of his best triremes.

Sending his negative uncle back to Susa to take charge at home, Xerxes summoned his kings and commanders and called on them to pray for Persia's success. The following day, the Persian army began to cross the Hellespont bridges with the Immortals leading the way. As the slow crossing was made over the coming weeks, troops used one bridge, while wagons, chariots, and animals traveled by the other. It was to take a month for the entire army to make the crossing. By June, the greatest army and navy on earth would be west of the Hellespont and advancing inexorably toward Greece by land and sea, creeping south in unison like a pair of giant tsunamis and gobbling up all in their path. And no earthly power seemed capable of stopping them.

9.
Athens's Floating Wall of Wood

With worried looks on their faces, delegates from the cities of the Greek coalition took their places in the meeting hall at Corinth. The Spartans, taking seriously their role as chosen leaders of the coalition and the threat from Xerxes, had called another summit. Themistocles again headed the Athenian delegation.

Sparta's chief delegate informed their coalition partners that Sparta had done all in its power to bring old rival Argos into the coalition. The Argives had learned of Xerxes's war plans very early on, and had sent representatives to the Oracle of Delphi seeking guidance. Despite the Oracle telling them to sit on the sidelines in any war between the Greeks and the Persians, the council of the Argives had responded to Spartan entreaties by proposing two conditions for joining the coalition. Argos would join if Sparta agreed to a thirty-year truce with Argos, and if Argos and Sparta jointly commanded all Greek forces in the Persian conflict.

Sparta had replied that it would agree to share command, but, as Sparta traditionally had two kings and Argos one, they would agree on the basis that Sparta had two votes when making command decisions and Argos had one. As this clearly left Argos as junior partners, and with a worthless vote, the Argives had rejected this proposal, and there was no chance of them now joining the war against the Persians. Likewise, Spartan and Athenian envoys had gone to Sicily and sought to bring King Gelo of Syracuse into the coalition.

Gelo had offered 20,000 infantry, 2,000 cavalry and innumerable support troops, plus 200 war galleys, but only on condition that Sparta and Athens bow to him and give him sole command of all coalition forces. His offer, like his condition, was rejected by the Spartan envoy. Gelo had then softened his demands, asking only for command of the coalition fleet. That too was rejected, this time by the Athenian envoy. So, the envoys left Sicily empty handed. King Gelo would bless the day his offer was turned down and he kept his army and navy at home, for that September, while the Greeks were busy fighting the Persians, a 300,000-man Carthaginian army invaded Sicily.

As the second Greek coalition summit meeting was taking place at Corinth, envoys arrived from Thessaly in northern Greece. The Thessalians had heard that the Persian army was about to cross the Hellespont, and they urged the coalition to send an army into Thessaly to block a narrow pass at Mount Olympus and prevent the Persians from entering Thessaly from Macedonia, a course the invaders would have to follow to reach southern Greece. Themistocles's policy throughout this conflict would always be that of taking the war to the Persians rather than sitting and waiting for them to come to him. He and the Spartans immediately agreed to the Thessalian request, and committed a combined force of 10,000 Athenian and Spartan hoplites to the task.

At Athens, the citizens from five or six regiments were called to arms, and these men who had been training as sailors for the past couple of years suddenly found themselves returned to the role of foot soldiers. The Athenians quickly donned their equipment and said farewell to their families. A vase painting from the fifth century BC shows an Athenian hoplite in full armor, shield on left arm and spear in left hand, using the right to shake his father's hand as his pet dog stands at his feet and his mother or wife waits with a jug and cup for the traditional farewell libation. In thousands of Athenian homes, just such a parting now took place.

These troops were conveyed part of the way north by sea on ships of Athens's new navy and those of coalition partners. The Athenian and Spartan forces landed and combined. With Themistocles in command of the former and Evaenetus, war archon of Sparta, commanding the latter, they marched inland together into Thessaly. Setting up camp in a mountain pass at Tempe that gave access into Thessaly from Lower Macedonia, they were joined by 2,000 Thessalian cavalrymen.

A few days later, a Macedonian envoy arrived at the camp. He warned Themistocles and Evaenetus of the enormous size of the Persian force now marching and sailing their way, and assured them that their meager force would be trampled by the Persian horde. The two Greek commanders then learned that there was another distant pass through the mountains, a pass that Xerxes would in fact use. Deciding against remaining where they were and risk being outflanked and cut off, Themistocles and Evaenetus withdrew their troops. They themselves returned to Corinth, where the other coalition delegates had continued to meet. Most of the Thessalians, feeling deserted by the southern Greeks, would now go over to the Persian side.

Back at Corinth, Themistocles joined in the strategy debate. Knowing that Xerxes was intent on close cooperation between his army and navy, it was obvious to the coalition delegates that once the Persian army had marched through Thessaly it would proceed on into Attica via a coastal route that put it in contact with and in sight of its fleet. That route would require the Persian army to use a narrow mountain pass in the territory of Thalcis at a place near the coast called Thermopylae, the Hot Gates. In that pass, Persian cavalrymen would have no advantage if opposed.

Themistocles led the summit in agreeing a two-pronged strategy. A mixed Greek advance force would occupy the pass at Thermopylae to delay Xerxes's land forces until a larger coalition army could take up station in Boetia behind it. Meanwhile, as many ships as possible of the combined fleets of coalition partners would meet at the port of Artemisium on the north coast of the large island of Euboea, forty miles to the east of Thermopylae, in support of the advance land force. Those coalition warships that could not be readied in time and could not reach Artemisium by a certain date were to instead assemble at Pogos, port of the city of Troizen, there to await further orders from the coalition.

Artemisium was selected as the forward assembly point partly because it could shelter a large number of vessels and offered abundant drinking water. Of equal importance was its strategic location in the path of the Persian fleet. That fleet would have to pass by there on its way south, whether it took the outer coastal route or slid down the narrow channel that separated Euboea from the mainland. Artemisium was also just several hours' row from Thermopylae, meaning Greek land and sea forces could maintain close communication.

Ten coalition partners volunteered their infantry for the Thermopylae operation, with Sparta and Corinth at the forefront. Command went to Sparta. This time, Themistocles didn't offer troops. For a decade, he had advocated that Athens become a naval power, and now he had the fleet to achieve that ambition. Apart from the 100 triremes built by the Athenians over 382–381 BC, Herodotus says that, following the Oracle of Delphi's prediction that Athens would be victorious via a wall of wood Athens's assembly had authorized the urgent construction of more warships. This program would, Herodotus wrote, increase the Athenian navy to a total of 200 warships. These latest triremes would be funded by the Laurium silver mine profits of 381–380 BC.

It seems that this batch of new ships had indeed been built over the recent winter, and that, as Themistocles was meeting with his coalition partners at Corinth for the final time before war broke out, those ships were still being fitted out and undergoing their sea trials. His new ships gave Themistocles the largest navy of any of the coalition partners, and gave Athens a powerful offensive force. This was an amazing turnaround for a city-state that, not long before, had let its one humble squadron of triremes rot on a beach. Having heard how massive the approaching Persian navy was from the Macedonian at Tempe, Themistocles was determined to commit every ship and every Athenian to fighting the invader on the water. Consequently, no Athenian foot soldiers would be going to Thermopylae.

As Athens now possessed the largest navy of any of the coalition partners, Themistocles had come to this summit prepared to let Sparta lead on land but with the intent that Athens command the combined fleet. But he soon found that a majority of coalition partners were averse to Athens taking the naval command. The feeling at the meeting was that Sparta should command on both land and sea, or no one should. Many coalition members even declared that if Athens were given the naval command, they would withdraw their ships from the coalition and go home. For, they declared, they would never serve under Athenian command.

We are never told by ancient sources why these other city-states were so antagonistic toward Athens. It is from Athenians and admirers of Athens that we know much about Greek history; perhaps, blinded by Greek arts, democracy, and generalship, these commentators were blind to the conceit of Athenians. Perhaps Athenians were so haughty, with their boast that they had taught all other Greeks how to make fire, how to draw water from springs, and how to sow corn, that they were insufferable. Or, was the Greek dislike of Athens in 480 BC aimed directly at Themistocles, this upstart commoner who, via the fledgling experiment with government by the people for the people called democracy, now commanded the largest navy in the region? It is quite possible that Athens at this time, and its elected leader, was held in the same suspicion by her neighbors that France would be in the eighteenth century following the French Revolution, and Russia after the revolution of 1917.

The other members of the Athenian delegation had come to the summit prepared to push for overall Athenian command at sea, but Themistocles, whose talent for statesmanship far exceeded his ego, convinced his fellow Athenians that this was not the time or place to assert Athens's leadership credentials. For the moment, Athens agreed to let Sparta command on both land and sea. With that settled and with the coalition being held together by Spartan glue, the delegates to the summit hurried away to their various capitals to mobilize their forces.

Despite the fact that the coalition was moving to confront the Persians on land and on sea, Themistocles returned to Athens convinced that, with the city's men at arms absent with the fleet, it would be necessary to evacuate the remainder of the population, just in case the Persians evaded opposing Greek forces. Themistocles, once back at Athens, joined a meeting of the governing council to report on all that had been decided at Corinth and put a motion for a military mobilization and evacuation decree to be issued at once. Evacuation of Athens would have been difficult for proud Athenians to stomach, particularly as they boasted that theirs was the first city in Greece. But Themistocles was able to remind his countrymen that both appropriate prophesies of the Oracle of Delphi had urged the emptying of the city in no uncertain terms.

As to where the women, children, and old men should be sent, the city of Troizen in the Peloponnese was chosen by the council. Troizen, an ancient inland settlement mentioned by Homer, and an Athenian ally, lay on the Argolid peninsula due south of Athens across the Saronic Gulf, and beyond the island of Aegina. The evacuation proclamation was duly issued, and it fell to every Athenian citizen to organize the evacuation of his family and possessions, including his slaves, and to himself to take up his assigned post in defense of Athens.

In 1847, a stone inscription was found on a large piece of marble in the village of Troizen. It contained what appears to be Athens's mobilization and evacuation decree of 480 BC, and came to be known as the Themistocles Decree of Troizen, or simply the Themistocles Decree. The physical inscription was later dated to two centuries after Themistocles lived, and for decades debate has raged between scholars who believe the inscription to be a genuine third-century BC copy of the fifth-century BC decree and those believe it to be a third-century BC forgery. No one in the latter camp has come up with a reason for such a forgery. And it is credible to believe that the people of Troizen, proud of the role they played in supporting Athens during the Persian invasion in times past and wishing to commemorate it, commissioned the inscription for public display.

According to the Themistocles Decree's inscription, the temple treasurers and priestesses of Athens were commanded to stay in the city and defend the holy Acropolis and its temples. All citizens of Athens and aliens living in the city were ordered, starting at dawn next day, to deposit their women and children at Troizen and their possessions and all men older than fifty on the island of Salamis. All Athenian men and alien men aged eighteen to fifty were commanded to then report for military duty. The year's ten elected regimental generals were to select two hundred leading citizens who possessed a house and land in Athens, men who were no older than fifty and had legitimate children, to serve as captains of the new navy's triremes. Using the voting rolls for citizens and the list of resident aliens held by the war archon, the regimental commanders were to then form the men of their regiments into companies of 200 men and allocate one company to each trireme. Those triremes included the 100 new ships built over the winter of 382–381 BC, the ships captured at Marathon and those built for Miltiades's failed invasion of Paros, plus the latest batch of new ships built over the winter of 381–380 BC.

The regimental commanders were ordered to post notices on the city's white notice boards showing the names of the navy's 200 triremes together with the names of their chosen captains and petty officers and to list the names of the individuals allocated as crewmen to each ship. From the company of 200 men assigned to every ship, 10 citizens between twenty and thirty years of age were to be chosen as marines, with another four men to serve as archers. With only 170 of the 200 men needed to man the oars, the balance would have been assigned to deck duties, as seamen. The next day, once all this had been done, the council and the commanders were required to perform the necessary sacrifices on the Acropolis to the gods Almighty Zeus, Athena, Nike, and Poseidon the Preserver, then take the crews down to port to embark on their ships.

The initial effect of this mobilization decree was, according to Plutarch, stupefying for the people of Athens, who were amazed by Themistocles's confidence in ultimate victory at sea and by the apparent rashness of abandoning their city to the enemy without a fight. They were standing around in disbelief when they saw twenty-seven year-old Cimon, the son of Miltiades, hero of Marathon, walk through the potters' quarter toward the Acropolis, accompanied by a number of his friends. Cimon didn't live in the potters' quarter. He may have had to pass through it from a home beyond it. Or, he and his friends may have just left a meeting at the home of commander in chief Themistocles, where Themistocles had appealed to his patriotism and urged him to bury the proverbial hatchet, just as Themistocles was doing in recalling Cimon's ostracized friend Aristides, and to lead by example.

Cimon was tall, athletic, and handsome, with long, curly hair that tumbled over his ears. A member of an aristocratic order of citizens who traditionally provided Athens's cavalry, Cimon carried his horse bridle, which, in the tradition of the day, would have been richly decorated with gold. Cimon took the bridle to a temple of one of Athens's female deities; it's likely, from previous events, to have been the Temple of Artemis. And there he dedicated his bridle to the goddess, leaving it with the other temple treasure.

Cimon then went to the temple wall, and took down one of the shields that had apparently been hanging there since being dedicated to the goddess following the victory at Marathon. This was quite possibly the shield of his late father. Plutarch would surmise that Cimon dedicated his bridle and took up the shield to show that, despite his long opposition to Thermistocles, he was turning his back on Athens's traditional reliance on a land army and becoming a mariner, endorsing Themistocles's naval policy in this time of great danger. For Cimon then led his friends down to the new ports at Piraeus, where they took their places on the waiting warships. Cimon himself apparently took up the post as a commander of marines on one of the triremes.

The example set by Cimon, up until now a firm adversary of Themistocles, gave confidence to fellow aristocrats, who set about emulating him. Tens of thousands of men chosen for naval service marched down to Piraeus, where they launched their ships. Most historians believe that Aeschylus the playwright was among the men who took their posts on Athens's triremes that morning. He joined fellow members of the eighth regiment, the Hippothontis, all of them residents of Eleusis, crewing one of the ships. Aeschylus was now forty-five and entirely bald. He was still of military age, although fifteen years too old to serve as a marine. He would have to occupy a bench as a rower, but his aristocratic family, combined with his fame as both a celebrated poet and a hero at the Battle of Marathon a decade earlier, would have elevated him to the top tier.

Aeschylus himself was to describe the first thing each trireme rower did once he took his assigned rowing bench as the ship prepared for action. After pushing his oar out through a leather rowing sleeve, he would lash the inboard part of the oar to a pin attached to the ship's superstructure. This pin was later called a thole by the Vikings, who used the same arrangement on their longships. Once tied to this pin, the oar could not slip from the rower's grasp, slide from its sleeve, and fall into the water. But neither could the oarsman rapidly withdraw the oar, a limitation that would prove hazardous when the ship was in close quarters with other ships, especially during battle.

Thousands of Athenians took their places aboard the new fleet. Yet, despite the turnout of citizens and aliens at Piraeus, overall the number of crewmen available for duty proved to be disappointing. Even now, says Plutarch, there was strong resistance from Athenians to a total reliance on defending Athens with the forward projection of sea power. The indications are that either the regimental commanders insisted on Themistocles leaving behind a large number of citizen soldiers to protect Athens from land attack, or many men did not answer the call-up.

For, when Themistocles reached the port, there were clearly not enough men available to crew the entire fleet. He could muster enough Athenian men to crew 127 warships, mostly triremes, to accompany him to Artemisium on the northern coast of Euboea. As events were to prove, even these 127 Athenian ships were undermanned by an average of 32 men per ship. Themistocles had promised the last summit at Corinth that he would bring a mighty fleet to Artemisium, and he was determined to keep that promise, even if it meant bringing undermanned ships. For, he was planning to snaffle more recruits to fill empty places once he reached Euboea.

Themistocles would have taken his motherless sons Archeptolis, Poleuctus, and Cleophantus with him to Piraeus, and put them aboard a boat for Troizen accompanied by household servants. He retained the boys' tutor, Sicinnus, on the staff that would sail with him to war. Sicinnus was a Persian slave, probably one of the Persian captives taken after the Battle of Marathon. His knowledge of both the Persian language and Persian ways could prove invaluable to the Athenian commander. Also joining Themistocles's staff as an advisor was his old schoolmaster Mnesiphilus, who had remained Themistocles's confidante throughout his political career.

At the port, Themistocles was joined by 4,000 foot soldiers from Athenian ally Plataea, who made camp as they awaited orders. Themistocles assigned the Plataeans the task of manning an additional 20 Athenian triremes; inexperienced as they were at rowing warships, they would have to learn to be sailors on the job, to bolster the perceived strength of the fleet that Themistocles took to Artemisium. While Themistocles sailed these 147 Athenian and Plataean ships to Artemisium for the rendezvous, he assigned the remaining 53 crewless warships of the Athenian fleet the task of ferrying the civilians of Athens across the Saronic Gulf to Troizen, once enough men could be found to crew them. It's likely that in the end, old men among the refugees were among those assigned to oars for the evacuation. Themistocles's orders to the commander of this ferrying operation were, once the city's refugees had been evacuated, to remain with his triremes at Pogon, port of Troizen, until Themistocles sent for them to join him.

Bearing in mind the Oracle of Delphi's prophesy about holy Salamis, Themistocles only saw the Artemisium operation as a forward probe designed to gain time while Athens was evacuated, and until the Olympic Games had run their course and more coalition troops and ships were available. Themistocles had always intended making a stand at Salamis. It's clear that he had convinced his colleagues not to send Athenian representatives to the Olympic Games this August, even though other coalition partners stubbornly persisted in participating in the Games.

This blinkered focus on the Olympics by so many of the threatened Greek city-states, even though Greece was being invaded, today seems as ludicrous as Americans ignoring an alien invasion to watch the Super Bowl! But to most Greeks, the Olympic Games were more than a sporting event. Dedicated to Zeus, principal god of the Greek pantheon, the Olympics were also considered a religious obligation by most deeply religious and superstitious Greeks. To them, ignoring the Games would be a sacrilege that invited the wrath of Zeus. And their fear of Zeus overrode their fear of Xerxes, a mere mortal.

Themistocles had a demonstrably healthy respect for Zeus, and his wrath. Yet even though Plutarch reports that Themistocles regularly paid for expensive animal sacrifices at the temples of Athens, these acts seem to have been more for show and reputation than out of any deep-seated religious belief. A thoroughly pragmatic man, Themistocles apparently observed the principal that, when it came to defending Athens and her interests, the gods helped those who helped themselves. And he now possessed the authority and the persuasive gifts to ensure that his fellow Athenians followed the same course.

Yet, while Athens stood ready to face the foe, there was nothing that Themistocles could say that would convince other key coalition partners to do the same. Only once the Games were over and their representatives had returned from Olympia would many of those partners have the men and the will to send their full complement of warships to join the coalition fleet. This meant that the Greek fleet that would gather at Artemisium late in August would only be about two-thirds the size of the one that would later come together.

In the last sitting of the council before Themistocles had headed for the port, he pushed through a decree assigning eight drachmas to every man serving in the fleet because the crews would have to provide their own rations. Amounting to a total of more than fifty talents once all Athens's ships were manned, this payout exhausted available government funds, indicating that the silver mine royalties had been roughly halved by this time. So Themistocles cast about for additional money to fund the war. Hearing a report from Athens's priestess of Minerva that the city's sacred golden shield, which bore the snake-haired Gorgon's image, had gone missing from the Temple of Minerva where it usually hung, Themistocles had the city ransacked in search of the shield. In the process, his men found large amounts of money hidden among people's possessions, which Themistocles confiscated for state use.

When Themistocles reached Piraeus, he boarded the ship that would carry him into battle, not as war archon alone now, but as admiral in chief—literally as Athens's *navarch*, or archon of the navy. Athens's flagship had been consecrated as a sacred vessel, and would have, uniquely, carried a golden statue of the goddess Athena, after whom the city was named and who was considered protector of the fleet, plus statues of other Athenian gods. This sacred galley differed from the other vessels in Athens's fleet in that only citizens were permitted to crew it, whereas aliens were included in the crews of other ships.

A decade or two earlier, Athens's sacred galley had been the *Theoris*, or Sacred Mission, a massive ship with five banks of oars. Slow and unwieldy, the *Theoris* had been captured by the Aeginetans off Cape Sunium in a commando raid. Now, Athens's sacred galley was a trireme just like the other ships of Themistocles's war fleet—fast, agile, and able to take care of itself in a fight. The captain of this flagship of Themistocles's new navy was named Architeles, and assignment to the sacred galley was an enormous honor for both Architeles and his crewmen.

As for this flagship's name, it has not come down to us, but we know that within several decades the Athenian navy's sacred galley was called the *Paralos*. This literally means "by the sea"; the Athenians came to use the Paralos as a term that referred to all the coastline of Attica, their homeland. In the same way, the sacred galley's name of *Paralos* symbolically encompassed all of Attica. The flagship's name became so revered among Athenians that Pericles, Athens's future general of great renown, who was to himself sail on this vessel during his long career, would name his first son Paralos.

Pericles was a teenager in 480 BC as the Athenian fleet prepared to sail with Themistocles to do battle with the Persians and the women and children prepared to evacuate the city. The sacred galley that led Themistocles's navy may well have been the same *Paralos* that would sail under Pericles's feet several decades later. If not, the ship's name may have been passed down from Themistocles's flagship to its successors. So, for the purpose of this narrative, Themistocles's flagship will be referred to as the *Paralos*.

Like all the other triremes in the fleet, the flagship was about 130 feet long and 18 feet across the beam. Eight to nine feet of its hull sat above the waterline. The modern replica *Olympias*, 35 meters long from tip of the sternpost to the prow, but excluding the ram, was built from the same type of timbers as the original triremes. It was found to weigh seventy tons, suggesting the lighter new ships of Themistocles's fleet weighed something less than that. From a staff jutting above the ship's sternpost fluttered a large pennant. Every vessel in the Athenian fleet flew the same pennant, identifying it as a ship of Athens. In the same way, the other ships of both the coalition fleet and those of the enemy fleet flew identifying pennants.

The nature of those pennants is unknown, but each Greek city-state had a symbol that was identified with it and that invariably appeared on its coinage. In the case of Argos, that symbol was the nine-headed Hydra. The city of Sicyon used the dove. Calydon in Aetolia used the lion for its symbol. Calydon's neighbor Corinth used Pegasus, the flying horse, while the running boar was the proud emblem of Thebes.

Mighty Sparta used an inverted "V" for its emblem; the Greek letter "L," it stood for Laconia, the territory where Sparta stood, and much of which it ruled. The island state of Aegina, Athens's new coalition partner and old enemy, used the turtle as its emblem. The symbol of Athens was the owl, which the Athenians believed represented wisdom. A later occurrence described by Plutarch indicates that the pennants of Themistocles's warships bore that owl symbol. The pennant on Themistocles's flagship, we are told by Herodotus, also identified this as the ship of Athens's admiral, and it was likely to have been a different color to those of the remainder of the Athenian fleet.

In the August sun, as civilians streamed down to Piraeus to board the ships allocated to the evacuation, Themistocles stood on the stern deck of the *Paralos* with his staff and the ship's captain and pilot as the sacred galley led a parade of 147 triremes and one or two smaller communications vessels out into the Saronic Gulf. With sails full and 170 oars pulling and dipping with the precision of a machine, the *Paralos* headed east for Cape Sunium, today's Cape Sounis. On every Athenian ship, marines and sailors were having to take places at vacant oars for the moment. Bringing up the rear of the fleet came the straggling ships crewed by the novice Plataeans, who, as they dragged their oars through the water, were finding muscles they didn't know they had, and creating blisters on hands more accustomed to spears than oars. Along the coast of southeast Attica the ships passed as on shore the residents of Themistocles's hometown of Phrearrhioi and settlements nearby hurried along the coast road northwest toward the evacuation point, taking with them all they could carry.

Once Themistocles had departed Piraeus with the fleet, taking with him his energy and his influence, the number of refugees following the council's command to give up their homes dwindled and then dried up. In this initial evacuation, thousands of Athenian refugees would be carried across the Saronic Gulf to Troizen, where by public vote the town would make a daily payment to every Athenian refugee and would pay for tutors for the education of children among the evacuees. Those children were also permitted to gather fruit wherever they chose without fear of prosecution.

But Athens then had a population of an estimated 150,000 to 160,000 people, plus an unknown number of slaves. Even with approximately 40,000 men serving in the navy, and perhaps 20,000 people answering the initial evacuation order and being carried down to Troizen in several waves of ships, as many as 100,000 other Athenian men, women, and children were refusing to budge. To them, deserting all that was valuable to them was unthinkable. Perhaps it had been Themistocles's infectious belief in his naval plan, linked with the Oracle of Delphi's assurance that Athens would be saved by a wall of wood, that made the majority of Athens's residents so intransigent. Now Athens's wall of wood was sailing away.

Aboard one of the triremes as it rounded Cape Sunium, Aeschylus and his fellow top-tier rowers would have turned their eyes to the Temple of Poseidon as it stood high on the point to their right, and offered silent prayers to the god of the sea for the deliverance of ship and crew from the storm of battle that lay ahead. There is no direct proof that Aeschylus took part in the sea battles of this campaign, but on circumstantial evidence, most historians believe that he did. Certainly, that is inferred by fellow playwright Aristophanes. And Plutarch credited Aeschylus with firsthand knowledge of the Battle of Salamis, details he would relate in his play *The Persians*, which would describe that sea fight with the accuracy of an on-the-spot observer. That play would be performed for the first time at Athens in 472 BC, eight years after the battle took place.

Aeschylus did not obtain those details from the history of the Greco-Persian War by Herodotus that serves as our principal guide today. Herodotus was just eleven years old in 472 BC, and it would be a number of years before he wrote his history. Yet, some of the details and the personalities in both men's work are identical, suggesting that Herodotus borrowed from Aeschylus's earlier work. In *The Persians*, Aeschylus has a character, the Messenger, report on Persia's disaster at sea, declaring that his words were not from the lips of others. He had been a witness of these events, he says, and had his share of them. As it was the custom for Greek playwrights to take the leading roles of their works on stage, it's likely that Aeschylus played the part of the Messenger when *The Persians* was first presented on the Athenian stage. In such a case, as a genuine participant in these battles, his words would have had a special relevance, and resonance, as his audience would have been very much aware.

It would be mostly young men in their twenties who would have direct contact with the enemy in the battles ahead, as marines. Now, middle-aged, Aeschylus used as a weapon a wooden oar rolling easily in its leather sleeve. With his fellow townsmen from Eleusis, he would turn his trireme into one large ramming weapon. Themistocles had briefed his crews and trained them on the tactics he expected them to skillfully employ. It would be up to them to put the commander in chief's once wild scheme into deadly practice.

Once around the cape, the pilot of Themistocles's flagship set a northerly course, and with the wind filling their sails, all the ships of the Athenian fleet scudded up the coast of Attica to confront the foe off a distant shore.

10.

The Battle of Thermopylae, and the 300 Spartans

As the fleets of Athens and other coalition partners made their way to Artemisium, the advance elements of the armies of a handful of Greek city-states began to arrive at Thermopylae. Many leading men of the coalition partners were at Olympia competing in or watching the games that would not close until August 19. As a consequence, each city was sending a token force to block the pass at Thermopylae and await the arrival of the bulk of their army once the games had ended. Sparta, which had command of all coalition forces, was not only hamstrung by the timing of the Olympics, but it also had religious commitments, just as it had ten years earlier at the time of the Battle of Marathon. This prevented Sparta from sending its full army until after the full moon that fell on August 19. But Xerxes and the Persian land army were likely to reach Thermopylae before then.

Because Sparta had command of coalition forces, one of its two kings, Leonidas, was determined to march to Thermopylae before the full moon, to show Sparta's commitment to the cause and ensure that other coalition partners didn't lose heart and the will to resist the invader. Apparently in his thirties, Leonidas had unexpectedly come to the Spartan throne when his two elder brothers had died a decade before. He had married Gorgo, daughter of his half-brother and former king Cleomenes. She had only recently given birth to Leonidas's only son. Under Spartan law, the kings were prevented from calling a mass military mobilization of their fellow Spartans until after the Carnea Festival. Sacred to Apollo, the Carnea ran over eight days leading up the full moon, during which all Spartan military operations were suspended. But those same laws did permit the king to recruit a special guard of 300 warriors, all having to be men with living sons. Leonidas would lead his 300 to Thermopylae.

Leonidas handpicked every one of his 300 Spartans for the Thermopylae mission, and once chosen they quickly gathered their equipment. The fact that these men all had children meant that they were thirty years old and above. Like Athenians, Spartan men did not marry before they were thirty. To be selected by the king from all the thousands of available Spartan men-at-arms, these warriors would have been fit and known for their military prowess. In the typical Spartan fashion, all had neat beards and all wore their hair long to their shoulders. Appointment to the king's guard was a huge honor, but on this occasion it also meant the chosen ones would soon be marching on a mission from which many would not return.

This was a potential fate that failed to concern the 300. For more than twenty-three years, since the age of seven, these men had trained daily for battle. They lived, ate, and slept athleticism and combat. The arts played no part in their lives, and their slaves performed all domestic, agricultural, and industrial work for them. All 300 would have had battle experience, and all had come through the highly disciplined militaristic upbringing of the Spartan male. To them, dying for Sparta alongside their king and the comrades they had been raised with would be an honor.

Now, King Leonidas bid farewell to his fellow king Leotychidas, his wife, Gorgo, and his only son, Pleisarchus, who was just a babe in arms. Leonidas then marched his 300 troops out of the city and up the north road. The king was accompanied by a lone advisor, Megistias, a priest and diviner of sacrificial omens from Acarnania in central-western Greece. The Acarnanians had a longtime connection with Apollo and the Carnea Festival, and it appears that Leonidas took Megistias along on the mission to carry out the necessary religious observations of the Carnea for the 300. The Acarnanians also had a longtime connection with Athens, and it was at Athens that Megistias had formed a bond of friendship with the poet Simonides, the close friend of Themistocles. It is likely, as a result, that Megistias and Themistocles knew each other.

Following along behind the king, the priest, and the Spartan warriors, and bearing their equipment and supplies, hurried 300 Helot slaves originally from the town of Helos in Laconia, which Sparta had long before conquered. Back at Sparta, it would be the job of Leonidas's fellow king Leotychidas to mobilize the entire Spartan army immediately following the Carnea Festival. After detaching a guard to garrison the city's citadel, Leotychidas would march the full Spartan army north, first to Corinth, the coalition command center, with all speed in support of his fellow king at Thermopylae. Sparta could field an army at this time numbering some 5,000 Spartan citizens and another 5,000 men from throughout Laconia, and, if necessary, could arm the Helots as skirmishers.

Leonidas marched to Thermopylae knowing that the Oracle of Delphi had predicted, when asked for a prophesy once it was learned that Xerxes was planning his invasion of Greece, that either the barbarians would overthrow Sparta, or one of her kings must die. That king, said the Pythia, would be a son of mythological hero Hercules. Leonidas, whose name means "son of the lion," claimed descent from Hercules. Without showing that he was the least concerned by the prophesy, and wasting no time, Leonidas marched his advance guard up to the Isthmus of Corinth then to Thebes in Boeotia.

The Spartan king deliberately went via Thebes because of strong Spartan doubts about the commitment of the Thebans to the war against Xerxes. Leonidas was determined, by his presence on their doorstep, to make sure that Thebes remained true to the coalition. Although many Thebans did have their doubts about the wisdom of fighting the Persians, they sent out their general Leontiades with an advance force of 400 hoplites to join the Spartan column, promising to send their full army once the Olympics had passed. With his force augmented by the Thebans, King Leonidas continued on to Thermopylae, on the Gulf of Malis.

Today, Thermopylae is quite a way farther from the water than it was in 480 BC. Back then, impassable marshes extended to the coast, so that the pass was literally between mountain and sea. When Leonidas and his combined force of 700 Spartan and Theban hoplites reached it, they found that the pass was just fifty feet wide at its broadest, and at one place above and below Thermopylae itself the pass narrowed even further. East of Thermopylae, lower down at the village of Alpeni, the pass was so narrow that just a single wagon could negotiate the road. Long before, there had been hot springs called the Cauldrons high in the pass. Long before, too, the Phocians had built three walls equipped with gates across the pass. The West Gate was at the Phoenix River at the western end of the pass. The Middle Gate was located halfway through the pass, near the Cauldrons. The East Gate had guarded the eastern extremity of the pass. Of these walls and gateways little remained. Gates and hot springs combined had originally given Thermopylae its Hot Gates name. Leonidas was determined that he would make the Hot Gates live up to their name. For Xerxes.

Camping near the village of Alpeni and emptying its grain stocks, the Greek troops set to work rebuilding the stone Phocian wall where the Middle Gate had once stood. As the Spartans and Thebans toiled, more and more coalition hoplite contingents continued to arrive to join them. From the city of Thespiae in Boeotia came 1,000 men. From Corinth, 400 men. From three cities in Arcadia, 1,120 men. From Phlius, 200 men, accompanied by another 80 from Mycenae. Leonidas also sent messages to the people living in the region of the pass, and as a result the Phocians sent 1,000 fighters and the Locrians of Ozolia provided all the armed men they possessed after crewing several warships that they had sent to join the coalition's fleet. The end result was that, by the time the Phocian wall had been rebuilt, Leonidas had about 5,000 infantry at his disposal to hold the pass until reinforced by the main coalition armies. Meanwhile, Leonidas's advisor Megistias discovered that his only son was one of the warriors from the other Greek states who had come to join the Spartans at Thermopylae.

News was brought by the Phocians when they arrived that Xerxes and an enormous Persian army was just a day or two's march away, having come down from the north through Thessaly and then swung east to follow the contours of the Gulf of Malis toward Thermopylae. On hearing this, the Greeks from the Peloponnese suddenly lost their courage, and wanted to withdrew back to their own cities to defend them. In a meeting of all the Greek commanders that night, it required all Leonidas's powers of persuasion to convince his faltering colleagues to hold their ground. If they could delay the Persians here long enough, he argued, they would give enough time for the expected Greek reinforcements to arrive. And then there at Thermopylae, Xerxes would be permanently halted in his tracks. At least, that was the plan.

Leonidas's Spartans were just as determined and confident as their king. When one of the fighters from another contingent said that the Persians were so numerous the sun would be blotted out when their archers filled the sky with their arrows, a Spartan named Dieneces cheerily declared that this was excellent news. "If the Persians blot out the sun," he said, "we'll be able to fight in the shade!"

Meanwhile, Leonidas, to his chagrin, learned in discussion with the Phocians that there was another way across the mountains apart from the Thermopylae pass. Running southwest of Thermopylae, and called the Anopaea Path, this was nothing more than a goat track, but it skirted the Greek position and came out to the east of Thermopylae behind Leonidas's force. If the Persians were to learn of it, they could send infantrymen via this path to attack the Greeks from the rear. Hoping that Xerxes was ignorant of this alternate route, Leonidas nonetheless detached the 1,000 Phocian troops and gave them the task of blocking the path. They withdrew back down the pass from the main force to fulfill their mission, and climbing up into mountains along the track selected a location that they could defend on the Anopaea Path and set up camp.

At the same time, Leonidas sent two of his Spartans away with the Phocians. The warriors Aristodemus and Eurytus had both developed serious eye infections that had left them close to blind. The nature of these infections has not come down to us, but the affliction mirrors the sudden blindness of Athenian warrior Epizelus on the battlefield at Marathon a decade earlier. Herodotus did not seem to think this disease of the eyes exceptional, and perhaps it was relatively common in those times. So severe was the affliction, the two Spartans could barely see, and, until they recovered, Leonidas sent the pair, each accompanied by his personal Helot slave, back to the town of Alpeni. That town, as it happened, sat at the terminus of the mountain path the Phocians were now assigned to block.

The combined Greek force camped on the eastern side of the rebuilt wall at Middle Gate, with a strong rotating outer guard camping on the western side. The Spartans pulled guard duty and were in the outer camp one August day when a lone rider came up the pass from the west. The rider, an advance scout sent by Xerxes, sat on the back of his horse and watched as some Spartans, stripped naked, carried out gymnastic exercises. Others were combing out and braiding their long hair. Turning his horse, the scout rode back the way he'd come.

Not many miles to the northwest, the scout rejoined the Persian army, which had overrun or incorporated every city and military force that had stood in its path into Thessaly. As the Persians were setting up camp at the West Gate, where there was plentiful water at the Phoenix River, the scout reported to Xerxes at his enormous headquarters tent. This fabulous pavilion was filled with couches and tables of gold and silver, and hung with rich Persian carpets of dazzling color. The prostrate scout told of seeing several hundred long-haired Greeks idling in the sun at a wall barring the pass at Thermopylae. He had failed to see the thousands of other coalition troops encamped the other side of the wall.

Xerxes scoffed on hearing that just a few hundred long-haired Greeks were daring to make a stand at the pass, but Demaratus, the exiled Spartan leader in the king's entourage, warned him that those long-haired Greeks were Spartan warriors, and that in grooming and adorning their hair they were ceremonially preparing to fight to the death. Still Xerxes was unimpressed. Many much larger opposition forces had run away when the Persians approached, and Xerxes was confident that these Greeks at Thermopylae would likewise lose their courage in the face of the Persian horde.

For four days, Xerxes remained where he was. But when, on the fifth day, his scouts reported that the impudent Greeks were still at Thermopylae, the king ordered his half-brothers Abrocomes and Hyperanthes to lead an assault against the Greek force. These two sons of the late King Darius were given a mixed force of elite Medians and men from the province of Cissia, which was home to Xerxes's capital Susa, and ordered to advance up the Thermopylae pass and clear the obstruction there. Xerxes gave express orders that his troops were to capture the Spartans alive, and bring them into his presence so that he could see what sort of men these reckless Greeks were.

Leonidas, meanwhile, had spotted the Persian scout and guessed that large Persian forces were not far behind. Hoping to draw more support from Greeks in Thessaly, he sent one of his Spartans, Pantites, hurrying along the pass before its western end was entirely closed off by the approaching enemy, to deliver messages to leaders of states in central and western Greece who had yet to go over to the Persians. Pantites would succeed in reaching western Greece, but would find no one there prepared to go against Xerxes now that his troops were in eastern Greece.

As the Medians and Cissians marched up the pass toward Thermopylae's Middle Gate, Leonidas instructed his troops to prepare for battle. Armor was strapped on, swords were draped over shoulders, helmet crests were affixed to helmets that were set on the back of heads, and shields and spears were taken up. Leonidas, like Themistocles, was an advocate of forward defense, of taking the battle to the enemy and surprising them. Instead of defending the wall, as Xerxes would expect as a result of the scouts' reports, Leonidas led all his troops out from their camp and along the road to the narrowest part of the pass west of Thermopylae, where it was just twenty feet wide. There, with Leonidas and his 296 remaining fellow Spartans taking the front position, the Greeks formed a series of close order phalanxes that stretched back along the narrow pass, with gaps between each. Shoulder to shoulder, the Spartans wedged themselves against the rock walls either side of them, and waited in tense silence.

When the Persian assault force came marching up, they were astonished to find a human wall of 4,000 men in front of them at the narrowest point of the pass, not just the 300 Spartans reported by the scout. The forepart of this human wall had a wooden and bronze facing of the interlocked circular shields of Sparta's finest fighters, all with the simple inverted "V" emblazoned on them. With their heads and faces covered by Corinthian helmets, every longhaired Spartan was anonymous. But the Spartans themselves knew that their king, Leonidas, stood in the first rank with them. Leading from the front, the professed descendant of Hercules was prepared to use Herculean efforts to hold the pass.

For as far as Median and Cissian eye could see, the pass was a sea of shields, poised Greek spearheads, and helmet plumes rustling in the breeze. Persian commanders Abrocomes and Hyperanthes ordered their Medians to charge. Eagerly, the self-confident Medians advanced to the attack. They wore the same outfits as their Persian cousins, with multicolored tunics covered with fish-scale armor, trousers, and flat turbans. They were armed with short spears and daggers, and carried light wicker shields on their left arms. The Cissians, who were held in reserve, were dressed and armed identically to the Medians, apart from wearing headbands on their heads instead of turbans.

The Medians crashed into the waiting Spartans. The spears of Leonidas and his men pumped from over their round Argive shields. These spears, in effect long pikes, were longer than those of the Medians, and the attackers were immediately at a disadvantage, being unable to reach over the shield line. Spartan spears lunged into Median necks and faces, and soon Median dead were piled high, while barely a Spartan was scratched. Bravely, more and more Medians charged the Greeks, and died. This slaughter continued through the morning and into the afternoon, and among those who were felled by the Spartans were Persian commanders, Abrocomes and Hyperanthes, the brothers of Xerxes.

In the meantime Xerxes himself had come up the pass accompanied by his bodyguard troops and the 10,000 elite Immortals. Xerxes had a raised throne set up, from where he watched the battle, and, enraged by the loss of his brothers and the failure of the Medians to defeat the Greeks, he called Hydarnes, commander of the Immortals, and instructed him to lead his men against the Spartans. The surviving Medians withdrew with their wounded, and the Immortals, the most feared unit in Xerxes's army, advanced machinelike to the attack.

The Spartans held off the Immortals for a time, then turned and ran back toward the next formation of Greek warriors. The Immortals, yelling victoriously at the top of their voices, broke ranks and gave chase. But, as one man, the Spartans suddenly stopped in their tracks, wheeled about, and drove back into the startled Persians, forcing them back the way they'd come, striking many down. This feigned retreat was a practiced Spartan tactic. Several times they employed it during the afternoon, and each time the Immortals fell for the trick, gave chase, and were lured into a bloody trap. Three times, Xerxes, watching this from afar, jumped up from his throne in anguish as he saw his men deceived. In the late afternoon, he had "Recall" sounded. Leaving thousands of his men dead in the pass, he withdrew his troops to the Persian marching camp at West Gate.

Leonidas meanwhile buried his mere handful of Spartan dead where they had fallen then withdrew to the camp at the wall for the night. During the night, Leonidas decided that it was time other coalition partners shared the blood and the glory. That day, he was to remark, he had possessed many combatants but few warriors. The next day, he would give his exhausted Spartans a rest, while the troops of other nations took a turn at the pointy end of the battle.

With the dawn, Leonidas again brought his combined force forward to take up a position west of Middle Gate. Throughout morning and afternoon, the warriors from other Greek nations duly took turns at the front of the battle formation, and after a day's fighting the Persians had once again been unable to dislodge the defenders. Throughout the two days of fighting, the Persians had lost thousands of men because of Xerxes's stubborn determination to capture the defiant Greeks alive. Had he permitted his troops to use their most effective weapon, the bow, the Persians would have truly blotted out the sun with their arrows, and would have destroyed the pass's Greek defenders by sheer weight of missiles. But Xerxes would not allow his men to use their arrows, for that would leave no Greeks alive to be interrogated or humiliated by the king. So for now, Xerxes's tactics were leading to the death and humiliation of his own best men.

Late in the afternoon of the second day of fighting, Xerxes called an end to combat and dejectedly withdrew his forces down the pass. On arriving back in his camp, Xerxes summoned his generals to a war conference, to discuss what should be done about the defiant Greeks. The conference had not long been under way when it was interrupted. A local man from the coastal town of Malis was brought to the king. Ephialtes by name, he had come to Xerxes in search of a large reward. For Ephialtes possessed valuable knowledge.

Ephialtes told the king about the Path of Anopaea, the mountain route around Thermopylae. Overjoyed by this revelation, Xerxes commanded

Hydarnes to lead the Immortals around Thermopylae via the pathway, and commanded the informant to be their guide. Ephialtes estimated that the men he led across the mountains would not be in position east of the Greek defenders of the pass until well after daybreak—about the hour that the marketplace of a Greek town or city was normally at its busiest, he said. It was then, Ephialtes suggested, that Xerxes should bring his main force up the pass from the west, to trap the Greeks between the two forces. Just as the sun was setting late that evening and the lamps were being lit in the Persian camp, Ephialtes led away Hydarnes and the now-replenished Immortals unit, which had been brought up to full strength again with the transfer of the best men from other Persian units to replace those who had fallen in the pass.

Crossing the River Phoenix in a single file, the Persians climbed up to a mountain ridge and found the path that Ephialtes had spoken of. With Ephialtes in the lead as their guide, the Persian force slowly followed the pathway along the ridge. Halfway along the path, the route passed under spreading oak trees. Autumn came early in the mountains, and a bed of dry fallen oak leaves covered the path here. As the Persians passed over them, the leaves crackled underfoot. The night was still, and the crackling leaves alerted the Phocians stationed on the path. The Phocians, who were almost asleep, sprang to their feet and took up their arms.

Immortals commander Hydarnes, at the head of the Persian column with the local guide, was alarmed at the sight of armed Greeks appearing ahead, and anxiously asked Ephialtes whether they were Spartans. Ephialtes, who recognized the Greeks' shield markings, replied that they were Phocians. Knowing that it was the Spartans in particular that his king wanted taken alive, not local farmers, the Persian commander ordered his men to fill their bows. Soon, hundreds of arrows were flying through the air. The Phocians were not fulltime soldiers like the Spartans. Terrified by the arrow showers, some threw away their shields and deserted, fleeing back along the path. Most withdrew off the path with their commander and climbed to a rocky peak where they could shelter from arrows. There they prepared to fight to the death.

But Hydarnes merely ordered his men to keep marching. The Phocians were left hunkered down and watching the enemy scurry by, knowing that they had failed Leonidas and failed the Greek coalition. It took all night for the Persian force to negotiate the path. As dawn was breaking, Phocian deserters arrived in Alpeni and gasped their story about the coming of the Persians. As several messengers were sent from the town to warn Leonidas at Middle Gate, the two blinded Spartans then in the town chose very different courses of action. Aristodemus, believing it pointless for a blind man to attempt to fight, decided to stay at Alpeni and went into hiding. The other Spartan, Eurytus, ordered his Helot to bring him his equipment and buckle him into his armor. Eurytus then instructed the slave to lead him back to Thermopylae.

At the Greek camp at Middle Gate that same morning, Megistias the priest carried out the normal dawn animal sacrifice. On consulting the entrails, he found them blemished. Word quickly spread through the camp that the omens for the day ahead were bad. A little later, the messengers arrived from Alpeni with the news that Persian troops were crossing the mountain path and would soon be behind Leonidas's force, cutting them off to the east. Before long, the Greeks would be sandwiched between Hydarnes's 10,000 Immortals and Xerxes's main force. Leonidas quickly called a conference of the contingent's commanders.

Most of the Greek commanders were in favor of pulling out before they were trapped. Only Demophilas, commander of the Thespians, agreed with Leonidas that a stand should be taken there, on principle, to show all of Greece what these men were made of. Demophilas vowed that he and his Thespians would stand beside the Spartans to the last. But he was the only commander to do so. Seeing the unwillingness of the other commanders to emulate the Thespians, Leonidas now ordered all contingents except the Thespians and the Thebans to withdraw. The Thebans, who had never been enthusiastic about this campaign, were ordered by Leonidas to remain with him. Megistias the priest also volunteered to remain, although he commanded his warrior son to retreat with his unit. The other contingents hurriedly packed up and marched back down the pass to the east. As they were withdrawing, lookouts came scurrying down from the heights to tell Leonidas they had seen Persian troops crossing the hills to the southeast. The Spartans, Thespians, and Thebans armed themselves and prepared for a final stand.

At the Persian camp, the Persian forces had formed up. But Xerxes held them back for several hours as Ephialtes had suggested, to give Hydarnes time to get into position. He then gave the order for a large detachment to advance with him up the pass toward Middle Gate. But the Persian force had not long been on the march when it was confronted by Leonidas and a phalanx of 1,700 men. To catch the Persians by surprise, Leonidas had advanced even farther west than he had on the previous two days, to a place where the pass widened considerably, with sheer cliffs on one side and marshland on the other.

Here, the two forces came together and became locked in bitter close-in fighting, although on a broader front today. As before, the closely packed Greek phalanx mowed down the Persians opposed to them. Now, knowing that their rear must have been sealed off by the Persians who had used the goat track and that survival was no longer an option, Leonidas and his men fought like demons. Determined to take as many opponents with them as they could before they themselves fell, they drove back the confused enemy lines. Many Persian troops were pushed into the marshy waters to one side of the road, where they drowned. A number of Persians were trampled to death by their own panicking comrades. Survivors, when they fell back, found their own officers armed with whips lashing them to force them to hold their ground or advance.

Leonidas, like many of his men, finding his spear splintered and broken, cast it away, drew his sword, and hacked at every Persian who stood in his way. It was here and now that Leonidas was felled and killed. Seeing him go down, the Persians gained new strength, and pushed back Leonidas's men. The Spartans, led now by Dieneces, the warrior who had joked about the shade provided by Persian arrows, and by two brothers, Alpheus and Maro, regrouped and charged the enemy until they once more stood over their king's body. The Persians, mounting a fresh drive, again drove the Spartans back. The Spartans, determined not to let Leonidas's body fall into enemy hands, charged again. A total of four times this drive and counterdrive took place, until finally the Spartans were able to lift up the corpse of Leonidas and carry it away as they fell back.

The Persian weight of numbers was telling, and the Greeks made a gradual fighting withdrawal back up the pass, until they reached the wall at Middle Gate and their camp. There, the Spartans and Thespians, still maintaining their national formations, retreated up onto a hillock above and to the west of the wall, which protected one of their flanks. There, Megistias the priest sheltered in their midst. The Thebans, who had never been willing partners in this battle, now hesitated. And then, as pursuing Persians troops came up, the Thebans suddenly threw down their weapons and with hands raised high to show that they were unarmed, they walked toward the enemy. As they did, they called out that they had been made to fight by Leonidas and had been nothing but hostages of the Spartans.

The first few unarmed Thebans were cut down and killed by the enemy, but then with Persian officers calling for the rest to be taken alive as Xerxes had commanded, most of the Thebans were made prisoner and hauled away. All would end up as slaves, and every one, starting with their commander Leontinides, would have his skin branded with a red-hot iron bearing the symbol of Xerxes.

This left the Spartans and Thespians clustered together *en masse* on the hillock. Now, Hydarnes and the Immortals arrived from the east. Breaking down the wall, they surged around the flank and rear of the Greek ranks on the hill. The encirclement of the Greeks was complete. Meanwhile, the blinded Spartan Eurytus had followed the Immortals up the pass, led by his slave. Now telling the terrified Helot to run for his life, Eurytus charged the Immortals blindly from the rear. Eurytus killed a number of the surprised enemy before, surrounded, he too fell. On the hill, the remaining Spartans and Thespians held their ground and fought off every assault.

Finally, Xerxes, now that he had made some of the Greeks his captives, ordered his men to pull back and for bows to be used at last. This sealed the fate of the Spartans and Thespians. The sun truly was blotted out by the clouds of arrows that now filled the sky. The Greek warriors held their shields above their heads to protect themselves and their near neighbors from the missiles, and arrows quickly filled shields, until those shields looked like porcupines and weighed twice their normal weight. But not every arrow could be fended off. Arms and legs were skewered. And, when a wounded man lost the power to continue to keep his shield aloft, and lowered it, even a little, more arrows got through and found necks, throats, shoulders. Minute by minute, the number of Greeks still standing was reduced, and the raised protective shields became fewer and fewer. And then not a single Greek was still on his feet.

Thirteen hundred bloodied Spartans and Thespians lay heaped in a mass that covered the hilltop. Their bodies, their shields, and the ground all around them were peppered with arrows. But still they were not all dead. Some moved. Some still defiantly gripped a sword in the right hand. The clouds of arrows ceased to fall. There was a silent pause, as Xerxes and his Persians surveyed the scene with a mixture of businesslike satisfaction and admiration for brave warriors who had fought to the last and caused them so much aggravation. And then Xerxes gave an order. At a trumpet call, the Immortals drew their swords and moved in for the kill.

The only image of Themistocles that has come down to us is this herm bust found at Ostia, the port of ancient Rome.

© Hans R. Goette.

An Athenian hoplite heading off to war farewells his father while his dog watches on and his wife or mother waits with jug and cup for the ritual departure libation. A fifth-century BC vase illustration.

The Soros at Marathon, where the Athenians who fell in the battle were interred, with Mount Kotroni behind it.

The remains of a monument raised on the Marathon battle site by the Athenians to commemorate their victory over the Persians.

© LOUISE DANDO-COLLINS.

A modern-day statue at the Marathon battle site represents Athenian commander Miltiades, helmet on the back of his head and sword in one hand while the other hand is raised to signify that here the Persians would not be permitted to pass.

© LOUISE DANDO-COLLINS.

The narrow beach at Marathon today. Most modern Greek vacationers enjoying this beach would have no idea that here thousands of Persians were slaughtered by the Athenians and Plataeans. © Louise Dando-Collins.

The beach at Artemisium. Where the boats of local fishermen lie today, hundreds of Greek triremes were beached in 480 BC. On these waters between Artemisium and the nearby mainland, three days of stalemated sea battles took place between ships of the Greek coalition and Xerxes's Persian fleet.

© Louise Dando-Collins.

The Treasury of Athens at the sanctuary of Apollo, Delphi, erected by the Athenians to house spoils from the Battle of Marathon and dedicated to the god Apollo. © LOUISE DANDO-COLLINS.

The remains of the Temple of Apollo at Delphi today. The Pythia, the Oracle of Delphi, received her clients in a cave beneath the temple. It was here that the Athenians received a baffling prediction from the Pythia that Themistocles interpreted as a forecast of Greek victory at Salamis.

© LOUISE DANDO-COLLINS.

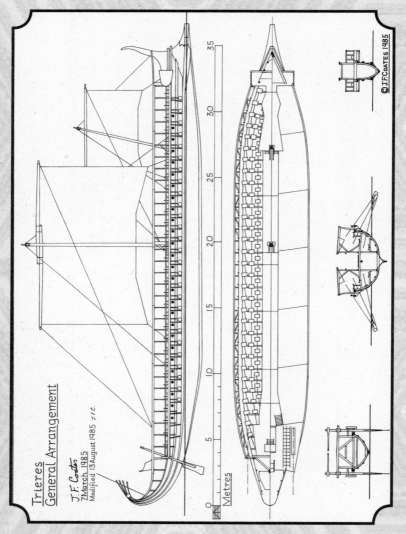

Trieres
General Arrangement

J.F. Coates
7 March 1985
Modified 13 August 1985 *J.F.C.*

Metres

© J.F.COATES 1985

Modern-day plans for a Greek trireme on which the *Olympias* replica was based.

The Greek trireme replica *Olympias* during sea trials in Greek waters.

The trireme replica *Olympias* arrives off Tolon during sea trials. A commissioned ship of the Helene Navy, she sits today in a naval museum at Piraeus. The Trireme Trust of the United Kingdom has plans to build a second trireme replica.

A close-up of the business end of a trireme—the ram of the Olympias. Themistocles urged his captains to focus on ramming the enemy rather than trying to board and capture them, and this tactic proved especially successful at the Battle of Salamis.

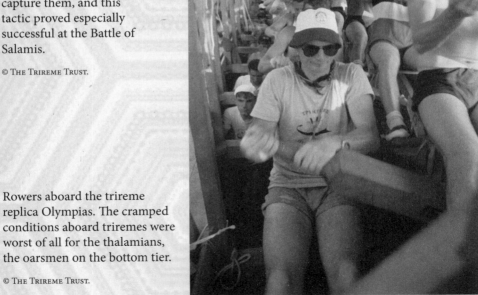

Rowers aboard the trireme replica Olympias. The cramped conditions aboard triremes were worst of all for the thalamians, the oarsmen on the bottom tier.

11.

Cut and Thrust at Artemisium

The sweeping Bay of Artemisium on the north side of the island of Euboea took its name from the fact that a temple to the goddess Artemis, also known as Diana, stood on a hill there overlooking the bay and the strait beyond. From there, the Greek mainland and the territory of Magnesia were clearly visible ten miles away across the water to the north.

In the week prior to the land battle at Thermopylae, and in sight of the shrine of Artemis, upward of 300 Greek coalition triremes and smaller craft had gathered. Some lay at anchor in the bay, but most were drawn up, side by side, along the full extent of the sandy beach. On the land had spread a city of tents of the various contingents, unloaded from the holds of their ships. Campfires smoked. There were some 55,000 Greek seamen, marines, and archers there, and most idled about the encampment, exercised, or prepared throwing spears and arrows for the expected battle ahead. Others ranged inland in search of provisions and wood for their cooking fires. Aristophanes, speaking from experience, said that a food-foraging mission ashore in a new land was often an adventure for young trireme crewmen, boys who had often never before been away from home.

Athenian commander Themistocles surveyed the scene at Artemisium with a mixture of delight and displeasure. He was delighted that his Athenian navy dominated the fleet here. He had arrived with 147 triremes, 20 of those manned by the unskilled Plataeans. With his own Athenian ships undermanned, Themistocles had handed 20 of his triremes over to Euboean islanders, the people of the city of Chalcis, which was then as now Euboea's largest city and chief port. Some Chalcideans were fishermen, with maritime experience. With Chalcis manning those 20 ships, Themistocles was able to move those ships' former crews over to his own remaining vessels, with the result that he had enough men to fully crew 107 Athenian warships there. Without a doubt, the forty ships that Themistocles gave away were the older triremes in his navy, those he had inherited from the Marathon and Paros campaigns. The new, light, fast triremes built to his specifications over the past two years he would reserve for his own crews, men who had been training in them for upward of twenty-four months.

But Themistocles would have been displeased with the number of other warships that joined the Athenian navy at Artemisium. And displeased with the fact that overall command of the entire coalition fleet was not his, but held by a Spartan, even though Athens's flotilla represented half the coalition fleet. The Corinthians had sent 40 triremes to Artemisium. From Athens's near neighbor in southern Attica, the prosperous port city of Megara, 20 triremes had arrived. From Sicyon had come 12. Epidaurus had sent 8 triremes, Eretria 7, and the Styreans 2. The Ceans had provided 2 triremes and 2 smaller penteconters, and another 7 penteconters had come from the Locrians of Ozolia. Sparta contributed just 10 Laconian triremes. Most annoying of all to Themistocles, Athens's old foe Aegina had managed to send a measly 18 triremes. Themistocles knew for a fact that, not long before this, Aegina's navy had consisted of at least 70 triremes. Clearly, Aegina was keeping most of its navy at home. Even the sparsely populated Athenian ally of Troizen had managed to send 5 triremes.

In all, there were some 270 Greek warships there. In itself, this was an impressive figure, but according to reports, the Persians were sailing south with more than 1,300 warships, outnumbering the coalition navy's ships by five to one. While many Greeks offered prayers to Boreas, god of the wind, to blow up a storm to wreck King Xerxes's fleet before it reached southern Greece, the same way that King Darius's fleet had been wrecked en route in 392 BC, Themistocles was a pragmatic man. He believed that Athens's fate and future lay in her own hands, and in her navy's hands. Not long after arriving at Artemisium and surveying the comparatively small coalition fleet, he sent one of the communications vessels scurrying south to Pogos, the port of Troizen, with orders for the 53 remaining Athenian triremes waiting there following evacuation duties to come with all speed to join him at Artemisium.

There was nothing that Themistocles could do about superseding Spartan command of the fleet. That post had been taken by Eurybiades, a Spartan who was to prove to be lacking in both imagination and strong leadership skills. But as Themistocles worked with Eurybiades and the other coalition admirals in agreeing to strategic and tactical plans, he asserted his influence and ensured that Athens played a key role in all developments. When two small, fast ships were assigned to serve as message carriers between the coalition sea and land forces, one was Athenian. A *triaconter* of thirty oars, it was stationed off Thermopylae, forty miles from Artemisium to bring communications from and news of King Leonidas and his force at the pass. The second vessel was kept at instant readiness at Artemisium, to take messages in the other direction, to Leonidas. Three triremes were also assigned to serve in the forward scouting role, to watch for the approach of the Persian fleet. One of these triremes was Athenian, another came from the quintet of ships from Troizen, and the third was provided by the Aeginetan commander. These three watch ships pushed well north together, with orders to sprint back to Artemisium as soon as they spotted the enemy fleet.

On the other side, a squadron of ten of the fastest sailing ships in the Persian fleet had also been sent ahead on scouting duty. And one summer's day, off the coast of Thessaly, this squadron was spotted by the coalition's trio of watch ships. With a strong wind behind them, the Persians were fast bearing down on the Greek trio. With their oarsmen straining at their oars and their deckhands trying to raise their sails while each vessel was under way, the watch ships fled south to alert the Greeks at Artemisium.

The lighter Athenian trireme soon pulled ahead of its two companions, as, with the tailwind filling their sails, the ten Persian sailing ships gradually hauled in the last of the fleeing ships, the trireme from Troizen. A Persian ship nosed against the stern of the struggling trireme. Grappling hooks trailing ropes of papyrus and flax flew across the gap. Once the hooks had bitten into wood, forty enemy marines dragged their bow closer to the Troizenian ship, then leaped aboard, quickly capturing the vessel without much of a fight. The most handsome member of the Troizenian marine detachment aboard, a young man named Leo, was disarmed and dragged to the prow of his own ship. There, the Persians slit his throat, sacrificing him to their god Ahura Mazda as their first captive of the campaign.

The nine other Persian ships continued to pursue the trireme from Aegina and the more distant Athenian ship. They overhauled the Aeginetan, but every time the Persians went to board, her pilot managed to turn the trireme away at the crucial moment. In the end, after giving its pursuers much aggravation, the Aeginetan ship was successfully boarded by marines from a ship from the city of Sidon in Phoenicia. The Aeginetan marines aboard put up a stiff fight, with one of them, Pytheas, only being subdued after he'd received numerous wounds. Pytheas's opponents were so impressed by his fighting spirit that they dressed and bandaged his wounds. When the Sidonian ship returned to the Persian fleet, Pytheas would be shown off as an example of a courageous Greek and feted by his captors. His Aeginetan crewmates were not so fortunate; they were dragged away into slavery.

The Athenian watch ship, one of Themistocles's fast new triremes, managed to keep the Persians at bay for some time. But the Athenian captain, Phormos, seeing that the enemy ships were gradually overtaking him, steered for the coast and beached his ship at a river mouth. As soon as their ship grounded, the Athenian crewmen leapt ashore and ran for their lives. The Persians captured their ship, but Phormos led his 200 crewmen overland through Thessaly, Magnesia, and Boeotia, and avoiding Persian troops eventually brought them home safely to Athens.

The fate of the three watch ships had been seen from the shore by local Greeks. Word was carried south to the island of Sciathus, modern Sciathos, and from its highest point fire signals were transmitted to nearby Euboea, warning that the Persian fleet was coming and the guard ships were lost. In fact, just three of the ten ships from the Persian advance squadron continued south, to lay a navigation marker between Sciathus and the mainland. The seven remaining Persian ships sailed back up the coast to rejoin the main invasion fleet with their three captured triremes and prisoners.

The news of the fate of the watch ships brought panic to the ranks of the Greek seamen gathered at Artemisium, and when their admirals met in conference that night Themistocles could not talk his colleagues into staying put. The majority of the admirals felt Artemisium was too exposed. They wanted to withdraw to the Euboean capital, Chalcis, and defend the long Euripus channel between the island and the mainland, which at its narrowest was just fifty feet wide. Rather than risk a split among the coalition partners, Themistocles went along with the majority. The camp at Artemisium was hastily packed up, and the coalition ships were heaved back into the sea to withdraw along the west coast of Euboea to Chalcis. It was pure fear, according to Herodotus, that drove the Greeks into withdrawing to Chalcis. Yet, considering what was about to follow this withdrawal, it's not unlikely that some old sailors in the Greek ranks, local men with a good weather eye and knowledge of the conditions around Euboea at this time of year, had an influence on the decision to seek a far more sheltered anchorage.

The Persian fleet, meanwhile, was so vast that at each overnight stop only so many ships could be hauled up onto a beach. The remainder had to anchor offshore, and as the fleet halted for the night off the Magnesian shore below Mount Pelion, between the city of Casthanaea and Cape Sepias, most had to be moored offshore in rows eight deep. It was here that the prayers of those Greeks who had sought the intercession of the wind god were answered, with a vengeance. The next day dawned deceptively clear and still. Deathly still. And then the sky in the east blackened, and a raging storm blew in across the Aegean Sea and swept the coast of Magnesia. The storm lasted three days. It sank or forced ashore 400 of the Persian vessels. Most of the more than 80,000 seamen from these ships survived because they were sheltering ashore at the time. So much wreckage was washed up after the storm there was enough wood for these survivors to build a tall wall of wood right around their encampment. Now, there were 400 fewer ships to menace southern Greece. But 900 warships still remained and would continue their progress south.

News of this Persian disaster was enough the buoy the spirits of the Greek sailors who at Chalcis had been untouched by the storm. Although no one at that time knew how many enemy ships had been lost, the expectation was that few could have survived the savage storm, and Themistocles was able to convince his fellow admirals that they should take advantage of Xerxes's misfortune by returning to Artemisium, from where they could confront what was left of his reduced fleet before it could pass them by. The coalition ships rowed back to Artemisium, and took up their previous position.

At the same time, the surviving ships of the Persian fleet advanced down the Magnesian coast, and, early in the afternoon of the same day that the coalition ships returned to Artemisium, ship after ship could be seen arriving and anchoring at Aphetae Bay, ten miles across the strait from the Greek fleet. It was abundantly clear to Themistocles and his fellow commanders that, despite the storm, the Persians still greatly outnumbered them, by at least three to one. Yet the gods seemed to smile on the Greeks when a squadron of fifteen Persian ships that had lagged well behind their main fleet came rowing toward Artemisium. The Persian commander of this tail-end squadron had not noticed that his own fleet was anchored at Aphetae. Seeing the mass of triremes ahead at Artemisium, he mistook those ships for his own fleet. Blithely, the fifteen ships came on, expecting a warm welcome at Artemisium.

They received a welcome, but not one they liked. Greek crews swiftly launched their triremes, which went surging out to surround the unfortunate Persians before they realized their mistake. The fifteen ships were taken without a fight. Among the more than 3,000 Persian prisoners taken from these ships were three leading nobles, generals in Xerxes's army. Under questioning, the prisoners provided Themistocles and his fellow coalition commanders with their most accurate picture yet of the makeup of Xerxes's land and sea forces. The prisoners were then taken away in chains to Corinth, which continued to serve as the coalition's center of operations.

Despite this easy success with the capture of the enemy squadron, the sight of the massive Persian fleet conglomerated across the water from Artemisium was a daunting one, and the confidence of many Greek captains and crewmen ebbed away like the outgoing tide. Talk around campfires was soon of withdrawing again from Artemisium, this time to the inner parts of southern Greece, to desert the sea and fight on land. The loudest voice in this negative talk was that of Adimantus, commander of the Corinthian squadron, who had considerable influence among his colleagues because of the central role that Corinth had played in the formation of the coalition, and continued to play as the center of resistance to the Persians.

This talk alarmed Themistocles, but it alarmed even more the men from Chalcis crewing twenty Athenian triremes for Themistocles—if the coalition fleet withdrew, their island of Euboea would be left virtually defenseless. The Chalcideans sent word to the leading men of the island, and that evening these local leaders descended on the Greek camp and sought a meeting with commanding admiral Eurybiades. In that meeting, the islanders begged the Spartan commander to command the Greek fleet to wait at least a few days to allow the islanders time to remove their children and their slaves to a safe place off the island. But Eurybiades only shrugged. Herodotus would accuse him of being fainthearted, an accusation Herodotus cast the way of many Greeks during his account of this war. But as was to be shortly proven, the Spartan admiral was merely weak. Eurybiades sent the Euboeans away, saying he would be guided by the will of the majority of coalition admirals.

The Euboean leaders then went to Themistocles's tent and put the same request to him that they had put to Eurybiades. To their relief, they found the Athenian commander determined to stay at Artemisium and risk a battle here in defense of Euboea. This was a far more attractive option for the Euboeans than evacuating the island. But, Themistocles lamented, convincing Eurybiades and the more outspoken admirals to adopt his point of view was almost impossible. The Euboeans would have to arm him for the task. The islanders got the message. They returned soon after with trunks full of silver coin—thirty talents' worth.

Themistocles then met privately with Eurybiades, and passed five talents in Euboean silver over to him. Weak Eurybiades took the bribe, and at that night's council of coalition admirals, he expressed his support for the course advocated by Themistocles, that of staying and fighting. This won over all the commanders but one. The odd man out was Adimantus, the Corinthian, who threatened to sail his forty triremes away without waiting for the other admirals to the do same. Knowing that such an act would sap the resolve of the other commanders and probably result in the complete breakup of the fleet, Themistocles took the Corinthian aside.

"Desert us, would you?" said Themistocles. "I do not think so! I will pay you more to remain with us than the Persians ever would for you to desert your friends."

Themistocles immediately ordered his staff to send a gift aboard the Corinthian flagship. A gift for Adimantus. When Adimantus returned to his ship and opened the delivery, he found the gift to be three talents of silver. The Corinthian admiral kept the money and ceased to call for the fleet to withdraw. Perhaps he chose to keep his mouth shut through the combined effects of the silver and the inference that Themistocles believed Adimantus capable of accepting a bribe from the Persians. That inference contained an implied threat that Themistocles would publicly accuse him of accepting money from the enemy. A little later in the war, Themistocles would use this same tactic to bring another straying commander back into line, only in that case he would articulate the threat to denounce the man as a paid agent of the enemy if he failed to do Themistocles's bidding. So, Adimantus kept the cash and his honor.

Both Adimantus and Eurybiades believed their bribes came from the Athenian treasury. Little did they know that Athens had spent her last talent on provisions for their sailors. The thirty-talent bribe paid to Themistocles by the Euboeans continued to be a secret known only to Themistocles and the islanders, with the latter no doubt thrilled with what Themistocles was able to achieve with that bribe. Themistocles, keeping the remaining of twenty-two talents as "working capital," soon had more use for that fund. He learned that Architeles, captain of his own sacred galley, was complaining about having no money to pay his men and was talking about upping anchors and taking the *Paralos* home.

Keeping other contingents at Artemisium after his own flagship had deserted Themistocles would be an impossibility, and he had to act fast. Unlike Themistocles, who lived ashore in his tent, Architeles lived aboard his ship. Themistocles now informed a group of his most loyal men of what Architeles was proposing to do. Furious, they stormed aboard the *Paralos* just as Architeles was sitting down to dinner. After roughing him up and threatening to do worse if he attempted to desert, the band of loyalists even took Architeles's supper. After Architeles complained bitterly to Themistocles about this treatment, Themistocles sent a chest full of provisions aboard the *Paralos*. Architeles emptied the chest and found at the bottom, beneath the foodstuffs, a talent of silver coin.

Architeles immediately went to Themistocles. Thanking him for provisions, he asked about the cash. The Athenian commander smiled, and told him, "Eat well tonight, and tomorrow pay your crewmen." Themistocles's smile faded. Now, he would expect to hear no more seditious talk from Architeles about taking the sacred galley away from Artemisium. "Or else I will spread it among the Athenians that you received the money from the enemy."

Every cloud, they say, has a silver lining. And the defeatist cloud hanging over the Greek fleet at Artemisium, now lined with silver, blew away. Themistocles had succeeded in committing the Greeks to battle, on the sea, on his terms. But it had been a monumental struggle for him to keep the fleet together, and to finally convince his colleagues and even one of his own captains to find the courage to do battle against the much larger enemy fleet.

Early the next morning, as ships were being prepared for action, a deserter from the Persian fleet arrived at Artemisium. His name was Scyllias, and he was a native of Scione in Chalcidice, to the north, a Greek-speaking territory originally settled by Euboeans from Chalcis. Scyllias was considered one of the most expert deep-sea divers of the era, with the ability to hold his breath underwater for an extraordinary length of time. Second-century AD Greek geographer Pausanias, who wrote during the reign of the Roman emperor Hadrian, was to claim that, the night the Persian fleet lay anchored off Mount Pelios, just days before Scyllias's defection at Artemisium, Scyllias and his daughter Hydna had swum around the Persian ships, cutting as many mooring lines as they could so the ships would be swept away by the storm then brewing. Statues of Scyllias and Hydna would be raised at Delphi by the coalition states, and according to Pausanias that was in recognition of their act of sabotage off Mount Pelion.

Historian Herodotus was to say that Scyllias had actually helped the Persians after the storm, diving for and recovering much treasure from their wrecked ships. But he added that Scyllias had also helped himself to some of that treasure. Herodotus also expressed doubt about another story he heard concerning Scyllias—that the defector swam all the way across from Aphetae to Artemisium underwater. Herodotus was convinced he'd used a small boat for the crossing. Not that the Greeks at Artemisium were concerned how Scyllias come to be there. Crowding around him on the beach, they plied him with questions. What he revealed excited the Greeks so much that Eurybiades called an immediate council of admirals to discuss this new intelligence. The defector detailed the Persian losses in the storm. More important, he said that the Persians had been keen to attack the Greek fleet at Artemisium at once, but had come up with a new strategy.

As Scyllias now told the Greek commanders, the previous night, 200 warships had been detached from the Persian fleet, and in the darkness they had slipped past Artemisium without the Greek fleet knowing. Those 200 ships were now making their way down the east coast of Euboea, with the intent of circling right around the island's south coast and coming up the Euripus channel from the south, behind the Greek fleet at Artemisium. Once these ship were in place, blocking any Greek retreat via the Euripus, they would signal their main fleet at Aphetae, which would engage the Greeks from the north. This meant that, in the interim, the main Persian fleet would sit at Aphetae for several days awaiting that signal, without seeking to engage the Greeks. Only once the Persian commanders knew that the blocking fleet was in place in the Euripus would they go to battle stations.

Themistocles and his colleagues would have acknowledged that this pincer movement was a well-thought-out Persian plan. It may well have worked, too, had Scyllias the defector not revealed it to the Greeks. For the 200 ships for the western arm of the pincer had already succeeded in slipping by the Greek fleet undetected. The council of admirals agreed to a counterplan. They would give chase to the 200 ships heading for the Euripus and engage them from the rear. Armed with the benefit of surprise and superior numbers, the Greeks would destroy the 200. It was also agreed that the Greek fleet should keep the appearance of inactivity at Artemisium during the hours of daylight that day, so the Persians would be lulled into a false sense of security. And then at midnight, the Greek fleet would sail in hot pursuit of the 200 ships. The council meeting broke up, and all at Artemisium seemingly went about their normal business.

By the afternoon, the mood had changed among the Greek commanders, and a different battle plan was devised and agreed. We are not told why. Perhaps some of the commanders were impatient for action. Perhaps the change in plan was Themistocles's doing—the new scheme has his ring of audacity about it. The coalition would attack the main Persian fleet that same afternoon, sailing toward evening and catching the enemy completely napping. For it was unheard of and totally impractical in these times for sea battles to be fought at night. The admirals also agreed to employ a fighting formation known as the cyclos, or kyklos in Greek—the circle. Once all the admirals knew their ships' place in the formation, they hurried away to put the plan into motion.

Before the sun had set over the Greek mainland, Greece's fleet would finally come to grips with the much larger Persian armada, and Themistocles, with his ships making up more than half the entire coalition fleet, would be proven a genius or a fool for turning Athens to the sea and turning Athenians from soldiers to sailors.

12.

The Battle of Artemisium

Two hundred and sixty-eight black Greek triremes slid across the water toward Aphetae with their oars lifting and falling with mesmerizing precision. Stripped of their sails, the warships had been lightened further by leaving surplus seamen back at Artemisium to join noncombatants such as slaves and locals, who would watch the battle from onshore. In August's late afternoon sun, the triremes cut through the placid strait leaving just a short wake and with their elegant shapes casting long shadows on the water to their starboard sides.

Standing on the poop deck in the stern of the Athenian flagship *Paralos* beside Architeles, the ship's captain, Athenian commander Themistocles proudly took in the impressive sight of speeding Athenian triremes fanned out to the left of his ship. As the war archon traditionally occupied the right of the Athenian line in land battles, so Themistocles's flagship took the right of the naval battle line. Behind and above him, the owl pennant of Athens fluttered from its sternpost jack, as it did on every Athenian ship. For more than a decade, Themistocles had been harping on about Athens becoming a sea power. Only for the last two years had Athenians taken his naval scheme seriously. But now, following month after month of ardent training driven by their commander in chief, tens of thousands of Athens's citizens were accomplished oarsmen. No longer did palms blister on oars. The Athenians' hands were now hardened, as was their determination to show friend and foe alike that they were the best in the business of naval warfare.

As the admirals had agreed, the Athenian ships were bringing up the rear of the coalition fleet, like shepherds herding their flock. The Corinthians were leading the Greeks out to battle, with the squadrons of the other allies advancing in between. Themistocles expected that, after his own fleet, the forty ships flying the Pegasus pennant of Corinth would prove the handiest in this battle. The Spartans were undeniably brave fighters on land, but their ten ships were unlikely to have much impact on the outcome of the fighting ahead. As for the Aeginetans, they worried Themistocles. On the strength of their island's past seago-ing reputation, the eighteen Aeginetan triremes should perform well there. But Themistocles had never entirely trusted Athens's powerful little near neighbor and old enemy. As was to come out before long, he feared the Aeginetans's changing sides and going over to the Persians, perhaps in the middle of a battle. The cyclos tactic that the coalition fleet would employ in this battle was probably Themistocles's idea. It offered protection to the novices from Plataea and Chalcis in their loaned Athenian ships. It was also a way of keeping the Aeginetans in forma-tion, giving them little opportunity to desert their coalition partners.

Looking toward the foredeck of the *Paralos*, Themistocles saw his fourteen armored, helmeted marines and archers on there, waiting to go into action. As ancient vase paintings show, the marines were kneeling with one knee on the deck and the heel of an upright spear also resting on the planking. On the foredeck of another Athenian trireme, Cimon, son of Miltiades, hero of Marathon, knelt with his marines, tense, ready to launch the collection of throwing spears that he and his men had prepared for battle. On another Athenian trireme, its captain, Callias, was enjoying the feeling of the ship he'd outfitted coursing across the flat sea under his feet. In full armor and with his helmet on the back of his head, far from being nervous, Callias was prepared for a good fight. He had fought well at Marathon a decade earlier, and now he was ready to deal death to the Persians again, and to secure another pile of booty. For Callias was as demonstrably greedy as he was brave.

On yet another Athenian trireme, forty-five-year-old Aeschylus the playwright was dragging on his top-tier oar. On every Greek ship, the close-packed oarsmen were in fluid, repetitive motion. Disciplined, obedient, well trained, they did not speak. Instead, they chanted mechanically to keep time. According to Aristophanes, sailors aboard Athenian triremes in his day, half a century after this, were too well educated for his liking, and would challenge and dispute the orders of their captain. They would even refuse to row if they disagreed with their orders, letting their ships drift aimlessly as they argued. By contrast, Aristophanes said, trireme crews in the time of fellow writer Aeschylus would only be heard when they called for rations, or when they sang "Rhyppapae," the rhythmic rowing chant that kept them working in unison as they pulled their oars through the waves.

Aboard the *Paralos*, Themistocles smiled to himself. Ahead he could see the Persians beginning to come out from Aphetae to meet the Greek fleet. Now Athens would prove herself to the invader and to her fellow Greek states. Seven hundred ships of the main Persian fleet came out to give battle. Herodotus says that their commanders and their crews were surprised by the audacious Greek attack so late in the day, yet more surprised that the Greeks were attacking at all. With their ships outnumbering the coalition vessels by more than two to one, the Persian commanders were confident of surrounding the Greeks and picking them off.

Those commanders were intent on capturing the Greek triremes intact rather than sinking them. Xerxes had promised them a bounty for every ship taken as a prize. Money, to them, was more of a motivator than glory. Of all the coalition ships, we are told, it was those of the Athenians that the Persians wanted to secure most of all. This was either because of Xerxes's determination to complete his father's mission to punish the Athenians for aiding the Ionians in rising against him and burning Sardis, or it was simply a desire to show Athens that it would take more than a large new fleet for her to rule the waves.

Most of the ships that sailed for Xerxes were identical in many ways to the triremes of the Greek coalition, only varying from the Athenian ships in that their decks were entirely planked over, as were those of the ships all the other coalition squadrons. There were in fact more Greek speakers in the Persian fleet than in the Greek fleet, and these crews were dressed and armed in the same fashion as their Greek adversaries. The Phoenician ships and the men who sailed them were considered the best in Xerxes's navy, by both sides. The Phoenician vessels differed from all the other ships in that they were taller, said Herodotus. With higher sides than the Greek triremes, they probably had better sea-keeping qualities. But, being larger, these ships would have been heavier and not as maneuverable as Themistocles's nimble, partly decked Athenian triremes.

The vessels of the Persian fleet fanned out, and midway between Artemisium and Aphetae they succeeded in surrounding the bunched Greek fleet. And that was exactly what Themistocles and his fellow Greek admirals wanted them to do. A signal was now given from the poop of the Spartan ship carrying coalition naval commander Eurybiades: "Form cyclos." According to Aeschylus, the Greeks' command signals were made in these battles by trumpet. At this signal from the admiral's trumpeter, all the triremes of the coalition fleet began to form a precise circle, with oars backing and pulling in a flurry of foam. With close to 270 triremes involved, that circle was vast, but once it was completed the sterns of each neighboring ship almost touched, making the formation impenetrable to the Persian ships.

The commanders of the 700 Persian ships, bamboozled by this tactic, circled the Greek formation or lay back, uncertain what to do. And then another trumpet call came from the Spartan flagship: "Attack." The Greek captains had been expecting this call. As one, all Greek oars hit the water, and all coalition triremes surged forward and charged. With oars pulling at the maximum rate, the Greek ships sped toward the circling Persians. First off the blocks was one of the Athenian triremes. Its captain, Lycomedes, had picked out a Persian ship and gave his pilot the target to steer for.

The Persians ships began to turn and wheel to prevent the speeding Greek ships from ramming them. So, Lycomedes had his trireme run up alongside his target, then, spear at the ready, he leaped aboard the enemy ship with his marines close behind. Despite being outnumbered by as many as four marines to one, Lycomedes and his boarding party fought like devils and succeeded in killing numerous enemy marines, whose bodies fell or were pushed or thrown into the sea. Lycomedes swiftly captured the Persian. Cutting down the enemy ship's pennant, said Plutarch, Lycomedes retained it to dedicate at a temple to the god Apollo. This was the first enemy fleet to be taken that day, but not the last.

The disorganized Persian fleet had lost the initiative. One after another, their ships were boarded and captured by fierce Greek fighters. In all, thirty Persian ships were captured intact by the time the setting sun signaled it was time for both sides to withdraw. Not a single Greek ship was boarded or sunk, although a number of ships on both sides received damage to one degree or another—mostly shattered oars destroyed when opposing ships ran close alongside each other from different directions and mowed down the oars of opposing ships, shattering them like matchsticks. The stunned Persians pulled back to Aphetae to lick their wounds, and the Greeks returned to Artemisium in triumph. The Greeks came back to their base towing their prizes and followed by a trireme from the island of Lemnos that was defecting to their side. The defecting captain would attach his ship to Themistocles's Athenian fleet, and would later be rewarded by Athens with a parcel of land on the Attic island of Salamis.

That night, as the Greeks celebrated back on shore, rain began to fall. Driven by a fierce wind from the northeast that came in over Mount Pelion, heavy rain lashed both fleets all night, accompanied by booming thunder and lightning flashes that scared the wits out of many seamen. The Greeks knew that any ship not in a sheltered harbor that night would suffer. Across at Aphetae, the Persian ships rode out the electrical storm, but on shore their crews spent a miserable night as swollen streams gushed into the sea and flooded parts of their camp. When the new day dawned, the storm had passed and the sun shone brightly. In the sunshine, the exhausted, saturated crews of the Persian fleet dried out and spent much of the day clearing away wreckage and bodies from the previous evening's battle, which storm and tide had washed in and which fouled their anchorage.

In the Greek camp across the water, the news was all good that day. During the morning, Themistocles's squadron of fifty-three triremes from Pogos arrived and joined the fleet. And then word arrived via locals that the 200 Persian ships that had been sailing down the coast of Euboea had been caught in the previous night's storm, and at a place on the rocky coast called the Hollows, every single Persian ship had been wrecked. With their spirits high, the coalition admirals met in council and agreed to launch a second attack on the Persians at Aphetae that afternoon at the same time as the previous day's attack.

During the late afternoon, led by the Corinthians, the Greek fleet again put out in battle order and made toward Aphetae, once more with each contingent in its usual station, and now with virtually the entire Athenian navy bringing up the rear. Themistocles, now bolstered by the ships from Pogos and the defector from Lemnos, had close to 160 triremes flying the Athenian flag. Once more, the Persians came out to meet the coalition fleet, despite the fact their crews were exhausted after the previous day's fighting and they had slept barely a wink all night. Chastened by the Greek successes the previous day, and fearful of Xerxes's reaction to the skirmish's result, the Persian commanders were intent on revenge.

In this evening's action, a series of dogfights no doubt took place across the broad expanse of water separating the two bases, as ships from either side tried to capture the other. But Themistocles had never been much interested in taking enemy ships as prizes. He had conceived his fleet of light, fast triremes as ramming weapons. And, this evening, his ships singled out for ramming an enemy squadron from Cilicia in Asia Minor. The seafaring Cilician people would in later times become the scourge of the Eastern Mediterranean as pirates. On this day, coalition ships succeeded in ramming and sinking several of the Cilician triremes before nightfall intervened and both sides returned to their bases.

In two days of sea fighting, the Persians had come off worst, with not a single Greek ship captured or sunk. When the third day arrived, the Persian admirals agreed they had to take the initiative. They had to give themselves enough time to finish off the Greek ships instead of being forced to end hostilities when nightfall came all too soon. As midday approached, the Persian fleet came out for battle. Arranging themselves in a huge hollow crescent formation to ensure no Greek ship could escape, the fleet crossed the strait with their commanders intent on fighting all afternoon if necessary, and this time destroying their opponents.

The ships of the coalition fleet took their appointed stations, but waited, motionless, in the bay at Artemisium for the enemy to come to them. Only when the Persians were close to the Euboean shore, maintaining their crescent in precise order, did coalition commander Eurybiades give the signal to advance and the Greeks rowed out to fight. This day's battle was long and bitter. The ships that fared best on the Persian side were those of the large Egyptian squadron, a squadron that had started out on this campaign 200 ships strong. In addition to thirty Persian soldiers, each of these triremes carried ten Egyptian marines equipped with throwing spears, swords, and huge poleaxes that were frightening to behold. In this third day of the sea battle, men from the Egyptian squadron succeeded in boarding and capturing five Greek ships and taking their crews prisoner.

The crews of Queen Artemisia's five triremes from Halicarnassus showed no less bravery this day, although they failed to capture any coalition ships. Artemisia herself commanded her little squadron from the poop of her flagship. Dressed in tunic, helmet, armor, and greaves in the Greek fashion, and with sword at her side, she looked for all the world to be a man.

For the coalition, the Athenians were in the thick of the action, and half their ships were damaged to one extent or another, although none was sunk. Of the Athenian captains, Callias distinguished himself above all his countrymen in damaging, destroying, and capturing enemy ships with his trireme and crew. By day's end, both fleets had returned to base. Many exhausted Greeks were now wondering how long they could keep this up. Already the battle had stretched over three days. If it were to last much longer and become a war of attrition, the Persians had the superiority of numbers that would surely allow them to prevail.

The next morning, as wreckage and bodies from the most recent fighting washed up at Artemisium, Themistocles sensed that his coalition partners had no more stomach for fighting and were ready to pull out and go home. Late that morning, going over the heads of Eurybiades and the other admirals, Themistocles called a meeting of the captains of all the ships of the coalition fleet. As a result, several hundred captains assembled on the beach to hear what he had to say. Meanwhile, all around the Greek camp at the cove at Artemisium were the sheep, goats, and cattle of the Euboean islanders, which had lately been herded here from all over the island for protection against Persian raids. The islanders, like the crews of the Greek ships, were anxious to learn what the coalition fleet would do now, and locals and crewmen alike crowded beyond the ranks of ships' captains to try to glean their fate.

Probably speaking from the stern of his beached flagship, Themistocles told the captains that he knew of a way to separate some of King Xerxes's most capable naval allies from his service and substantially reduce his fleet, thus allowing the Greeks to fight the enemy on more even terms. Privately, Themistocles felt that the Ionians and Carians in the Persian fleet, who had Greek roots, might be convinced at least to remain neutral if approached by representatives of Athens. After all, Athens had gone to the aid of their cousins the Ionians during their revolt against Darius two decades earlier, even if that revolt had not turned out as hoped. For the moment, Themistocles did not identify those in the Persian fleet he felt could be swayed, but many of his listeners had a good idea to whom he was referring.

Not for the first time, Themistocles was trying to keep the Greek coalition together. To his mind, every additional day spent by the coalition fleet at Artemisium could result in a decisive victory over the Persians. Besides, Themistocles was determined to keep faith with Leonidas and the Greek troops at Thermopylae—a withdrawal by the sea force would be a betrayal of the land force. So, Themistocles told the gathered captains that, as regards the coalition fleet withdrawing from Artemisium, he would take personal responsibility for determining the right moment for such a withdrawal and for managing an orderly pullout that ensured every ship got home safely.

This was music to the ears of the Greek captains. Themistocles sounded as if he supported a pullout, yet promised that it could be achieved without the enemy falling on the withdrawing fleet and creating havoc among the Greek ships at a time when they might be disorganized and vulnerable. To take the captains' minds off withdrawal for the time being, Themistocles pointed to the Euboean cattle grazing around the cove.

"Considering the circumstances in which we all now find ourselves," he said, "I advise you to slaughter as many cattle as you like. After all, it is surely better that our own men enjoy them rather than the enemy do. Go ahead, and tell your men to light their cooking fires as usual."

The captains happily went away, and instructing their crews to light their campfires, proceeded to have cattle rounded up and butchered. The entire camp would dine on prime beef that night. Themistocles had gained another day. Meanwhile, he hurried to console to the Euboeans, telling them that the loss of many of their cattle was a small price to pay for keeping the Greek fleet at Euboea. Throughout the remainder of the day, Themistocles maintained a close watch on the Persian ships across the water at Aphetae, hoping they would come out and challenge the Greeks again. But the Persians, like the Greeks, were exhausted and had lost the taste for battle for the moment. All through the day, their ships remained at their moorings.

In the early evening, as the Greeks were enjoying their steak at Artemisium, the thirty-oared Athenian ship that had been stationed off Thermopylae came sliding into the cove. The ship's Athenian captain, the aristocrat Abronychus, a man sufficiently senior and influential to later be a candidate for ostracism, landed and quickly made his way to the tent of Themistocles. Grimly he passed on the news that Leonidas and the Spartans and Thespians with him had perished at Thermopylae after a three-day battle, and that Xerxes and his army now occupied the pass. By coincidence, the sea battles off Artemisium had taken place on exactly the same three days as the fighting at Thermopylae.

Themistocles's heart sank. Not only had many brave Greeks fallen at Thermopylae, but there was also no longer any excuse to keep the coalition fleet at Artemisium. On land, nothing now prevented the Persians from taking all of Boeotia and advancing through Attica to the gates of Athens. Boeotian cities such as Thebes would now go over to Xerxes, and the residents of other cities of the region would flee south overland to the Peloponnese. That the coalition fleet would now pull out was a foregone conclusion. But Themistocles was determined that the fleet be kept together, to again challenge the Persians when time and place were right.

Calling a meeting of the coalition admirals, Themistocles passed on the grim tidings about the Battle of Thermopylae and the Greek defeat. There was no debate in this meeting. The worried admirals would remain at Artemisium no longer. The best that Themistocles could do was to get his colleagues to agree to rendezvous off the island of Salamis, in sight of Piraeus and Athens. Salamis had been in his thinking ever since the Oracle of Delphi's second prediction. We don't know whether he genuinely believed in the prophesy or whether he felt he could use it to manipulate the hearts and minds of his fellow Greek naval commanders to stage a last stand there. Events before and after this would suggest that it was the latter. In addition, in promising to cover the others' withdrawal by being the last to withdraw, Themistocles was also able to convince his colleagues not to leave pell-mell, but to make an orderly departure, based on the stations each contingent had occupied during the battle, one contingent at a time.

That night, the crews of the Athenian ships discussed who they thought should receive the prize as the bravest man among them in the battle that had just passed. This was an age-old tradition. Following the Battle of Marathon, it had been the Athenian commander Miltiades who had been awarded this honor by his men. Out of the three-day struggle, two men emerged as leading contenders in the vote. One was Lycomedes, the swashbuckling captain who had led the capture of the first Persian ship on the first day of battle. The other was Callias for his courageous work on the last day of the battle. In the end, neither man could be separated in the opinion of their countryman, so both received the acclaim and a symbolic palm frond award. The real prize was the glory that would accompany both men for the rest of their days, and long after.

That night, too, Themistocles summoned all those men from his Athenian crews who were stonemasons in civilian life, and from them he separated those who were experts at chiseling inscriptions. To these men he gave pieces of papyrus, each of which contained the same short message. In the light of handheld oil lamps, those stonemasons chiselled the message on large rocks edging the beach at Artemisium. Addressed to the men of Ionia, it urged them not to fight against their Greek cousins and to come over to the Greek cause. If they could not do that, it went on, then the Ionians should at least refrain from fighting, and should convince the Carians to do the same. If the Persians forced them to fight, the message continued, then the Ionians should only pretend to do so. Themistocles ended up by reminding the Ionians that it was because the Athenians had helped Ionia two decades earlier that Xerxes was bent on destroying Athens.

After three days of battle, Themistocles had gauged which of his ships had the fastest rowers. Selecting these ships and assigning stonemasons to each, he instructed their captains that, once the Athenian triremes had pulled out of Artemisium next day, they should put in everywhere along the Euripus where streams flowed into the sea, and where Persian ships might be expected to put in for fresh water for their crews. There, the captains were to set their stonemasons to work chiseling the same message on stones there, where Ionian and Carian crews might see it. Once the Greeks had completed their withdrawal next day, the Ionians would be among the first crews from the Persian fleet to land at the deserted Greek campsite at Artemisium and would find the message waiting for them.

Some would dismiss this message as a pointless waste of time. Yet, there was genius in this tactic by Themistocles. It was a brilliant piece of psychological warfare. He knew that there was a small chance some of the Ionians and Carians would be encouraged by Themistocles's plea to defect. On the other hand, some might indeed put up a sham of a fight the next time the two sides met in battle. Even if none of these things were to happen, the possibility that they might was now planted in the minds of the Persian commanders, who would begin to lose faith, and maybe even trust, in their allies the Ionians and Carians, and perhaps even exclude them from further participation in the war for fear of them turning against them in midbattle.

Two other episodes in Themistocles's life illustrate that his primary intent here was indeed to plant the seeds of doubt in the minds of the people on the receiving end of his tactic. One example relates to the coming battle at Salamis. The other was quoted by Plutarch. He wrote that before this Persian War, when Themistocles was building his political career and his wealth, his eye was taken by a particular colt. But when he asked the horse breeder Diphilides for it, Diphilides refused to sell it to him; probably because the horse breeder supported a political faction other than that of Themistocles.

"Then, before much time passes, Diphilides," Themistocles responded, "I will turn your house into a wooden horse."

The horse breeder knew exactly what Themistocles meant. He was referring to the Trojan Horse, the huge wooden horse left at the gates of Troy when the Greeks besieging the city appeared to withdraw. Thinking the horse a gift from the gods, the Trojans had pushed it inside their city walls, unaware that Greek soldiers were hiding inside. Those Greek soldiers had subsequently emerged at night and covertly opened the city gates from within, letting the waiting Greek army into the city. And thus Troy was defeated from within. In the same way, Themistocles was threatening to cause dissension within the horse breeder's family.

Themistocles did not have to do a solitary thing to follow through on this threat. He had planted the destructive thought in the mind of Diphilides, after which the horse dealer was likely to misread and misconstrue everything that Themistocles and his own family members said or did. We are not told whether Themistocles's ploy worked with the horse dealer. But the episode clearly demonstrates that Themistocles knew how to play with people's minds.

At dawn on the day following news of the fate of the Greek troops at Thermopylae, the Greek naval pullout began at Artemisium. The same stations occupied by the coalition contingents during the three days of battle were occupied in the withdrawal. The Corinthians went first, followed by the other, smaller contingents, pulling around the northwest coast of Euboea and then down the Euripus channel, heading for Attica. The Athenian fleet covered the withdrawal, occupying the most honorable but most dangerous position at the rear of the fleet. Once the Athenians got under way, their exposed backs would be to the enemy.

We hear nothing of the fate of the fifteen Persian ships captured prior to the battles, or those taken during the fighting. While their crews had been sent away in chains to Corinth, the ships themselves were apparently burned on the beach at Artemisium, just prior to the Greek pullout, along with wreckage washed ashore. The captured ships would have been stripped of their oars and other useful fittings before the vessels' destruction. Burning of captured vessels was not unusual. The following year, the Greeks would burn all captured Persian ships following the Battle of Mycale rather than retain them for their own use.

Those ships and that wreckage would certainly have made a grand funeral pyre for the few Greek dead from the three days of battle. And Plutarch reports that when he visited Artemisium hundreds of years later, there was a mound of sand on the beach, like the funeral mound at Marathon. When Plutarch's hosts dug into the mound, they revealed a black base of ash, which Plutarch supposed to be the remnant of the burned shipwrecks and Greek bodies from the Battle of Artemisium.

As the other Greek ships pulled away from Artemisium's shore in their squadrons, the Athenian triremes waited in the cove, at battle stations, ready to go into action should the Persians attempt to intervene in the fleet's withdrawal. But the Persians were delighted to see the Greeks depart. To them, this signaled the disintegration of Greek opposition at sea. They felt no need to give chase. The Persian admirals would now rate the Battle of Artemisium a victory for their side, firmly believing that from now on they would be able to gobble up the Greek fleet piecemeal, with each Greek contingent worrying about its own city and its own people and deserting the united front.

The latter proved correct in one instance. Once the Athenian triremes left Artemisium and followed the other coalition ships down the Euripus toward Attica, bringing up the rear of the departing fleet, Themistocles discovered that, as they'd been rowing down the Euripus, the twenty Athenian triremes crewed by Plataeans had put into the mainland opposite Chalcis. There, the Plataeans had abandoned the Athenian ships and hurried inland to reach their home city before the Persian army did. Their intent was to supervise the evacuation of Plataea and then escort their people south to the Peloponnese.

Themistocles could not blame the Plataeans for putting their own people first. Their city would be burned to the ground by the Thebans, acting on behalf of the Persians, after the residents fled. But neither would Themistocles thank the Plataeans. If every coalition city-state emulated their action and put themselves first, the coalition would crumble and the war would be lost. Forming skeleton crews from men detached from other ships of the Athenian fleet and putting them aboard the triremes abandoned by the Plataeans, Themistocles added these ships to his fleet and continued south for Salamis.

Ahead lay the battle that would decide the fate of Athens, and Greece as a whole. But before that battle could take place, Athens would have to suffer her greatest humiliation at Persian hands.

13.

After Thermopylae

Xerxes was in no hurry to push on, after his troops finally overcame Leonidas and his Greeks at Thermopylae. So vaunted had the Spartans been as warriors, the Persian king wanted to show that even they were no match for Persian force of arms. To emphasize the point, he had trenches dug beyond the pass for the burial of all but a thousand of the Persians who had fallen taking Thermopylae. In reality, the Greek troops at the pass had killed 20,000 Persian troops over the three days of fighting. Once 19,000 of the Persian dead were interred in the mass graves, those graves were filled in and then covered with foliage to hide their very existence.

The Persian king then sent a messenger to the Persian fleet at Aphetae, inviting all crewmen who were interested in seeing the fate of the Greeks at Thermopylae to come by water to view the battle site. Herodotus wrote that the Persian admirals were overwhelmed by requests from their men to take up the offer. When sightseers from the fleet came to Thermopylae, they found the bodies of a thousand Persian troops and, heaped around the hillock where they had fallen, the bodies of the 1,300 Spartans and Thespians. A number of the Helot slaves of the Spartan warriors had also been caught by the Persians; these men had been executed, and their bodies were mixed with those of the Greek fighters to visually inflate the Greek death toll. Following the battle, the body of King Leonidas had been located among the Spartan dead. Xerxes had had Leonidas's head lopped off and displayed on a pole. Leonidas's headless body was raised on a large cross for all to see. The bodies of his men would be left to rot.

Following this war, the Amphictyons, the representatives of the Greek coalition's city-states, would have a monument erected at the site of the Battle of Thermopylae, celebrating the fight put up by 4,000 Greeks against a Persian force that they estimated to number 300,000 men. Sparta would erect a separate monument to its fallen at the site of the battle. A third monument would be erected to Megistias the priest, paid for by his friend Simonides the poet, who also composed the epitaph. It is one of those twists of fate that, even though a thousand Thespians died alongside the Spartans at Thermopylae, fighting just as bravely as their comrades from Laconia, it is the 300 Spartans that popular culture has remembered, in several feature films and numerous books.

Aristodemus, the Spartan warrior afflicted with blindness who hid out at the village of Alpeni at the time of the Battle of Thermopylae, would succeed in returning home. There, he would be shunned by his fellow Spartans for not having emulated his comrade Eurytus and died fighting alongside the other members of the 300. Aristodemus, who recovered his eyesight, formed a determination to find a way to prove to his countryman that he was no coward. But courier Pantites, another member of the 300 who had also missed the battle and was equally shunned by his fellow Spartans, could not take the cold shoulder treatment when he got home. Pantites was the messenger sent by King Leonidas to try to round up more allies for the Greeks at Thermopylae. He too managed to return to Sparta. Even though he'd been obeying orders when he missed the battle, like Aristodemus, he was also reckoned by fellow Spartans to be a coward. The disgrace proved too much for Pantites; he hanged himself.

Xerxes, meanwhile, was concerned by the astonishing courage and determination he had seen exhibited by the Spartans at Thermopylae. Demaratus, the former king of Sparta, continued to be a member of Xerxes's entourage, and Xerxes acknowledged that Demaratus had spoken truthfully when he'd warned that Sparta's fighting men made tough adversaries. When Xerxes wondered aloud whether the 300 had been exceptional men and whether the rest of the men of Laconia would put up such stiff resistance, Demaratus replied that every warrior of Sparta was exceptional and would fight as hard as Leonidas and his 300. So, Xerxes sought Demaratus's advice on how to defeat his own countrymen. In response, Demaratus advised Xerxes to seek to take the Spartans out of the coalition by sending 300 warships to take the Spartan-controlled island of Cythera (modern-day Kythera). He guaranteed that the Spartans would be so intent on regaining their island they would divert all their attention, and their forces, away from the coalition cause.

Xerxes's brother Achaemenes was also in this meeting. He was one of the admirals in chief of Xerxes's fleet and had come with the sightseeing sailors from Aphetae. He counseled vehemently against Demaratus's suggestion, claiming that Spartan Demaratus did not have Xerxes's interests at heart, and that it would be unwise to break up the fleet any further by detaching 300 ships for the Cythera operation. Achaemenes was afraid that in doing so, Xerxes would reduce his main fleet to just 400 warships. Achaemenes knew that, should the Greeks again come out united, as they had at Artemisium, they had the capacity to muster upward of that many ships themselves, eliminating the Persians's numerical superiority.

While not believing that Demaratus was working against him, Xerxes agreed with his brother—the fleet had been reduced enough by storm and battle, and it would be unwise to break it up to take Cythera. With all the cities of Boetia, led by Thebes, submitting to Xerxes following the Battle of Thermopylae and doing his bidding in the region, the king now set his sights firmly on Athens. Xerxes had dreamed of taking all the people of Athens back to Persia in chains, leaving their city in ruins. In doing that, he would be fulfilling his father's failed ambition and showing the world the foolishness of opposing Persia.

For the march into Attica, Xerxes would take the advice of his cousin Artaphernes, who had led troops into Attica once before. This was the same Artaphernes who, with Datis, had commanded Persian forces at the time of the Battle of Marathon. Ten years older now, he had been given command of the Persian army's Lydian and Mysian troops for Xerxes's campaign, and he was determined to make amends for the Marathon disaster.

Xerxes now issued movement orders for his army and navy. He would march the army south into Attica to take Athens. The fleet was to continue to shadow the land army south and to then anchor at Phalerum Bay, Athens's old port. Athens would be sandwiched between the land army and the fleet, and the escape route for Athenians would be cut off. The fall of Athens, Xerxes was determined, would be achieved before summer's end.

14.

Abandoning Athens

The Athenian fleet coasted past the beach at Phalerum Bay and put into the new ports at Piraeus, just a stones' throw from Salamis Island. After fighting the much larger Persian fleet to a draw at Artemisium, the Athenian crews returned home in high spirits, said Plutarch, and unafraid to go against the "barbarians" again. To Themistocles's relief, the coalition admirals had all kept their word—the remainder of the Greek fleet had arrived ahead of the Athenians and lay at the agreed-on rendezvous point of Salamis Island. Most of the coalition ships were drawn up on the shores of the island's Ambelaki and Paloukia bays. Other ships were moored on the bays themselves. Coalition officers and crews could be seen ashore, busily making camp on the island, which became the coalition fleet's headquarters, and hard at work repairing the damage done to their ships in the Artemisium battle.

Themistocles's first imperative now was the safety of Athens's civilians. As soon as he landed at Piraeus, he was greeted with the news that in his absence the majority of Athenians had ignored the evacuation decree and had not budged from their homes. Leaving orders for twenty-one trireme crews to be formed from the Athenian hoplites who had remained at Athens, to man each of the twenty triremes that had formerly sailed under the Plataean flag and the ship that had defected from Lemnos, he hurried up to the city. Themistocles knew that advance elements of Xerxes's army would be outside the gates of Athens within six or seven days. He also knew that the city was indefensible from an attack by so large an army as Xerxes possessed. The Athenian commander in chief had to find a way to get the stubborn population to move, and fast, if Athens's women and children were to be saved from becoming captives of the Persians.

Prior to this, reason had succeeded in convincing only a small part of the population to evacuate. So Themistocles now turned to superstition to aid him. There was a belief among Athenians that a huge holy snake lived in the inner sanctum of the Temple of Minerva in the city—snakes and the Gorgon, being closely associated with that particular deity in Greek mythology. Once every month, honey cake was left out by the chief priestess of Minerva for this snake to eat, and sure enough the cake would always disappear. The common people believed that the snake ate the cake. Themistocles was a pragmatic man, and he knew that it was the priestess who was removing the honey cake every month to sustain the myth. Themistocles now prevailed on the chief priestess, with bribe or threat, or both, to announce that this month the cake had not been eaten. This, Themistocles declared to the people, was proof that Minerva had abandoned Athens and fled south from the invader toward the sea, giving the lead to the people of the city.

Themistocles also reminded the people that the Oracle of Delphi had called on Athenians to give up their city, with the assurance that the invader would ultimately be defeated by a wall of wood at Salamis. The coalition fleet lay anchored off Salamis, ready to fulfill the prophesy, but first, the Oracle's instructions must be obeyed by Athenians and Minerva's example followed. This achieved the result. Evacuation now began in earnest, and in a rush. A number of "old" men fifty and older would still resist the evacuation order. Claiming that the wall of wood referred to the wooden palisade that had anciently surrounded the Acropolis, they defiantly stayed behind and joined the temple attendants in erecting a wooden barricade around the 500-foot Acropolis mount in emulation of that ancient wall. Creating a citadel, the old men prepared to defend it.

Tens of thousands of Athenian noncombatants and slaves flooded down to Piraeus, where they were loaded aboard the waiting Athenian fleet. Because time was now of the essence, only some ships involved in the evacuation went all the way down to Troizen, via its port of Pogon, where the first batch of evacuees now were. One of the ships taking Athenians to Troizen also carried orders from Eurybiades for all coalition warships that had lately gathered at Pogon to come at once to join the Greek fleet at Salamis.

Other ships taking part in the evacuation took evacuees to Athens's new ally Aegina, which was closer to Athens than was Troizen. And a number of refugees were also carried the much shorter distance across to Salamis Island. The original evacuation decree had stated that only old men were to be sent to Salamis, but with time running out before the Persians were expected to arrive, women and children were also packed off to the island in their thousands. As the Persians were to learn, these additional evacuees sent to Salamis would tax the ability of the island to feed them, as no store of foodstuffs had been built up on Salamis in expectation of such numbers.

The timeline provided by Herodotus allows for only three days of evacuation following the return of Themistocles and the fleet from Artemisium. They were three hectic, dramatic, emotional days for the Athenians. The evacuation proceeded with men who were remaining behind to fight putting their wives, children, and elderly parents aboard ship, producing a spectacle that, Plutarch wrote, was both pitiable and admirable, with sad parting calls and tears mixed with the stoic resolve of those who were staying behind.

Among the more than 100,000 Athenians evacuees was a handsome sixteen-year-old youth by the name of Sophocles, who would go on to gain fame as one of Athens's most celebrated dramatists, learning his profession under none other than Aeschylus. In years to come, the prodigious protégé would beat his instructor to first prize in the City of Dionysia contest, after which Aeschylus would leave Athens and never return. Sophocles's father, Sophillus, was a wealthy businessman, thought by some historians to have been a manufacturer of hoplite armor. Sophillus is likely to have been serving at this time in the Athenian fleet. Which of the three evacuation destinations Sophocles and his mother were sent to is unknown.

Another evacuee was the heavily pregnant Cleito. Daughter of an aristocrat, she was the wife of Mnesarchus, a wealthy merchant. Mnesarchus apparently dealt in fresh farm produce, because the comedians of Athens would later joke that Cleito herself sold inferior greens. Mnesarchus would have been in military service under Themistocles when his wife was evacuated. Mnesarchus's family is believed to have owned several rural properties, including one on Salamis, and one tradition holds that it was on Salamis shortly after the evacuation from Athens, and around the time of the battle that followed, that Cleito gave birth to a son. That son was Euripides, who in adult life would become yet another of Athens's great writers. Euripides would include the great philosopher Socrates among his friends.

Some historians believe that Euripides was actually born four years prior to this, making him four years of age at the time of the 480 BC evacuation. Even if that were the case, Euripides's mother would have taken him with her to Salamis in the evacuation. In later life, Euripides would live a hermit's life in a cave on Salamis, a cave that had two entrances and a beautiful sea view. If the first tradition is correct, that Euripides was in fact born on Salamis in September 480 BC, he may have born in that very same cave that later became his home. For historians marvel at how sleepy Salamis could have supported tens of thousands of evacuees, the 76,000 crewmen from the Greek fleet that ultimately gathered at the island, and several thousand Athenian hoplites who also took station on the island's shores in August and September of 480 BC. It is highly likely that when Cleito arrived on the island it was to find her husband's property overrun by refugees and sailors, forcing her to resort to a cave for shelter. And there, surrounded by servants and evacuees, she gave birth to Euripides.

Another Athenian who evacuated to Salamis was Xanthippus, the aristocrat and accused friend of the tyrants who, under ostracism, had been exiled four years before this. Under the recall initiated by Themistocles, Xanthippus had only recently returned to Athens. His family had a large rural property just to the north of the city and would also have kept a city house from which they now hastened to Piraeus. With Themistocles keeping any real power out of the hands of the ostracized men, Xanthippus, his wife Agariste, their children and their slaves now joined the throngs rushing down to the sea and crowding onto the waiting ships. Once aboard, they would have to sit on an exposed deck or cluster in the hold on top of the ballast for the brief voyage across to Salamis.

One of the children of Xanthippus was a son, Pericles. Aged about fifteen at this time, Pericles would one day become one of Athens's most famous sons. Writing would not be his metier. War would provide his road to fame. Pericles would become arguably Athens's most famous general. Leading Athens to numerous naval victories and expanding her empire before leading her into a calamitous war with Sparta, Pericles would be elected Athens's military commander in chief a record nineteen times.

A teenager now, Pericles is likely to have been impatient to join the men manning Athens's triremes so that he could prove his worth. For he was the butt of jokes among schoolmates and had a lot to prove— he possessed a very high forehead, which seemed to make his head too large for his body, and gave rise to an unflattering nickname: "onion head." Once Pericles was famous, all portrait busts of him would show him with a helmet on the back of his head, deliberately disguising his overlarge forehead. But Pericles was three years short of military age, and his father would have made sure the family kept together as they took part in the evacuation. Before many years had passed, Pericles would have his chance to row and command Athenian triremes.

In the haste of the evacuation, Xanthippus and his family had to leave their pet dog behind. Like the dog on the vase mentioned earlier, the dogs bred by the Greek elite at this time tended to be slender, long-limbed, and lithe in the mold of today's greyhound, with long, curving tails that ended in a point. Aristides, another of the ostracized politicians recalled by Themistocles—unlike Xanthippus, he had yet to return to Athens and was still on Aegina—had once owned a very handsome dog with a fine long tail. One day, Aristides had lopped off the dog's elegant tail. His friends were horrified and asked Aristides why he'd done such a thing. This was at a time when Aristides was in office and deliberately looking the other way when other politicians stole from the Athenian treasury. In answer to his friends' question, Aristides had smiled and said that he'd cut off the dog's tail so that people would criticize him for that rather than for his more serious misdemeanors.

It seems that one of Xanthippus's children, quite possibly Pericles, had brought the family's pet dog down to Piraeus in their baggage. But the marines assigned to each trireme would have had strict orders from Themistocles to prevent pets and other excess baggage being carried on board the ships of the evacuation fleet, which could have overloaded them. Xanthippus's dog was forcibly removed from the family and left on the dock. But the plucky mutt plunged into the water and swam alongside the ship as it pulled away. The dog kept pace with the galley, swimming the strait to Salamis. But the ship's captain would not stop to pick it up.

Once Xanthippus landed, he reunited with his pet. But the swim had been too much for the dog, and, exhausted, it died in its master's arms. Xanthippus reverently laid his loyal dog to rest in a tomb on a cliff overlooking the Salamis Strait. As a consequence, the place would gain the name of Dog's Tomb. In telling the story of Xanthippus's dog, Plutarch was to add that one of the saddest things about the evacuation of Athens was the number of abandoned pet animals left wandering about the deserted streets and howling for their owners.

And then it was done. Athens had been emptied. Apart from the wandering pets and those men and women who had remained at the Acropolis to guard the temples and their holy treasures—which, once consecrated to the gods, could not lawfully be removed by mortals—Athens was a lifeless city. With the evacuation complete, Themistocles had the Athenian fleet join the remainder of the coalition ships at Salamis Island. With their few penteconters and smaller-oared vessels added to their trireme squadrons, the Athenians had approaching 200 warships at Salamis. As Themistocles that same afternoon landed on Salamis and entered the coalition camp, he had no plans to go anywhere. He had always set his sights on fighting it out with the Persians there off Salamis.

With the commander of the fleet's single-largest naval contingent now among them, Eurybiades called a war conference of all his senior commanders. There were more admirals in this meeting than had attended similar meetings at Artemisium, for the warships of several more coalition partners had by this time come up from Pogon to join the fleet. Their arrival had brought the total number of Greek ships drawn up on the beach and at anchor around the Spartan flagship to upward of 400. Despite this impressive size of the reinforced fleet, Themistocles found the mood at the admirals' meeting somber and negative. Most coalition commanders had arrived at Salamis expecting a large Greek army to be in place in Boeotia by this time, standing in Xerxes's path north of the Peloponnese. Instead, they found that many Greeks from the Peloponnese, including the Spartans, had congregated like frightened chickens at Corinth, the coalition headquarters, joining the Corinthians and evacuees from Plataea and Thespiae.

Under the leadership now of Spartan leader Cleombrotus, brother of the late King Leonidas, the chief men of the coalition cities represented at Corinth had changed the Greek war plan. They had decided that instead of going forward to engage the Persians in Boeotia, as had originally been agreed when Themistocles had been involved in the war planning at the earlier Corinth summits, they would rebuild and fortify an ancient wall that stretched across the narrow Isthmus of Corinth and defend it against the Persians. Tens of thousands of hoplites, old men, women, and children had eagerly joined in the wall building. Using cut stones, boulders, bricks, baskets full of sand, and wood, they soon completed the work along the five-mile length of the wall, which they felt sure would hold the Persians back.

To Themistocles and one or two other coalition admirals at Salamis, trying to hold a defensive line at the isthmus wall was a total waste of time. While the Persians had a strong fleet, they could land behind the defenders at the isthmus, outflanking them and making a joke of the wall. But other Greek admirals began to fret that they too should take their men to the isthmus to support their countrymen there. To Themistocles's relief, Eurybiades recognized that never again would so many coalition ships be available to sail for Greece, and that it was now or never. To his mind, it was not a question of *whether* the enlarged coalition fleet took on the Persian armada, but *where*. Aware of the discontent among his colleagues, the Spartan admiral quickly opened up the meeting to debate. Expressing the view that Attica could not be saved from the invader, he invited every one of the admirals to offer their opinion on the best place to fight a deciding sea battle.

The admirals from Corinth and other Peloponnese cities were quick to speak up, and one after the other they declared that the fleet should sail around to the Isthmus of Corinth and link up with their countrymen there and then draw the Persian fleet into battle off the isthmus. The great concern expressed by these commanders was that if their ships came off the worst in the narrow confines around Salamis Island, they and their crewmen would be trapped on the island. On the other hand, off the isthmus, if the coalition fleet was defeated, the waters were much more open, and Greek ships would be much more likely to escape and return to their home cities. Themistocles detested this defeatist talk, and the glass-half-empty attitude exemplified by these commanders. Instead of considering the narrow straits around Salamis a negative, Themistocles saw them as a way for the coalition to negate the Persian fleet's superiority in numbers. Forced to fight in such a narrow waterway, the enemy would be limited by the number of ships it could throw into battle at any one time.

As the Peloponnese admirals were speaking, an Athenian messenger arrived. Brought into the tent where the conference was taking place, he breathlessly delivered news of the advance of the Persian land army. After pushing through Boeotia and plundering its way down into northern Attica, the Persian spearhead division, under Xerxes himself, had arrived outside Athens. The Persians had quickly scaled the walls of the undefended city and set up camp on the Areopagus Hill, facing the Acropolis and the wall of wood built by the old men who had voluntarily stayed behind to defend their citadel.

This news, while painful to Themistocles, was not unexpected. Yet it shook the already-shaky confidence of many of his fellow admirals. Some rattled admirals hastily departed the meeting before Eurybiades even called for a vote on the course of action to be followed by the fleet. Boarding their ships, these commanders ordered sails raised. They intended sailing west for the Isthmus of Corinth at once. The wind god and other coalition ships had other ideas. With not a breath of wind and apparently with the last-to-arrive ships of Athens occupying the outer limits of the cage and refusing to let them pass, the deserters could not move.

Those admirals who had remained at the meeting cast their vote. Themistocles was for staying and fighting off Salamis, but he was in the minority. The majority vote was for departing for the isthmus. With night about to fall, Eurybiades issued an order for the entire fleet to sail with the morning tide, then boarded his own ship and commanded it be readied to sail. When Themistocles dejectedly returned to the *Paralos*, he was met by Mnesiphilus, his old friend and advisor.

After Themistocles passed on the outcome of the meeting with the admirals, Mnesiphilus shook his head. "Themistocles, if you allow these men to sail away from Salamis," he said, "you can forget a united fight for one homeland. They will scatter to their own cities, and neither Eurybiades nor anyone else will be able to stop them!"

Mnesiphilus went on to urge Themistocles to do all he could to persuade Eurybiades to reverse the decision, and Themistocles, motivated by his old tutor, immediately left his ship and hurried to Eurybiades's vessel. In the dying light of the day and looking up to the stern of the Spartan flagship, the Athenian commander called for an audience with the admiral in chief, saying that he wished to discuss a matter of public service. Eurybiades invited him aboard. Greeting Themistocles once he clambered up one of the stern boarding ladders, he bade him sit beside him on a bare bench on the ship's deck and speak his mind. Themistocles and Eurybiades sat down together, and Themistocles now repeated Mnesiphilus's sentiments and added arguments of his own, declaring that Greece would fall if allowed to be divided by unwise words. He beseeched the Spartan to call a fresh meeting of the admirals and put the case for all the Greek partners to remain at Salamis and, united, fight the Persian fleet there in the narrow straits.

Eurybiades, persuaded by Themistocles, sent for the other admirals. Even as many were still boarding the admiral in chief's flagship and before Eurybiades had called the meeting to order, Themistocles moved among his fellow commanders, lobbying them to keep their ships at Salamis and do battle there.

The Corinthian admiral, Adimantus, was incensed by this. "Themistocles, you realize that, at the Olympic Games, those charioteers who start before the rest are liable to be lashed?" He meant lashed with wooden rods on the order of the games' judges.

"That is true, but those who start too late do not win the crown!" Themistocles quickly retorted, referring to the leafy crown awarded the winner of each Olympic event.

Once Eurybiades had formerly convened the meeting, he called on Themistocles to address it. Although Themistocles had in his private meeting with Eurybiades criticized their fellow admirals, now he focused his words on Eurybiades, declaring that the future of Greece lay in the Spartan commander's hands. He spoke of how unwise it would be to enter a sea fight at the Isthmus of Corinth, in the open sea, and outnumbered. Herodotus was to record what he claimed were Themistocles's exact words in this address, but at this point he put a single word in Themistocles's mouth that has troubled scholars for two and a half thousand years.

"Our ships are *heavier*" is what Themistocles is supposed to have said. Such a statement seems at odds with the evidence. The Phoenician ships, for example, sat much higher in the water than Greek ships, according to Herodotus himself. Plutarch described them as having high sterns and lofty decks, and sitting higher in the water than the Greek ships. This would have involved more timbers, which would have made the Phoenician ships heavier than the normal trireme. In fact, Plutarch added that because of their size, these ships were particularly cumbersome. Two hundred and seven of the triremes in the original Persian armada of close to 1,300 were considered to be especially fast, and may have been, like the Athenians ships, only partly decked. How many of those fast triremes had survived the two storms and three days of battle that had deprived the Persians of more than 600 warships to this point, we do not know. Even if all 207 had survived to this time, the majority of triremes in the Persian fleet, apart from those from Phoenicia, were identical to the full-decked ships sailed by most of the Greeks.

To explain Herodotus's reference to heavier Greek coalition ships, modern maritime experts have suggested that perhaps the Persian ships had been out of the water for some time prior to this campaign, which had allowed their timbers to dry out. This would have made them lighter than the Greeks ships. But there is no evidence to support this. And why would the entire Persian fleet, made up of squadrons from many nations throughout the Mediterranean and Aegean, have been out of the water for some time and the Greek ships not? The sailing season in the Mediterranean ran between spring and autumn, with the last sailings taking place by the end of October. Over the winter months, when the winds were adverse, *all* ships were traditionally removed from the water.

Perhaps this head-scratching quote came as a result of an error by a secretary or later copyist. But more likely it was an error by Herodotus himself, a misquote. Perhaps what Themistocles actually said was, "*Your* ships are heavier," and he was focusing on the previously expressed desire of the Peloponnese admirals to be able to flee if the battle turned against them. Quite possibly what Themistocles was talking about was the fact that the fully decked ships from the other Greek coalition partners were heavier than most of those from Athens, implying that those ships would not have as much of a chance of escaping the Persians as the lighter, partly decked Athenian triremes.

That Herodotus could make mistakes in his narrative is made clear not many pages earlier in his *History*. For example, in summarizing the outcome of the Battle of Thermopylae, he wrote that 4,000 Greeks had fallen there. Yet not long before that, he had made clear that it was the 1,300 Spartans and Thespians who fell on the last day at Thermopylae, after 4,000 coalition Greek troops had fought there over the previous two days, before 2,300 of them pulled out. This reference to 4,000 Greek dead was a simple slip of the tongue, literally; ancient authors tended to dictate their books to secretaries.

So dismissing a pullout to the isthmus, Themistocles put his case for remaining at Salamis and doing battle with the Persians there where the Persian advantage of numbers was nullified. For another thing, he said, if the coalition fleet pulled out, that would leave the islands of Salamis and Aegina and the city Megara—which stood to the west of Athens on the gulf midway between Athens and Corinth—open to easy capture by the approaching Persian fleet. That would result in the loss of tens of thousands of women and children sheltering there. On the positive side, he said, by choosing to fight there at Salamis, they could turn the narrow waterway to their advantage. And if they fought there, he said, they were defending the Peloponnese just as effectively as they would at the isthmus, but with a much greater chance of victory over the Persians.

"If things work out as I plan," Themistocles went on, "and we defeat them by sea, then we'll have kept your isthmus free from the foreigners, and they will have advanced no further than Attica. From there they'll flee back in disarray. And we will have saved Megara, Aegina, and Salamis—where an oracle had prophesized we'll overcome our enemies." He mused, "Reasonable counsels breed reasonable chances of success, but when men reject reason, Zeus rejects them, and their human frailties."

Adimantus had heard enough. "We do not have to listen to you, a man without a house or a city!" Adimantus had argued against Themistocles ever since the war began. He seems to have done so, like many Athenian politicians in the past, on principle—the principle that Themistocles was a commoner and not worthy of being treated as an equal. Turning to Eurybiades, the Corinthian noble said, "You cannot put a question to this meeting at the behest of a man who is stateless. Let Themistocles prove what state he represents as envoy here before we count his voice with the rest."

At this, the admiral of the squadron from Eritrea echoed Adimantus's view. Themistocles glared at the Eritrean. "Have you anything to say of war that does not sound like the tactics of an ink-fish!" he snarled, his usually well-contained temper finally getting the better of him. By ink-fish he meant the squid and the octopus, which eject a cloud of black ink into the water around them as a defense against attack. And the symbol of Eritrea now flying on their warships' pennants was the octopus. Themistocles was saying that in speaking against him and for a withdrawal to the isthmus, the Eritrean and Adimantus were both only clouding the issue and preventing the others from seeing the situation clearly.

"I have a sword that will speak for *me!*" Adimantus apparently declared, grabbing the hilt of the sword at his side.

"You have a sword, but no heart!" Themistocles retorted.

Adimantus's eyes flared. It seems that as he went to draw his sword against the Athenian commander, others grabbed his arm to restrain him.

"Go ahead, strike me if you will," Themistocles countered, "but give me a hearing."

Eurybiades had to step in, raising his staff of office to separate the two men, before inviting Themistocles to continue.

"We have indeed left our houses and our walls, you scoundrel," said Themistocles to the Corinthian, "rather than become slaves for things that have neither life nor soul. *Here* is our city, the greatest in all Greece." He spread his hand to the Athenian warships, anchored on the periphery of the beached coalition fleet. "A floating city made up of 200 galleys—which are here to defend you, I would remind you. But if you flee and betray us, as you did once before, the Greeks will soon hear of the Athenians possessing as fine a country and as large and free a city as the one they've lost." Themistocles's inference, Herodotus was to point out, was perfectly clear to all present. Should Themistocles choose to do so, he, his 200 ships, and his 40,000 men could descend on any Greek city, be it Corinth or Sparta, and take it for the Athenians, and no other Greek power had the capacity to stop them.

This implied threat was a sobering thought, and it silenced Adimantus. When Eurybiades now asked Themistocles to say what he would have him do, Themistocles, his hackles now raised, said, addressing the Spartan commander in chief directly and ignoring Adimantus and the other admirals, "If *you* remain here, everything will be all right. If you do not, Greece will be ruined. The whole outcome of this war depends on Athens's ships."

No one could argue with that. Athens's navy represented half the coalition fleet. Remove them from the equation, and the coalition fleet would be down to fewer than 200 warships, against 700 Persian vessels, odds of more than three to one. With the Athenians, the odds were halved.

"But, if you are not persuaded by what I have to say, Eurybiades," Themistocles went on, "then we'll take our families, load them aboard our ships, and sail to Siris in Italy. Siris was settled by our people long ago, and there are prophesies that we'll settle there someday. Then, when you've lost allies like us, you'll have good reason in the future to remember what I've said here today."

Eurybiades thought for a moment, and as he did someone pointed to a bird flying in the evening sky. Coming in over the fleet from the east, it landed on top of the mast of the Spartan flagship. Birds were seen by both the highly superstitious Greeks and Romans as harbingers of things to come, as messengers from the gods. And as the admirals craned their necks, this bird looked down inscrutably at them from the mast top. It was an owl. The symbol of Athens, the symbol that flew on the pennants of the many Athenians warships in the fleet.

The majority of the highly superstitious men on the deck of the Spartan trireme took this as a good omen, and a sign that the gods were with Athens. Eurybiades certainly did. His appointment as admiral in chief had given him the power to command his colleagues to obey his orders, but knowing how divided the other admirals were, Eurybiades had up until now always put major decisions to the vote, siding with the majority decision. This time, he feared that unless he sided with the Athenians, Themistocles would take Athens's ships from the fleet, which would perish without them. Rather than bring disaster down on the coalition, Eurybiades made a solitary decision. He announced that as Themistocles proposed, the fleet would remain at Salamis and do battle there with the Persians.

There were no arguments. Like the decision or not, these men had all vowed to submit to Sparta's orders in this war, and now they must remain faithful to that vow. The admirals all hurried away to prepare their squadrons for battle. The Aeginetans even sent a trireme scurrying south to their island to fetch statues of descendants of mythological hero Aecus, so that they could carry them into battle there. According to legend, the Greek hero Ajax, son of King Telemon, had descended from Aecus. And Ajax had been born on Salamis. The Aeginetans hoped their own people and their fellow Greeks would recognize the statues and the symbols of Greek heroism they represented as they went into battle off Ajax's birthplace.

Themistocles returned to the *Paralos* a happy man. His argument and his war strategy had prevailed. All he had to do now was keep the fleet together long enough to bring the enemy to battle there off Salamis. The rest, he was confident, would take care of itself.

15.

The Salamis Trap

As dawn was breaking, an earthquake shook southern Attica and the nearby islands. This unsettled the Greeks at Salamis, who immediately made prayers and offerings to all their gods, being unsure of which of their deities to credit with the earthquake or to divine what message they should take from it. Some Athenians would have thought Athena responsible, now that her city had fallen and her holy precinct was in flames. It was if she was registering her anger.

For two days, Xerxes troops had attempted to overcome the wooden barricade built around the Acropolis and defended by old men and priestesses, who hurled stones down onto the attackers. Unable to storm the barricade, the Persians had resorted to firing fire arrows into it, arrows dipped in tow and lit. The defenders had put out every fire, and when offered the opportunity to surrender and save their lives, they had turned it down. A small party of Persian soldiers then found a secret entrance to the citadel at the Sanctuary of Aglaurus, and via this had been able to climb all the way to the top of the Acropolis.

Some of the defenders, seeing the enemy among them, committed suicide by throwing themselves from the heights. The Persian infiltrators were able to open the citadel gates from the inside, allowing thousands of their comrades to rush in. Every Athenian man and woman they found within the citadel, many of them taking refuge in Athena's temple, was put to death. That temple to Athena on the Acropolis, like the other temples near and below it, was looted of its treasures, and then set on fire. This sacked temple was not the famous Parthenon—that would be erected by Pericles some forty years after this to replace the one destroyed by the Persians.

Xerxes was now able to dispatch a mounted courier back to Persia to deliver the news to his uncle Artabanus at Susa, for distribution throughout the empire, that Athens had fallen and her treasures were in Persian hands. At Susa, which had been denuded of its young men for the Greek campaign, this news would be greeted by the mothers, sisters, wives, children, and grandparents of the men serving in Xerxes's army and navy with joyous celebrations in the streets and victory feasts.

The same morning that Athens fell, the Persian fleet arrived and put in at Phalerum Bay. It had set off from Aphetae three days after the coalition fleet departed Artemisium and had taken three days and nights to come down the coast. The ships of the fleet were so closely packed as they now lined the beaches around the bay, Plutarch was to say, the entire coastline had disappeared. Xerxes camped outside Athens, now with his complete army, which had been reinforced by a number of Greek cities that had recently come over to him. These Greek reinforcements, said Herodotus, had more than made up the Persian losses at Thermopylae. Now even the Thebans and the Locrians, who had fought with the coalition against Xerxes at Thermopylae, were a part of the Persian army. To complicate matters, seven Locrian pente-conters still sailed with the coalition fleet. Xerxes, seeing his own vast fleet arrive, decided to go down to the bay to pay it a royal visit and confer with his admirals and captains.

Xerxes was not a sailor. He never ventured on board a ship. At Phalerum, his naval conference was held on shore in the open. At Susa and then at Sardis, Xerxes had met with his subordinate rulers in audience halls out of the public eye, and there all his subjects involved in the interview were required to prostrate themselves before him. On the shore, in view of thousands of Persian and allied soldiers and sailors, Xerxes decided that the only way for him to preserve his dignity was not to meet with all his subordinates in person. He sat well back on a throne, and benches were provided for all his satraps, commencing with the Phoenician ruler Testramnestus, King of Sidon, who sat looking at him in all their finery.

Xerxes then sent his brother-in-law and chief deputy Mardonius around all the dignitaries, one at a time. Mardonius put the same question to each, asking whether he felt the fleet should risk a sea battle here with the coalition fleet that now lay at anchor just a few miles away to the west. Every one replied that Xerxes should engage the Greeks there and put an end to the threat posed by the coalition fleet. Just a single leader spoke against doing battle. This was Queen Artemisia. She began by telling Mardonius to remind King Xerxes that she and her little squadron had fought at Artemisium and had performed better than most other contingents. So she was speaking from the point of view of a combatant, not an outsider.

"This is what I advise," she went on. "Save the ships. Do not risk a battle. These Greeks are better seamen than your people, just as men are better than women. Why risk a sea battle when you have conquered Athens? Was not that the very reason for this campaign?" She predicted that if Xerxes kept his fleet close to the shore and marched his land army to the isthmus, the coalition fleet would break up with the different contingents scattering to defend their home cities.

The other royals knew that Artemisia was a favorite of Xerxes, and those who disliked and were envious of her hoped that in expressing this contrary view the queen would incur the wrath of the king. But once Mardonius reported the views of all the assembled leaders to Xerxes, the king was pleased with Artemisia above all the rest for her refreshing honesty. Still, he decided to go with the majority view. He commanded that the Persian fleet launch an attack on the coalition fleet off Salamis at once. And he announced that he would be taking up a viewing position overlooking the Salamis Strait, from where he would watch the battle.

As Xerxes and his entourage departed, the Persian admirals agreed on the sailing order of their fleet, and squadron by squadron the ships were heaved into the water all around Phalerum Bay and cleared for action. But by the time the entire fleet was on the water, night was coming on, so it was agreed that the Persian naval attack would commence at first light next day.

*   *   *

On Salamis, although the coalition ships were prepared for battle during the day, no sailing order was forthcoming from the admiral in chief. This delay allowed the coalition admirals who were opposed to fighting off Salamis the time to grumble to each other about the folly of Eurybiades's decision to fight there, to complain about Themistocles's influence on Eurybiades, and to agree that they had no desire to fight this war for Athens's sake. Up until this time, all decisions had been made on the vote of the majority. The admirals now decided among themselves that they should call for another naval war council where they would demand a vote. That vote, they knew from their lobbying efforts, would be strongly in favor of pulling out and sailing to the isthmus. A deputation from these admirals convinced Eurybiades to convene a meeting, and the summons went out to all coalition admirals to meet in the headquarters tent that evening.

Themistocles, meanwhile, waited all day for Eurybiades to issue the order for the fleet to launch into the attack against the Persian fleet at Phalerum Bay, only for the Spartan to find minor reasons to stall. Eurybiades had lost the courage of his newfound convictions. Now he would order neither an attack nor a withdrawal. The frustrated Themistocles decided to take matters into his own hands and force the coalition fleet into battle there at Salamis. Taking aside his Persian servant Sicinnus, he gave him a secret mission. It seems that Themistocles had treated Sicinnus very kindly during his years in his service, and, according to Plutarch, Sicinnus had become devoted to his Athenian master. Conversely, Themistocles trusted the Persian implicitly. He needed to if this mission was to succeed.

In the fading evening light, Sicinnus boarded a merchant vessel, which put out from Salamis, passed through the coalition fleet, and disappeared into the night. The ship worked its way east to Phalerum Bay and the anchored Persian fleet. There, Sicinnus was conveyed aboard one of the Persian flagships and brought before the four commanding Persian admirals.

"I have been sent here in secret, without the knowledge of the other Greeks, by the Athenian commander, Themistocles," Sicinnus told the Persian admirals. "He favors King Xerxes's side, and would rather that you were successful than his countrymen. He has instructed me to inform you that the Greeks have been overcome by fear and are planning a fast escape. If you prevent them from escaping, you'll win the greatest victory you have ever achieved. They're now arguing among themselves, and it is likely those who favor you and those who oppose you will end up fighting each other."

This news was so welcome to the Persian commanders that they thanked Sicinnus and let him depart, possibly in the expectation that he would become their agent behind enemy lines and continue to provide information. Sicinnus reboarded the merchantman and sailed away to rejoin Themistocles. The slave could have remained with the Persians and regained his freedom, but he was so loyal to Themistocles that he returned to his service. Later, Themistocles would reward Sicinnus by giving him his freedom, by making him a rich man, and by having the city of Thespiae admit him to Thespian citizenship.

Every successful lie needs to contain an element of the truth, and the news that Sicinnus delivered about the coalition admirals were fighting among themselves and planning to flee from Salamis was truthful. That Themistocles favored Xerxes was the hidden untruth. So convincing was Sicinnus's delivery, the Persian commanders decided to take advantage of this fresh intelligence and act immediately to blockade Salamis Island, trapping the coalition fleet there.

All the ships of the Persian fleet weighed anchor and quietly slid through the night in their allotted sailing order to Salamis. By midnight, most of the Persian warships were at their new stations east and south of the island and slowly cruising back and forth, ready to go into immediate action against the Greek fleet, which they believed from Sicinnus's information could attempt a breakout in the night. At the same time, 400 Persian troops were landed on the small, rocky, uninhabited island of Psyttaleia, which lay east of Salamis, between it and the mainland. It seems their commanders were three of Xerxes's nephews, three young men who were the sons of his sister Saundice and her husband Artayctes. These troops lined Psyttaleia's shore. They had orders to save the lives of any Persian seamen who came ashore there after losing their ships in battle and to kill any coalition seamen who did the same.

Back on Salamis, it was well into the evening by the time Themistocles and the other admirals joined Eurybiades in the headquarters tent for the latest council of war. In the light of flickering oil lamps, the admirals took their seats. Once again, Eurybiades invited the admirals to speak their minds. A tempest of words was unleashed by Adimantus and the numerous other admirals who supported him, with each giving a lengthy speech in support of his view. All advocated a pullout to the isthmus at dawn the next day. Only the admirals from Aegina and Megara joined Themistocles in speaking in favor of remaining at Salamis and fighting there. Both these two commanders had realized that Themistocles was right—if the fleet did withdraw to the isthmus, Aegina and Megara would be easy prey to the Persians and would quickly fall.

The meeting dragged on for hours. As midnight approached, and with heated words still flying, a message was brought to Themistocles informing him that Aristides was outside and asking to see him urgently. This was the first that Themistocles had heard of Aristides's being back in Athenian territory. Curious, Themistocles slipped from the meeting as the speeches continued, leaving his few supporters among the admirals to keep up the argument for remaining at Salamis. Outside the tent, Aristides was waiting. He had only just landed on Salamis after traveling up from Aegina, and on learning the situation from friends among Athenian commanders on the island and being told that Themistocles was currently at the war council, he had come directly to find him. Apparently, the flood of Athenian refugees to Aegina had given Aristides the courage and the impetus to venture back to Athenian territory. And, quite possibly, he had learned from refugees on Aegina that members of his own family had evacuated to Salamis.

"Themistocles, let us forget the vain rivalry that has extended back to our childhood," Aristides began, "and team up to form an honorable partnership in an argument that concerns the preservation of all Greece. You as the commander, and me as the advisor."

Although this would have surprised Themistocles, it was he who had taken the first step of reconciliation in recalling Aristides, so he had to give the man the benefit of the doubt. Despite being suspicious of Aristides, Themistocles knew that he was still well connected among Athenian aristocrats and the leading men of many Greek cities and could be a valuable ally in the war. He asked Aristides to suggest how he proposed to advise him.

"I understand that you have urged the council to follow the wisest course—engaging the enemy here in the straits, without delay," Aristides went on.

Themistocles answered that was the case, but Adimantus was leading calls for withdrawal to the isthmus, in opposition to Themistocles's advice. Worst of all, he said, Eurybiades seemed to be now siding with those advocating withdrawal.

"No matter how much the Corinthians or even Eurybiades may wish it, the fleet cannot retreat now," said Aristides. When Themistocles asked why that was, Aristides replied, "What I'm about to describe to you I've seen with my own eyes."

Aristides went on to explain that he had just come up from Aegina by small boat, and as that boat approached Salamis Island in the darkness it had come upon the Persian fleet spreading through the Salamis Strait, blocking all exits. It had been only with great luck that Aristides's boatmen had discovered a small gap in the blockade and slipped through it while the Persians were looking north and west and not expecting any vessel to try to run the blockade from the south.

"We are now enclosed on all sides by the enemy," Aristides declared. "Go in to the others, and tell them what I have told you. Tell them that we will all have to prove ourselves brave men and fight here whether we want to or not. For there is no opportunity left for escape."

"You have excelled yourself in coming to me, Aristides," Themistocles responded. "After this good beginning, I will do all in my power to exceed your spirit of goodwill through my actions. Your news is good, and what you have seen occur is precisely what I wanted to occur. You should know that what the Persians have now done was at my instigation." When Aristides frowned at this, Themistocles explained, "It was necessary to make our people fight here, whether they wanted to, or not." Behind them, voices were being raised in the tent. "But you will have to come into the meeting with me. Without you, they're unlikely to believe me when I tell them what you have seen."

So Aristides walked at Themistocles's side when he rejoined the council of war. Much would have been the surprise of the other admirals to see Themistocles now accompanied by the man who had famously been his most bitter rival at Athens for decades past. Eurybiades now gave Themistocles the floor, and Themistocles proceeded to relay all that Aristides had told him and to repeat his own earlier advice to Eurybiades that he order the battle in the strait to begin the next morning. As Themistocles had expected, he was met with disbelief by many of his listeners.

Predictably, Adimantus suggested that Themistocles had actually invented this story that they were now surrounded. Pointing to Aristides, he said, "Not even Aristides likes your advice, Themistocles. Look, he is present, but says not a word in support of you."

Themistocles now invited Aristides speak.

"As Themistocles said, I have come from Aegina, and barely escaped the ships of the blockade," Aristides informed the admirals. "Xerxes's ships entirely enclose the Greek fleet here at Salamis. There is no way out." Having said his piece, he withdrew from the meeting.

Some of the admirals believed Aristides. But most did not, believing instead that his tidings about the relocation of the Persian fleet were an invention, an Athenian trick designed to keep the fleet there. The meeting had become just as volatile as before, when another man was brought into the tent. He was Panaetius, captain of a trireme from the island of Tinos in the Cyclades, a ship that only a short time earlier had been a part of the Persian fleet. Panaetius had defected to the Greek cause with ship and crew, and as he was questioned urgently by the admirals he revealed the full extent of the Persian fleet's blockading movements, which were still going on as they spoke.

The information provided by the timely defector convinced a solid majority of those who had doubted Themistocles and Aristides. When Eurybiades now called for a vote, the admirals elected to take the battle to the enemy the next morning in the strait. According to Aeschylus, the fleet had been divided into squadrons of thirty ships apiece, and before the meeting broke up the admirals agreed to the battle order the squadrons would follow next day. Finally, Themistocles urged all his colleagues to employ the same tactic they had used on the first day of the Battle of Artemisium, backing water in a defensive formation to lure impatient enemy captains into breaking their own formation and making solo charges that could be easily dealt with by several coalition ships at a time. The admirals then bustled away to issue their orders.

It was the early hours of the morning by the time Themistocles returned to his own tent and informed his waiting staff that the battle was just hours away. As he tried to get a few hours' sleep, he was content in the knowledge that, by hook and by crook, he had managed to wrangle the entire coalition fleet into fighting where and how he wanted. He had also succeeded in luring the Persians into the narrow waterway. The Persians now believed they had the Greeks trapped at Salamis. It was just the opposite. The trap was in fact of Themistocles's making, and the Persians had sailed right into it.

16.

The Battle of Salamis

It was the day of decision—by the calculation of some modern historians, September 25, 480 BC. Before dawn, the crews of the Greek coalition fleet prepared their ships as they lay on the beaches or sat anchored around Salamis's Ambelaki Bay and Paloukia Bay. Before dawn, too, assisted by priest and diviner Euphrantides, Themistocles conducted the ritual sacrifice that preceded a battle. Plutarch says that the altar used by Themistocles was located close to where Eurybiades's flagship lay and that the flame from the altar rose especially high in the predawn darkness as the animals killed for the sacrifice were burned.

Plutarch, in his biography of Themistocles, also related a story by a philosopher from the island of Lesbos, who claimed that as Themistocles was sacrificing, three sons of the Persian commander Artayctes, brother-in-law of Xerxes, were brought to him as prisoners. Themistocles was supposedly convinced by Euphrantides that these Persian youths had to be sacrificed to satisfy the gods and ensure victory, which Themistocles did, although reluctantly.

Not only was human sacrifice alien to the Athenians, but this story was contradicted by Plutarch himself in his *Aristides*, where Plutarch relates that the sons of Artayctes were actually captured by Aristides on the island of Psyttaleia toward the end of this day as the battle was winding up, not prior to the battle. He said that Aristides sent the prisoners back to Salamis for Themistocles to decide their fate, after which Euphrantides took it upon himself to order the sacrifice of the three Persian youths. Why would Plutarch tell the story two ways in two different books, with the first reflecting badly on Themistocles? Plutarch clearly had his favorites among his biographical subjects, and Themistocles was not one of them. Plutarch's praise of Themistocles's achievements was begrudging, and he lost no opportunity to paint Themistocles in a bad light.

The omens from the predawn animal sacrifice proving favorable, Themistocles held a series of meetings in his tent. Plutarch, in his *Themistocles*, said that Themistocles enjoyed packing a lot of meetings into a short period just prior to battle to increase his self-importance. More likely it got his adrenaline pumping. In their ten regimental groups, the captains of the Athenian navy would have come to their commander in chief in quick succession and received his orders for the day—most important, all ships were to back water and keep close defensive formation until Themistocles ordered otherwise. Once the "attack" was signaled by Themistocles's trumpeter, the Athenian captains were to concentrate on ramming the enemy's ships rather than attempting to board them.

Themistocles also issued one other, special order: "A reward of 1,000 drachmas for the captain who takes Queen Artemisia of Halicarnassus alive."

As dawn broke, and the beached ships of the Greek fleet were launched by their oarsmen and deckhands, all the marines of the fleet were called to mass assembly to be addressed by the coalition admirals. As Themistocles strode to the assembly to deliver his speech, he cast his eyes out over the bay. The Persian fleet was clearly visible across the Salamis Strait just where Themistocles wanted it to be. It was a fine morning, but a firm westerly breeze was blowing, sending whitecaps scudding across the waters of Salamis Strait toward the Persians.

This strong morning breeze, and the chop it created in the channel, was a regular summer occurrence at Salamis. Themistocles was well aware of this—it had figured in his two-year-old determination to stage a morning battle here. That breeze would increase the effort required for the coalition ships to back water during the initial phase of the battle, but would force the Persians to advance through the heavy chop, making navigation less precise for them. In the second stage of the battle, when the coalition went on the attack, the Greek ships would have the wind behind them, adding to their speed and their ramming momentum.

As Themistocles joined the assembly of marines, Eurybiades and the other coalition admirals were addressing their gathered men-at-arms to spur them to glorious deeds this day. Among the close to 2,000 Athenian marines in the largest assembly stood twenty-seven-year-old Cimon, at the head of his marine detachment. He would have been both nervous and eager for battle, hoping to emulate the glory of his famous father Miltiades. Cimon's commander in chief Themistocles gave the last, and according to Herodotus, the best address of the day to his marines.

It had been ten years since Themistocles had commanded a regiment at Marathon. Now, he was forty-four years old, paunchier, his hair graying, but a man made wise by years of political in-fighting. Over the past decade he had never deviated from his belief that Athens's future lay on the water, nor from his determination to make his fellow Athenians lords of the seas. He had never taken the easy route in walking that road, as difficult as it had been. Looking out over the ranks of thousands of Athenian hoplites as the westerly breeze rustled the crests on the Corinthian helmets sitting on the back of their heads, Themistocles contrasted the simpler but dishonorable choices a man could make in life with the honorable, more difficult choices.

"Fleeing the fight is dishonorable, standing to fight for your country is honorable," he concluded. "I call on you, today and in the future, in everything that your nature and your ability permit you to do, always do the honorable thing. Go now, board your ships, and do your duty to your country."

Across the water, the Persian fleet of 700 ships was already in motion. The crews were in good spirits and supremely confident of winning a crushing victory today. Their admirals had passed around the encouraging intelligence that the vastly outnumbered Greeks had been trapped at Salamis, that they were squabbling among themselves and did not want to fight there, if at all. Herodotus says that the Persian crewmen were also burning with a desire to prove themselves while King Xerxes was watching, especially after the generally poor performance of most Persian crews at Artemisium. Encouraged by Xerxes himself, the crews of the Persian fleet had set their sights on taking every single coalition ship before the day was out.

By Aeschylus's account, the Persian ships advanced to their battle stations with precision. Most of the Persian captains, he wrote, were under orders to form three attack divisions, line abreast. The Phoenicians would form the north division, taking the honored right wing of the Persian battle line. The Ionians and the Carians were to form the middle division, with a mixture of contingents making up the most southerly division, on the left wing. The ships of the remainder of the fleet were assigned guard positions off the south coast of Salamis, to block any possible Greek escape. Spirits were high. Aeschylus wrote that the previous night, as each Persian squadron slid past others waiting their turn to move or already in their allotted position, the crews of each shouted a greeting, which was returned with boisterous enthusiasm by their comrades.

On the mainland shore opposite Salamis Island, men of the massive Persian army spread along the coast, to deal with any Greek seamen who attempted to land. As dawn broke, behind his army, King Xerxes ascended to a viewing platform that had been created for him on the slopes of Mount Aegialeus above the coastal site of a Greek temple to Hercules. On that platform sat a hugely expensive and immensely heavy throne of pure gold, with silver feet and a crimson shade cloth stretching over it. With a golden crown on his head and his golden scepter of kingly office in his right hand, Xerxes took his seat. Members of the king's royal entourage gathered around the throne, but those closest to him were slaves, secretaries sitting cross-legged on the ground with clay tablets and writing styluses at the ready. Xerxes would dictate to the secretaries during the course of the battle, to record the deeds of those of his commanders who did well and were worthy of reward and those who failed him and deserved punishment.

In front of the king spread the white-capped strait of Salamis, with the Persian fleet moving into position in front of him, and a mile away across the water, Salamis Island, with its two principal bays lined with

Greek warships still waiting to take up their battle stations. Making himself comfortable, Xerxes prepared for the entertainment to begin.

Themistocles followed his marines as they boarded the *Paralos* and then instructed the Athenian flagship's captain, Architeles, to get the ship under way. Commands rang out, boarding ladders and anchors were hauled in, the musician piped the rowing speed, oars dipped into the water, and the sleek *Paralos* eased forward. With the addition of the ship from Lemnos that had been incorporated into Themistocles's navy at Artemisium, and that made up for the loss of the watch ship prior to the battle there, the Athenian squadrons numbered 180 triremes and some 20 penteconters. Once again, the men from Chalcis crewed the 20 Athenian triremes that Themistocles had lent to them. Their ships sailed as part of the Athenian formation and under Themistocles's command.

In all, according to Herodotus, the coalition fleet that now put out from Salamis numbered 380 warships, including the trireme from Tinos that had defected the previous night and that now sailed for the coalition under its own flag and with its own crew. As the Greek ships got under way, thousands of fully armed Athenian hoplites spread along the eastern shoreline of Salamis Island. As many as 20,000 Athenian citizens remained for military service after Athens's fleet was manned by citizens and aliens on Themistocles's command. As these men took their stations on Salamis's beaches and rocky promontories, from where they and tens of thousands of Athenian civilians would watch the coming battle, they would have cheered the departing warships.

Corinth would have again claimed the right to lead out, and Adimantus and his forty triremes pulled away from the shore and passed through the Athenian ships now upping their anchors to take up their agreed-on station on the northern, left-hand side of the coalition fleet. The Athenians followed, with the *Paralos*, carrying war archon Themistocles, taking its place on the right of the Athenian battle line. Aeschylus, hauling on his oar aboard one of the Athenian triremes with his comrades from Eleusis, observed that the Greek left wing extended out into the strait like a huge horn. The left-wing squadrons set out first because the Corinthian and Athenian ships had the farthest distance to go to occupy their allotted positions. Once that horn was in position, the Corinthian and Athenian ships forming the tip of the horn would be the closest Greek ships to the Persian fleet. The admirals had agreed to this attacking formation for the fleet the previous night; a curving, concave battle line that blocked any escape by Persian ships to the north into the Bay of Eleusis then ranged down to cover the east coast of Salamis and confront the Persian fleet head-on.

Now the remainder of the Greek squadrons moved out to occupy their positions in the line. Various Greek contingents, many of them of just one or two ships from small Aegean islands, would fill in the center of the coalition line. A number of those contingents had been enlarged by the addition of ships that had joined them from Pogon. Some of the smaller islands had only been able to contribute pente-conters, but four triremes had recently come in from the island of Naxos. The participation of the contingent from Naxos went against the wishes of the island's leaders. Their ships had been dispatched to join the Persian fleet, but once they left the island, the captains had headed for the coalition fleet, to join it in the fight against the Persians.

Eurybiades's Spartan squadron had grown from ten to sixteen triremes, and as admiral in chief , he claimed the place of honor, the right wing of the coalition fleet, for his ships and himself. The position that the Spartans took up put them due west of Piraeus. Since reaching Salamis, the seventeen-ship contingent from Aegina had been bolstered by the arrival of another thirteen triremes, bringing their squadron up to thirty ships. Even though the Aeginetans claimed these thirty were the best ships in their navy, Themistocles knew that they were keeping many more triremes back at their island. Aegina's admiral Polycritus had also insisted that his squadron be allowed to take up the most easterly position of all the Greek ships as a last line of defense. His stated objective was to intercept Persians ships that attempted to escape the battle.

That positioning of the Aeginetans at the bottom of the strait had bothered Themistocles. For one thing, it allowed the Aeginetans them-selves to turn and flee homeward if the going got rough. It also reached the ears of the captains from Aegina that Themistocles had wondered out loud whether the Aeginetans would not prove firmer friends to the Persians than to Athens and the coalition in this battle, by deliberately permitting Persian ships to escape the net that Themistocles had worked so hard to cast. As twenty-nine Aeginetan triremes were taking up their position, the thirtieth arrived back from Aegina, carrying the statues of the sons of Aecus that it had been sent to fetch. It was to arrive just in time to rejoin its squadron for the battle.

Themistocles, aboard his flagship as it eased out of the bay with its oars rising and falling in slow time, noted from the motion of his admiral's pennant on its jackstaff that the westerly tailwind was holding and making the going easy for his rowers. On the foredeck, his marines and archers were kneeling, ready for action. His entire crew was chanting, as were the crews of all the ships around the *Paralos*. One of those rowers, Aeschylus, would record that chant, a mixture of a hymn and a war cry that followed the rhythm of the dipping oars and rolled like thunder across the waves to the ears of the Persian crews: "Forward, sons of Greece! Free your land, and free your children and your wives!"

The sound of the chant rising up from the Greek fleet echoed off Salamis's rocky headlands, said Aeschylus. And then, from the Persian fleet, the chant was answered by an almighty roar in Persian from the throats of Xerxes's marines. Now a trumpet call sounded from the ships of the Greek admirals, rippling around the fleet from right wing to left, and the coalition oarsmen began to back oars. The Greek advance came to a halt, and for a time the Greek fleet was stationary. As one, the Persian fleet eased forward in good formation, the westerly chop breaking over their extended beaks as they advanced. The Greeks ships, maintaining their places in line, gradually backed away into the wind. For a time, the Persians ships followed, keeping strict formation until their admirals, fearing being lured into a trap, ordered their own vessels to hold their positions—not an easy task in the conditions.

To the southeast, the Aeginetan trireme returning with the statues from Aegina was spotted by ships of the Persian left wing as it came up the Saronic Gulf to rejoin its sister ships. A single straggling Greek ship was too inviting a target for several Persian captains, who had their eye on a large reward from King Xerxes for being the first to take a coalition ship. Breaking formation, they turned their bows toward the lone Aeginetan and ordered maximum speed from their oarsmen. Seeing this, a number of other ships of the Aeginetan squadron also broke ranks, and, leaving their guard post, surged forward to support their comrade. As a result, the Aeginetans would later claim that it was they who launched the coalition attack at the Battle of Salamis.

Yet, the honor for the first Greek ship to physically attack the enemy fell to an Athenian. He was Aminias, a native of the inland Attic town of Pallene, which lay midway between Athens and Marathon. A rural noble he may have been, but Aminias was smarting at the fact that his family property, his home town and his capital city had been ravaged by the invading Persians. With his family refugees at Troizen or elsewhere, all Aminias had to think about now was revenge. With the coalition fleet backing water, those ships directly opposite the Salamis shore had reversed so far their sterns were almost touching land. Aminias ran out of patience. Instead of waiting for Themistocles's trumpeted order to attack, Aminias gave the order that men of Athens's sixth regiment, the Oineis, crewing his ship had been waiting for.

"Rowing master, order attack speed!"

Aminias's trireme sprang from the Athenian line like a runner from the blocks. All the other Athenian captains kept their places and watched Aminias's ship streak forward toward the Phoenician ships opposite with a mixture of admiration and dread. Aeschylus described what happened next. Aided by the tailwind, the attacking ship picked up speed. With its rowers heaving with all their might and their oar blades creating foaming wakes and flashing in the morning sun each time they dipped to take a new drive, the ship was soon probably traveling at ten to twelve miles per hour—breakneck speed for a trireme. Ahead, a Phoenician ship was also leaving formation and charging forward, intent on capturing an Athenian vessel. Aminias instructed his pilot to head in its general direction but to steer as if to pass it.

As the bows of the two ships passed, Aminias bellowed, "Now!"

The pilot pushed his steering oars hard over. The trireme swung as if on a dime, and, bronze beak leading, the warship plowed through the water. With a bone jarring shudder, the Athenian thudded into the Phoenician's stern quarter, where its construction was weakest.

194

The impact almost knocked the men on the Athenian's fore- and stern decks from their feet. Pent-up Athenian oarsmen below, most of them blind to their target until the last few moments, knew at once what had happened and let out a huge cheer. The Athenian's beak not only holed the Phoenician ship—the impact was so great that, with the shriek of breaking timbers and the screams of Persian crewmen, the entire stern broke away from the Phoenician.

"Reverse!" yelled Aminias.

His oarsmen dug deep, and the Athenian quickly backed away from its foundering victim. The Phoenician's stern went under within seconds, spilling yelling, panicking crewmen into the water. Persian officers and marines, clad in helmets and armor, fell into the water and sank like stones. The bow angling skyward, the rest of the ship quickly filled with water. Aminias didn't wait to watch what was left of the enemy ship follow the stern under.

Surveying the scene, Aminias saw that the other Phoenicians to the east were still attempting to hold their station, but that was being made difficult by the swell driven by the westerly wind, which was pushing their bows around so that they, as Plutarch would remark, were presenting their sides toward the Greeks, toward Aminias. These inviting targets begged a visit from the now-blooded trireme. Aminias pointed out these fresh targets to his pilot, who would have smiled, nodded, and adjusted his course.

As soon as a crewmen in the bow yelled that the ship's prow was clear of the sinking Phoenician, Aminias again ordered full speed ahead. Oars dug into the water, the trireme began to move forward, the pilot pushed his helm over, and the bow came around. As the Athenian ship quickly gathered speed, another Phoenician loomed up, its side presented to the Athenian ram as it struggled to maintain station. The Athenian ship surged toward the luckless victim, and for a second time that morning its beak bit into Persian wood. Again Aminias ordered his rowers to reverse away. But, try as they may, they could not free the ship from its victim. With the two vessels locked together, the officers and marines on both began exchanging spears and arrows at close range.

Back at the Athenian line, Themistocles had watched Aminias score his victory, the first victory of the day for the coalition fleet.

That victory had brought a mighty cheer from the marines watching from Athenian ships, but Themistocles would have cursed Aminias for disobeying orders and breaking ranks. But then, looking down the strait, he could see that several of the Spartan ships had also jumped before "Attack" was signaled by Eurybiades and were surging toward the enemy in their sector. There was no point holding back any longer. Within seconds, the entire coalition line could break up. Turning to his trumpeter, the Athenian commander in chief ordered, "Sound 'Attack!'"

The admiral's trumpeter put his instrument to his lips and blew the much-anticipated call. Within seconds, every ship in the Athenian line was in motion. The sound of that trumpet, Aeschylus was to say, set Athenian hearts on fire. As the Athenian triremes surged forward, several of them pointed their bows toward Aminias's now stranded ship and sped to his aid. Before long, they too had joined the fight.

The Athenian charge ignited the other squadrons into action. Rowers on ships from more than twenty nations dragged on their oars with all their might as they competed to be among the first to get a piece of the action. According to Simonides the poet, the third coalition warship to ram an enemy vessel that morning was captained by Democritus, master of one of the four triremes that had defected to the coalition from Naxos. In Simonides's words, Democritus's victim split asunder after the ship from Naxos hit it. Like a log cleaved end to end by a single blow from an ax, the enemy ship split in two, and its horrified, terrified crew spilled into the water.

It did not take long for the strait to fill with dog fighting ships. Some Persians charged forward, like the Greeks, and picked specific targets, seeking to board rather than to ram. Other Persians held station, unsure what to do. For aside from a general strategic order to capture every Greek ship, the Persian admirals had not issued any tactical orders. As far as the Persian captains were concerned, it became a matter of every man for himself.

As battle was being joined, the courage of the admiral of the Corinthian squadron failed him. This was Adimantus, the loud-mouthed, snobby admiral who had argued loudest against Themistocles and so adamantly advocated a coalition pullout to the Isthmus of Corinth. His argument, it was now proved, had been based on fear, not on strategy.

For without explanation, Adimantus ordered the sails raised on his flagship then turned away from the fight and set a course up the strait toward the Bay of Eleusis, hoping to sail right around Salamis's north and west coasts and escape to the Isthmus of Corinth. It could be argued that it was in Adimantus's mind all along not to fight at Salamis but to retreat to the isthmus no matter what the other coalition contingents did. But the fact that he did not order the other ships of his squadron to withdraw with him suggests that his decision was spur-of-the-moment and driven by a desire for self-preservation.

The remaining Corinthian captains, seeing their admiral sail away, followed his example, put on sail, and, steering for the north, fled from the fight. Herodotus would say that, later, the Corinthians would deny they deserted the coalition fleet. But the Athenians who took part in the battle saw it with their own eyes. The Corinthians were occupying the same wing as the Athenians, and their departure exposed the Athenians on the left wing. It would be Themistocles and his Athenians who would do all the fighting there for the next few hours.

Some distance along the northeast coast of Salamis, probably as he was entering the Bay of Eleusis, Adimantus encountered a sail-powered merchant vessel coming the other way. Those on board this vessel shouted across to Adimantus, telling him to turn back, as the Greeks were winning the battle in the strait. There was no way these seamen could have known the state of the battle, so Adimantus took them on board his trireme to question them. They challenged him to return to the battle and see if they were not correct, taking them along as hostages. Adimantus had a change of heart. Turning his ship around, he set a course back to the battle. The other Corinthian captains again followed suit. It would be the afternoon before the Corinthians straggled back to the coalition fleet and joined the fight, and by that time the tide of battle would have decidedly turned in favor of one side.

Meanwhile, back in the strait, the battle was now at its hottest. In the middle of the Persian line, a number of Ionian captains excelled their fellows with their exploits. Some Ionians did follow the advice etched on rocks at Artemisium and along the Euripus by Themistocles's stonemasons, and avoided fighting. But most, aware that Xerxes was watching them, fought like demons and captured a number of coalition ships from the smaller Greek states. Herodotus would single out two Ionian captains from the island of Samos who were particularly successful in ramming and boarding Greek ships.

But not all the Ionians fared as well. The ships of the Persian fleet were crammed so thickly together in the narrow waterway many of them ran out of sea room, as Themistocles had planned. Those Ionian ships on the most northerly part of their formation, their bows driven around by the swell, began crashing into their Phoenician neighbors. With screams from below deck, oars were mashed, ships were holed. And in turn, the impact of each collision pushed the damaged Phoenicians into the next ships in line, which caused more mayhem. The result was a logjam of oarless ships, some sinking, some capsized, others powerless to move. And a tumult of cries in many tongues. Athenian ships now circled this tangle of hundreds of enemy vessels, pouring missiles onto their decks, and, when the opportunity presented itself, dashing in to ram and sink a defenseless victim. The Phoenicians, once struck by a well-aimed beak and split in half, quickly filled with water and sank to the bottom of the strait.

This was one of the hottest days of the year, and the afternoon was the hottest part of the day. Aboard one Athenian trireme in the blistering heat and in the thick of the fight, Aeschylus was bending his perspiring back and dragging on his oar. On deck close by to him, Athenian marines were launching their javelins and yelling excited narrations, describing what was going on around them. A tall, powerful Persian commander, a black man with a bushy red beard, was seen to tumble overboard from his ship, impaled by a spear. This, Aeschylus would later learn, was Magus, an Arabian noble who had come to the campaign at the head of 30,000 cavalrymen.

From an Egyptian ship, three noblemen were seen to fall into the sea at once. One of them, Pharnacus, was wearing immense iron armor, and weighted down by that he stood no chance of surfacing once he hit the water. On another ship, a Persian commander threw away his spear in terror. Marines would tell Aeschylus of seeing the speared Dadacas, a commander of 1,000 Persian troops on land, drop into the water with the graceful elegance of a diver. Aeschylus was to learn that his comrades considered the King of Cilicia, commander of the large Cilician flotilla in the Persian fleet, the bravest of all the enemy fighters during the day. It was reckoned that he cost the Greeks more blood in this frenetic battle than any other Persian commander. But eventually the Cilician sovereign went the way of many of his comrades, surrounded by Greeks, fighting gloriously to his last gasp.

Athenian captain Aminias, who had achieved the first "kill" of the day for the coalition, had, after a lengthy struggle and aided by other Athenian captains, finally freed himself from the second Phoenician to feel the bronze of his ram. Leaving his second victim to sink, he had gone in search of fresh custom. Eventually, he found himself a pretty target, an elegantly adorned Greek-style trireme that had initially made a foray against the Athenian ships but was now retreating toward the other triremes of its own squadron. Aminias gave chase. He knew the pennants of all the coalition ships, but he could not recognize the distinctive pennant of the trireme running before him. Ahead, toward the southeast side of the strait, other ships of the same enemy squadron were moving into the path of Aminias and his prey. The trireme the Athenian was chasing was blocked by one of its own ships, which lay broadside to it.

But the ship ahead of Aminias didn't deviate from its course. At full attacking speed, it charged its colleague, and, to Aminias's amazement, rammed it amidships. Deciding that his prey was in fact a Persian ship that had changed sides—perhaps one of the Ionians that his commander Themistocles had hoped would defect to the coalition in the heat of battle—Aminias ordered his pilot to steer away and went in quest of another target. As the Athenian trireme came about, his former prey was backing away from the ship it had just rammed.

The ship that Aminias had been chasing was in fact one of the five triremes from Halicarnassus, and it carried none other than Queen Artemisia. Dressed in helmet and armor, she was indistinguishable from the fleet's male commanders. The ship that Artemisia had just rammed was not only on her own side and from her own little kingdom, it carried her deputy Damasithymus, ruler of the city of Calydna. The ramming was no accident. There was a rumor that Artemisia and Damasithymus had argued after their ships joined the Persian fleet at the Hellespont. Herodotus would say that he could not confirm that, but he surmised that either Artemisia had a grudge to settle against Damasithymus or she simply rammed one of her own ships to clear an escape path. It seems it was the latter. Once Artemisia had reversed away, the Calydnian ship sank quickly, going down with all hands, including Damasithymus, without Artemisia making any attempt to save the crewmen struggling in the water. Her path now cleared, Artemisia pointed her ship for the waters of the Saronic Gulf, and safety.

From his viewing platform on land, Xerxes was tensely watching the battle take place on the strait in front of him, agonizing and raging over each Persian loss.

"Look master!" one member of his entourage called, pointing. "Look how well Artemisia is fighting! She has just sunk an enemy ship."

Xerxes squinted in the direction of the man's pointing finger. "Is that really Artemisia's ship?" he queried.

"Oh, yes, master," came the reply. "I recognize her ensign."

Others around the throne agreed and assured their king that it was a coalition ship that Artemisia had just dispatched.

Convinced by this weight of opinion, Xerxes declared, "My men act like women, my women like men!"

The officers of a number of Phoenician ships lost in the logjam on the Persian right wing managed to reach shore, and they now reported to Xerxes. The demise of their ships had occurred right under the nose of the king, and he was not happy. When he demanded an explanation, the Phoenicians, prostrate before the king, blamed others for the loss of their ships.

"It was all the fault of the Ionians, majesty!" wailed one.

"The Ionians are traitors, master!" declared another. "They deliberately destroyed our ships."

Just as Xerxes was about to order the execution of every Ionian captain who survived this battle, Ariaramnes, a Persian and a senior member of the king's court, directed Xerxes's attention to a dogfight taking place close by. An Ionian trireme from Samothrace had just rammed an Athenian ship. With the royal party watching, the Samothracian attacker reversed away, leaving the Athenian sinking. A ship was at its most vulnerable when it backed away from an attack like this, with little speed and virtually no maneuverability. Another coalition ship, from Aegina, spotted the reversing Samothracian and came rushing to the attack. To the horror of those watching on shore, the Aeginetan rammed the Samothracian. The two ships became locked together.

The men of Samothrace were famed for their skill with the javelin, and the Ionian marines on the crippled ship now let fly at the Aeginetan before it could reverse away and killed every Aeginetan in sight, clearing its decks. The crew from Samothrace then leaped from their ship to the one from Aegina and captured it. The Samothracian captain transferred his flag to the Aeginetan trireme, and, leaving his own ship to sink, returned to the battle in the captured ship.

This fight had transfixed the king and his entourage. Thrilled by the outcome, Xerxes was easily persuaded by Ariaramnes, who was a friend of the Ionians, that, seeing such a display of Ionian bravery, initiative, and loyalty, it was impossible to believe that Ionians would have deliberately sunk Phoenician ships. The Phoenicians, blamed with poor seamanship, were saddled with the blame for the loss of their owns ships, and Xerxes ordered the offending Phoenician officers taken away and beheaded.

Although many of the Phoenicians's ships had been caught up in the logjam to the north, a number had still managed to escape that death trap and, with seaway, continued to take part in the battle. One of these latter Phoenician ships was the flagship of the most senior of Persia's admirals, Ariabignes, the bravest and worthiest of King Xerxes's brothers, in the opinion of Plutarch. Right now, Ariabignes was being stalked by one of the coalition admirals.

Plutarch says that throughout the battle, eyes in the coalition fleet were frequently on Themistocles. The Athenian commander in chief had fought a long and loud war of words in the councils of the admirals to ensure this sea battle took place here and now, and his example could make or break the spirit of coalition commanders. Fully aware of that, Themistocles went in search of his opposite numbers, the four commanding Persians, to take them on, ship to ship, as he would on the battlefield.

Eventually, among the Phoenician ships, Themistocles found his target. In recounting this encounter between the two admirals, Plutarch misnamed this Persian prince as Ariamenes, confusing Ariabignes's name with that of Ariaramnes, the senior Persian, who, according to Herodotus, was on shore with Xerxes at this time. Themistocles had the agile *Paralos* circle the huge but unwieldy Phoenician flagship as his marines and archers showered its decks with missiles. All the while, said Plutarch, Ariabignes could be seen on the enemy's poop deck, which had high wooden sides like the walls of a castle tower, throwing spears and shooting arrows at his attackers.

But while the pilot of the Persian flagship was concentrating on avoiding Themistocles's ram, he failed to see another Athenian trireme bearing down on his vessel at ramming speed until almost the last moment. The captain of the charging trireme was none other than Aminias, the Athenian commander who had launched the battle by sinking the first ship of the day, also Phoenician, and who had given chase to Artemisia before unwittingly letting her go. Aminias had already racked up an impressive tally of sinkings, and he was intent on adding Ariabignes's flagship to the list.

The prow of Ariabignes's lumbering ship came around just in time. The Athenian charge was now head-on. With a splintering of oars and hulls on both ships, and screams from oarsmen bludgeoned by oars that were wrenched from their grasp and driven into them, the bronze rams of Athenian and Phoenician plunged into each other's timbers. The two vessels were joined, stem to stem. After the initial impact had almost knocked them off their feet, the captains of both ships bellowed for their oarsmen to back water to free their vessels. But with many forward oars on both ships made useless in the collision, neither vessel had the power to extract itself. The two ships were locked together in a death embrace.

Both Aminias and Ariabignes ran forward to where their two ships were connected. With a yell to his Persian marines to follow him, the prince of Persia vaulted over the side of his ship and dropped onto the forward deck of the Athenian below. Waiting for Ariabignes were Aminias and, at his side, the Athenian sixth regiment marine Sosicles. With their pikes leveled, Aminias and Sosicles ran at Ariabignes together. The force of their charge drove Ariabignes back. There was no rail bordering Athenian triremes' decks. Ariabignes was pushed from the open deck and over the side by the combined rush of the two Athenians. Ariabignes plunged into the sea.

Weighed down by expensive clothes, gold jewelry, and armor, Xerxes's brother would quickly drown. The story would be told that Queen Artemisia later recognized the body of Ariabignes among the wreckage and thousands of corpses littering the strait, hauled it aboard her vessel, and delivered it up to Xerxes. As can be seen, the timelines involving Artemisia's escape from Aminias and the subsequent death of Ariabignes at the hands of Aminias and Sosicles make that tale highly unlikely. Although, it is possible that the captain of another of the ships from Halicarnassus who had also escaped the strait retrieved the body of Ariabignes from the water and later passed the prince's body over to Artemisia, who in turn passed it onto Xerxes.

With Themistocles ordering his flagship's captain, Architeles, to find him another admiral to fight, the *Paralos* moved on, leaving Aminias and his marines to board and capture the Persian flagship now that the loss of Ariabignes had destroyed the fighting spirit aboard. Aminias, with his trireme and the captured Phoenician locked together, would not be able to stage any more daring ramming attacks. Like many other Greeks that day, he and his crew would spend many hours, as Aeschylus describes, using broken oars and splintered spars as they leaned over the side of their drifting ship, breaking the heads and backs of the crews of sunken enemy ships who struggled in the water trying to swim to them for safety or clung to floating wreckage.

In this way, the battle, the longer it lasted, changed from a glorious adventure in the morning to a barbarous slaughter in the afternoon. Aeschylus was to write that, in places, it was now impossible to see the water in the strait for bodies and wreckage, most of both being Persian. As Aeschylus's own trireme coursed through the debris, he and his fellow oarsmen would at times struggle to find the water with their blades.

As Aminias and his crew went about their gruesome butchery of enemy survivors, Themistocles turned the *Paralos* away and went in search of enemy ships and intelligence of the course of the battle. Soon, as the *Paralos* was in pursuit of a Persian and driving it southeast, Themistocles saw the flagship of the admiral of the coalition's Aeginetan squadron, Polycritus, making a failed ramming run at an enemy trireme from Sidon. Polycritus, recognizing the pennant of Athens's admiral, steered close by the stern of the *Paralos* as he brought his ship around for a fresh attack on the Sidonian.

As the two admirals' ships passed within a stone's throw of each other, Polycritus yelled in a sarcastic tone to Themistocles: "Don't the Aeginetans show themselves strange friends of the Persians!"

Themistocles no doubt smiled to himself. Polycritus had heard the rumor that Themistocles had complained that the Aeginetans, in occupying the guard position at the south of the strait, would show themselves to be friends of the Persians by letting the latter's ships escape. As Themistocles watched, the ship with a turtle pennant made another run at the Sidonian, this time successfully. Polycritus led his marines in boarding and capturing the enemy ship. And when they did, they discovered and released an Aeginetan prisoner aboard—none other than Pytheas, the Aeginetan marine captured aboard the watch ship from Aegina taken prior to the Battle of Artemisium. Pytheas would be returned home safely to Aegina.

It was clear to Themistocles that the Athenians' ships were now in command in the middle of the strait. To the north, the Corinthians, now that they had returned to the battle, were busy capturing disabled Phoenician ships caught up in the entanglement that had destroyed their squadrons's effectiveness as a fighting force. One Corinthian captain, Diodorus, would dedicate Persian armor that his crew took from Persian marines in the battle to the goddess Leto at her temple at Corinth. Notably, there would be no record of any Corinthian ships actually sinking any enemy vessels.

Themistocles, turning his eyes to the bottom of the strait, could see that the Aeginetans were doing their job of cutting off enemy vessels attempting escape. While Athenian captains went hunting for and continued to ram fresh victims, their attacking forays were driving many Persian craft, like sheep, southeast toward the gulf and the waiting Aeginetans or forcing them to beach themselves on the strait's mainland shore. With so many Persian commanders lost, there was no semblance of organized Persian resistance now, no neat ranks of ships standing their ground. With so many Persian ships lost, the early morning Persian confidence had shattered. Now, as fear began to take hold in Persian ships, so too did exhaustion; many of these crews had been at their oars most of the night patrolling the exits of the strait and had managed to get little or no sleep. The only recourse for many captains whose oarsmen no longer had the strength or the will to row was to raise sail, and, with the wind behind them, attempt to steer their ships eastward to safety.

Some brave Persian captains whose ships occupied the rearmost Persian line and had yet to engage did try to fight for honor, even though victory had clearly slipped from Persia's grasp. They pushed forward through the mass of capsized vessels and floating debris to engage the Greeks. But many more enemy captains already in the fight no longer cared what Xerxes thought of them. Taking advantage of the westerly wind, they were raising their sails, turning away, and running for the gulf. And as they did, they obstructed the progress of the last line of Persian ships attempting to push forward into the fight, and more entanglements ensued.

Those that evaded these encounters only ran into waiting guard ships from Aegina, which had a merry afternoon dashing out from behind Psyttaleia Island at the southern entrance to the strait and taking escaping enemy ships by surprise. Coming up on them from their port quarter, they rammed them amidships while enemy eyes were on the open waters ahead. The Aeginetans would claim the most Persian ships sunk in this battle with the Athenians a close second.

Back on Salamis Island, the hoplites and civilians there had been watching the battle play out before them. Thousands of men had been deployed along the island's shoreline to help coalition seamen swimming to shore after their ships were lost and to dispatch Persian survivors who attempted to make it to the island. As it happened, there were few of either. Greek casualties were much less than those of the enemy, and, said Herodotus, most of the Persians could not swim, and once in the water drowned. The westerly wind cast many Persian dead on the mainland shore, some opposite Salamis, some as far east as Point Colias beyond Phalerum Bay. Only when the wind changed, come the evening, did Persian bodies begin to wash up on Salamis.

Young Pericles was among the spectators on Salamis, standing on a promontory with his father Xanthippus, exulting in the Athenian successes and wishing that he could be out there in the fight. Eight years later, although just twenty-three years of age, Pericles would gladly fund the production of Aeschylus's play *The Persians* at the 472 BC City of Dionysia competition. That play, telling the exciting story of the Battle of Salamis, inventively from the Persian perspective, would win Aeschylus first prize in the competition. It would also add a gloss to young Pericles's reputation and create a solid foundation for his own future political career.

Another of the spectators on Salamis was Aristides. As he watched Aeginetan ships dart out from behind Psyttaleia Island and deal death to escaping enemy ships, Aristides must have seen the glint of sunlight on the helmets and armor of the Persian troops that had been occupying the island since the previous night. To Athenians, the island was sacred to the god Pan. Perhaps Aristides now reminded his countrymen that prior to the Battle of Marathon, Pan had declared to Philippides that he favored the Athenians. Certainly Aristides was determined to play a part in the day's victory and to grab a piece of the glory for himself. Although he held no position of command, Aristides used his powers of persuasion and his reputation to assemble an assault force of perhaps a thousand Athenian hoplites and archers, many of them no doubt men from his own tenth regiment, the Antiochis.

Aristides then organized boats to carry the troops: fishing boats and merchant vessels. After loading the troops into the motley little fleet, late in the day Aristides set sail with his assault force. The boats landed the Athenian fighters all around rocky Psyttaleia's shores, and these men attacked from all sides the Persians holding the island. Most of the 400 Persians were wiped out. Only a few high-ranking Persian officers were spared—among them Xerxes's nephews, the sons of Artayctes and Saundice—and taken prisoner. According to Aeschylus, the Athenians even used stones to batter the Persian troops and finished them off with bow and arrow. Aristides achieved his objective; for his assault on Psyttaleia, his name would be recorded among the heroes of Salamis.

By late afternoon, the fighting was at an end. The Battle of Salamis would be celebrated for all time, in the words of Themistocles's friend the poet Simonides, as a noble and famous victory. The Strait of Salamis had been cleared of enemy fighting ships. Only flotsam, jetsam, and drifting wrecks remained. Even Xerxes had fled his royal viewing platform, fearing that the Greeks might land and come after him personally. He and his troops withdrew to Phalerum Bay, where most of the surviving ships of the Persian fleet would also put in for the night. Xerxes departed the platform on Mount Aegialeus in such a hurry he left behind his fabulous but weighty golden throne. As Themistocles had planned and predicted, the Battle of Salamis had resulted in a stunning victory for the Greek coalition. Four hundred Persian ships had been destroyed. Little more than forty coalition triremes had been lost. Xerxes's navy had suffered ten times the losses of the opposing fleet.

The surviving ships of the coalition fleet put back into their base at Salamis, towing wrecks and a few intact enemy ships—three captured Phoenician galleys would be retained for dedication to the Greek gods in thanks for the day's great victory. Aeschylus was among the many Athenians who had survived the battle and who now, exhausted, helped haul their boats up onto the shore. Aeschylus would put the victory down to a single man, a man he was to describe as a genius of wrath. That genius was Themistocles.

When Themistocles, too, landed back at Salamis, he would have been surrounded by ecstatic Athenian captains keen to slap him on the back and to relate their part in the day's crushing victory. About 7:00 P.M., in the light of the setting sun and trailed by staff and officers, Themistocles walked along a beach as the incoming tide brought Persian bodies rolling in through the frothing surf. Greek soldiers moved among the bodies, identifying and stripping them. Ten percent of all booty resulting from the battle would be dedicated to the gods. The balance would be divided among the victors. Those troops reverently stood back when the Athenian commander in chief came and paused to look down at drowned Persian officials.

Themistocles recognized some of these lifeless men from their faces or their attire, and he was sad, not elated, to see them. Many of them were fellow Greeks, and the most surprising thing was the number of men of rank who were among the dead. The Persian world had been deprived of many of its satraps and kings. As Themistocles looked down at several regal bodies adorned with golden bracelets and necklaces, one of his advisors, possibly Mnesiphilus, suggested that Themistocles take the jewelry for himself.

"You take those things," he said. "For you are not Themistocles." He would not soil his hands with booty from honorable enemies. With that, he moved on.

That evening, as he dined in his quarters and his men boisterously celebrated their victory in the camp outside, he received reports of the deeds of his various captains and marine commanders and a list of noble Persians taken captive during the day's fighting. The opinion of his Athenian captains was that two of their number deserved the prize of valor as a result of the battle. One was the dashing Aminias, whose work Themistocles had seen firsthand. The other Athenian captain to catch the eye of his countrymen was Eumenes, a member of the first regiment, the Erechtheis, from Anagyrus, a seaside community just outside Athens and today a suburb of the city.

Just how many enemy ships Aminias and Eumenes accounted for is not recorded. But Simonides the poet would record that Democritus of Naxos sank five Persians at Salamis and recaptured a coalition ship that had been earlier taken by the other side. So the two Athenian captains must have racked up quite a tally, for only they, along with Polycritus of Aegina, were singled out by Herodotus for praise for their achievements in the battle. A vote among all the citizen crewmen of the Athenian fleet in days to come would formalize the Athenians' choice of Aminias and Eumenes as their champions. Marine commander Cimon, son of Miltiades and a vehement political opponent of Themistocles prior to the war, had also acquitted himself gallantly in the battle, said Plutarch, and gained great credit for it among his fellow Athenians.

Following dinner, Themistocles joined a meeting of his fellow admirals. Every one of them had survived the battle, and every one of them, including the cowardly Adimantus, would have claimed a share of the glory for the victory. Meanwhile, it was reported that Persian troops were at work digging on the far side of the Salamis Strait and dumping rock and earth into the strait. It appeared that Xerxes meant to build a causeway across the strait to Salamis Island, and that he intended to continue the battle on land and sea. Based on this, Eurybiades told his fellow admirals that Xerxes would assuredly resume naval operations next day and urged them to be ready to fight the Persian fleet all over again come the new dawn.

17.

Pursuing the Persians

In the vast Persian military camp at Phalerum Bay just to the south of Athens, Xerxes was sliding between anger and depression and back again. In anger he had ordered a causeway built between the mainland and Salamis Island, supposedly to continue the war against the Greeks. But his dejection was such that he was already thinking about going home. Lurking in the back of his mind was the dread that the now-victorious Greek fleet would sail to the Hellespont and destroy the bridges there, cutting him off in Europe, just as his uncle Artabanus had warned him when he first contemplated this campaign.

Xerxes's brother-in-law Mardonius had come to know the king well and could almost read his mind. Fearing that he himself would be blamed for talking Xerxes into this campaign in the first place, Mardonius now spoke in private with the king. Promising to win the war on land for Xerxes, he asked for a sizeable portion of the Persian army with which he would conquer the Peloponnese for Persia, while Xerxes went home to Susa. Queen Artemisia was in the camp at Phalerum Bay. Xerxes, still believing that the queen had sunk an enemy trireme in the Salamis Strait, and considering her one his bravest commanders, summoned her to an audience to take her advice.

Artemisia advised the king to return home. He had burned Athens, she said, which had been his principal objective. And if Mardonius kept his word and conquered all of Greece, Xerxes would have the glory, without the danger, of such a victorious campaign. And if Mardonius failed, no one could blame Xerxes. This advice pleased Xerxes, and he allowed his brother-in-law to select the units that would remain in Greece while he went home. Herodotus claimed that the army retained by Mardonius numbered 300,000 men, but modern historians believe the total was between 100,000 and 200,000. The Immortals would head Mardonius's force, although their commander, Hydarnes, refused to leave his king's side, and would return to Persia with Xerxes. The other units being left with Mardonius were primarily Persian, Median, Sacae, and Bactrian, with a strong emphasis on cavalry.

To Artemisia, Xerxes entrusted his youngest sons, who had accompanied him on the expedition, with orders to speed them home by sea. Xerxes himself, apparently afraid of water, would go back to Susa overland. That night, Xerxes issued orders for what remained of his fleet to sail for the Hellespont to protect it from coalition attack and for his army to march for Thessaly. In Thessaly, Xerxes would part from Mardonius, leaving him with his chosen troops to continue the war against the Greeks on land.

Word had reached Salamis that the remnants of the Persian fleet had put out from Phalerum Bay and headed east. Eurybiades immediately ordered the coalition fleet to give chase. That fleet sailed to Andros, the island at the southern tip of Euboea. Andros had supported the Persians in this war, and it was thought the Persian fleet might have put in there. With no sign of the enemy fleet, the coalition force had landed at Andros, and Eurybiades had convened a council of the Greek admirals to decide their next course of action.

When it came Themistocles's turn to speak, he put the view favored by his fellow Athenians, who, said Herodotus, were the most annoyed of all the coalition members that the remnants of the Persian fleet had escaped. The Athenians were prepared, Herodotus said, to sail on alone and break down the bridges over the Hellespont to trap Xerxes in Europe. So Themistocles proposed to his fellow admirals that the coalition fleet pursue the Persian ships all the way through the islands and also hasten to the Hellespont to destroy the bridges.

But Eurybiades opposed Themistocles. His view was that Xerxes and his army should be permitted to return home. If trapped in Europe, Xerxes might redouble his efforts to conquer the Greeks, he said. Later, the Greeks could take the war to the Persians in their own land. In the meantime, Eurybiades proposed to lay siege to Andros Town to punish the islanders for supporting the Persians.

When Adimantus of Corinth and the other Peloponnese admirals predictably spoke in support of Eurybiades and against Themistocles, and the majority of the others indicated they felt the same way, Themistocles bowed to the will of the majority. Knowing that some hotheads among his captains were all for sailing off to the Hellespont to break down the Persian bridges, whether the rest of the coalition fleet accompanied them or not, he now had to talk his own commanders around to the council's view. Themistocles had spent years building this coalition and had almost sweated blood to hold it together in recent weeks. There was no way he was going to allow it fall apart now.

So Themistocles called an assembly of all Athenian crewmen and convinced them that they should return home to Attica, rebuild their homes, and sow the next crops for their families. In the following spring, he said, the coalition would sail to the Hellespont and Ionia in Asia Minor to take the war onto the Persians's doorstep. The Athenians, acknowledging that it was through his strategic genius that they had overcome the Persians to this point, accepted Themistocles's advice.

Now that it had been resolved not to pursue Xerxes, Themistocles wanted to be certain that the Persian king did leave Greece after all. And the best way to do that was to give him a scare. Themistocles now instructed his Persian servant Sicinnus to carry out another secret mission. Sicinnus and several other of Themistocles's most loyal staff members set off from Andros in a small boat and sailed back to Attica. All these men had to be loyal enough not to crack under Persian torture, if it came to that, said Herodotus. According to Plutarch, another member of this party was Arnaces, a eunuch who had been high in the Persian royal court before being made a prisoner by the Athenians. It is likely that Arnaces had been captured when Ariabignes's flagship was taken.

The boat sent by Themistocles put in at Phalerum Bay, where Xerxes and his army were in the final stages of their preparations to depart.

The other men with Sicinnus nervously waited at the boat once it made landfall, while Sicinnus boldly demanded to see King Xerxes. The king, remembering the last visit from Sicinnus, who had, he believed, brought valuable intelligence—intelligence that his fleet had been unable to capitalize on in the Battle of Salamis—agreed to see him. Sicinnus declared that his master Themistocles, commander of the Athenians, had sent him here to inform Xerxes that he had restrained his fellow Greeks from sailing to the Hellespont and breaking down the bridges there, and he wished him a leisurely trip home. Again Xerxes permitted Sicinnus to depart, and Sicinnus and his companions sailed back to Andros and rejoined the coalition fleet.

As he did so often in his career, Themistocles the master tactician had brilliantly planted the seed of doubt in his opponent's mind. Again he had sold the enemy a lie, but a lie containing a major element of truth. Although the coalition as a whole had no intention of sailing on to attack the bridges, this was something the Athenians were especially keen to do. It's possible the prisoner Arnaces had told Themistocles that the destruction of the Hellespont bridges represented Xerxes's greatest fear. Now, Xerxes knew from "informant" Sicinnus that this was something the Greeks were discussing.

Later, when this story came out, many Greeks would accuse Themistocles of a traitorous act in passing information onto the enemy. But, as psychologists will tell you, Themistocles's latest covert exercise was a classic case of reverse psychology. When someone you have suspicions about assures you they are *not* going to do a particular thing, many people begin to fear that this is exactly what they *will* do.

If Xerxes had held any doubts about the wisdom of hastening to the Hellespont prior to this, now he was spurred into heading home without delay. This was Themistocles's objective, an objective wholly consistent with the coalition admirals' agreement to let Xerxes cross the Hellespont and return home. After receiving this visit from Sicinnus and just a few days after the Battle of Salamis, Xerxes and his army were on the move. Retracing their steps of a month before, the Persians hurried out of Attica and up into Boeotia, planning not to stop until they reached Thessaly, where Xerxes would part with Mardonius and that portion of the army remaining with him.

When Sicinnus arrived back on Andros, he found Themistocles in negotiation with the local people. In these times, one way to end a siege was for the besieged party to pay off the attacking party. Nine years earlier, Miltiades had attempted just such a resolution of his Paros campaign. In approaching the Andrians with his proposal, Themistocles famously said that he had brought two powerful gods with him to Andros—Persuasion and Necessity. Just as famously, the Andrians responded that two equally powerful gods resided on the island—Poverty and Helplessness. Andros refused to pay up and prepared to sustain a long siege. Meanwhile, the pro-Persian island of Paros and city of Carystus in southern Euboea agreed to Themistocles's demands for payment to prevent the coalition fleet descending on them.

With the end of the sailing season looming, the coalition fleet abandoned the unsuccessful siege of Andros, sailed to Euboea, ravaged Carystian cropland for supplies, and then sailed back to Salamis. There, the spoils of the Battle of Salamis were divided, with the "first fruits" sent to the sanctuary of Apollo at Delphi. In the dedicatory inscription on a golden tripod set up at Delphi in commemoration of the victory over the Persians by the Greeks, thirty-one coalition states were named. Diplomatically, Sparta was listed first, Athens second, and Corinth third. One of the captured Phoenician galleys was dedicated at Salamis and put on display there, another at Cape Sunium. The third was taken with the fleet as it sailed to the isthmus, where it too would be dedicated, by the Corinthians.

At Corinth, Eurybiades and his admirals reported to the overall coalition commander in chief, Cleombrotus of Sparta, and delegates of all the coalition city-states. They then met to decide among themselves which admiral should be awarded the crown as most deserving. Each admiral was entitled to two votes, in two ballots. The first would decide the most deserving, the next the second most deserving. In the first secret ballot, every admiral received one vote, with most voting for themselves. As to the second most deserving, the majority of votes went to Themistocles. With the admirals unable to compromise on a first place winner, the prize was not awarded.

The admirals and their squadrons now dispersed and went home. The Athenian ships would commence the task of bringing Athens's refugees back home. Although, with homes throughout Attica sacked and destroyed by the invader and needing to be rebuilt, and with a Persian army still in central Greece, it seems that a number of refugees remained at Troizen and on Aegina at least until the following spring. In contrast, Salamis, unable to feed its thousands of refugees, probably disgorged many temporary residents quite quickly.

In the admirals' vote for first place in the award-giving, it is likely that Eurybiades had voted for Themistocles and Themistocles had voted for Eurybiades. For the Spartan commander now invited Themistocles to accompany him back to Sparta to receive the thanks of the grateful Spartan people. Themistocles accepted the invitation and traveled to Sparta with Eurybiades. Sparta was now being jointly ruled by King Leotychidas and the late King Leonidas's nephew, Pausanias, whose father, Cleombrotus, had died suddenly just after bringing Sparta's troops back from the isthmus. Pausanias was acting as regent for Leonidas's young son Pleisarchus. In front of an applauding crowd, Leotychidas and Pausanias presented first Eurybiades and then Themistocles with the victor's crown and then awarded Themistocles the finest chariot in Sparta and the unprecedented honor of a cavalry escort of 300 Spartan citizens while he was in Spartan territory.

By the time that Themistocles arrived back in Athens, the city had been reclaimed by a number of its residents, who were beginning the task of rebuilding their destroyed homes and interrupted lives. The reconstruction of the temples on and around the Acropolis would be a long-term task. It would be some years before the new temple to Athena was erected—the Parthenon. Themistocles himself personally funded the erection of a new temple to Diana that was built close to his house in his home deme, near the Hangman's Gate. He would dedicate it to Diana of Best Advice. His aristocratic adversaries would claim this was to advertise that Themistocles felt that it was solely through his best advice that Athens had defeated the Persians. As evidence of his supposed conceit, they would point to a small golden statue of himself that Themistocles deposited at this temple.

But this was still some way in the future as the autumn of 480 BC came to an end. For the moment, Themistocles was the hero of the common people of Athens, which only annoyed the aristocrats all the more. Even through the war with Persia was not yet over, some Athenian aristocrats would now look for every opportunity to find fault with Themistocles, to lessen his popularity and his power. Already they were complaining about the way he had been lauded by the Spartans. Others among the nobility now fawned on him outrageously. One handsome young aristocrat named Antiphates had studiously avoided courting Themistocles prior to the war. Now he wanted to be Themistocles's best friend.

This would have brought a wry smile to Themistocles's face and educed the comment, "Time, young man, has taught us both a lesson."

The necessities of life and the fact that Persian troops were still on Greek soil meant that there were no extravagant victory celebrations. Those would come the following year, on the anniversary of the Battle of Salamis, when, says Aeschylus, there was a public holiday during which there were sporting competitions: athletics and horse and chariot racing. Athens's Boys Chorus would lead the religious celebrations of the anniversary, and leading the singing and dancing of the Boys Chorus in those inaugural celebrations would be the teenage Sophocles, the future writer of renown, whose later patron would be Cimon.

Xerxes had departed Thessaly and hurried toward home with the troops of his escort suffering malnutrition and dysentery along the way. Reaching the Hellespont, he found that his bridges had been destroyed after all—not by the Greeks but by a storm. Reluctantly, Xerxes boarded a ship to cross the Hellespont, and he and his troops were ferried across to Asia. The King of Kings would be joyously welcomed home to his capital Susa by his subjects, and there he would await news of Mardonius's campaign in Greece.

Mardonius, meanwhile, decided to wait until the spring of 479 BC to launch his offensive. Wintering in Thessaly, he and his troops lived off the people of the subjected Greek territories. Mardonius was determined that come the spring Athens, Sparta and the Peloponnese city-states would be defeated on land, and all of Greece would come under Persian control.

18.

The Battles of Plataea and Mycale

Over the winter of 480–479 BC, Athens received an envoy from Mardonius. This was King Alexander I of Macedonia. Although a Persian ally, Alexander had a longstanding compact of friendship with Athens, and relying on this he sought to address Athens's board of archons. The Athenians, almost certainly on the advice of Themistocles, put off granting Alexander an audience, stalling until envoys had also arrived from Sparta. With the Spartans present to hear their answer to Alexander's address, Alexander was invited before the nine archons.

Alexander delivered a message from Mardonius. Xerxes would forgive Athens for opposing him and would allow her to occupy her lands and rebuild her homes in peace if Athens entered into an alliance with Persia. In answer, the Athenian archons declared that the sun would have to change its course before Athens allied itself with Xerxes, a man who had desecrated their gods and destroyed their homes. Athens, they said, would never cease to oppose Xerxes. As Alexander departed to deliver this message that was sure to anger Mardonius, the archons urged the Spartan envoys to hurry home and call on their people to lead a coalition army north into Boeotia before Mardonius could enter Attica.

As the Spartan envoys headed home, Athens staged her annual election for tribal regiment commanders. Quite probably to the displeasure of Themistocles, two of the ten generals elected for the year were returned-exiles Aristides and Xanthippus. Themistocles, still war archon and now at the height of his power, had two of his greatest political adversaries among his military deputies. How much influence Themistocles had over the specific appointments of this pair is unknown, but Aristides was appointed commander of Athens's land forces and Xanthippus admiral of her fleet, with all generals expected to lay down their commands the following winter in the usual manner.

It was clear that the coalition would have to fight Mardonius on land, but the Persian fleet, although greatly diminished in the battles and storms of 480 BC, was still sizeable and still posed a significant threat to the coalition states. This meant that Themistocles had to divide Athens's military forces between land and sea. The result was the formation of an Athenian force of 8,000 hoplites under the command of Aristides that would join a coalition army against Mardonius. That army would again be commanded by the Spartans, this time in the person of the Spartan regent Pausanias. This left enough Athenians of military age to crew a squadron of its triremes, which Xanthippus would command as admiral.

Before spring arrived, Xanthippus sailed Athens's squadron down to Aegina, where it joined a reduced coalition fleet totaling 110 triremes and commanded by the Spartan king Leotychidas. There at Aegina, Ionian envoys arrived. They wanted the coalition to free Ionia of Persian rule and urged Leotychidas to sail against the Persian fleet, which was then at the island of Samos. As a result, the coalition fleet sailed for Delos as the first leg on a voyage to Samos.

Come the spring, word reached Athens that Mardonius was on the march down into Boetia, where his army was joined by Thebes's best troops. At Athens, alarm increased as it became clear that Sparta's army was not on the march to join the Athenians against Mardonius. The Spartans were celebrating another religious festival. Once again, Athens was evacuated. This time there was neither the time nor the vessels to ferry evacuees as far as Troizen and Aegina. The entire city population was carried the short distance to Salamis Island.

In June, Mardonius's army entered the deserted Athens and overturned the restoration work that had been going on since the Battle of Salamis. From Athens, Mardonius sent another envoy to hugely crowded Salamis Island, again offering the Athenians a treaty of alliance. One archon who urged his colleagues to consider the proposal was stoned to death when angry Athenians heard of it, as were his wife and children shortly after. Now word arrived that the Spartan army led by Pausanias was at last on the march in support of the Athenians.

The Peloponnese city of Argos had promised Mardonius it would stand in the way of any Spartan army, but now it sent him a message warning that the Spartans were on their way but declaring that Argos was too weak to stop them. With the Argives deserting their alliance with Persia, Mardonius leveled Athens's city walls to the ground and then pulled out, leaving Athens in flames. In July, sending his cavalry to devastate Megara, Mardonius marched away, heading for his ally Thebes in Boeotia.

From the isthmus, Pausanias's Spartan force, accompanied now by contingents from Corinth, Tegea, and other Peloponnese cities as well as from Megara, marched east. Once the army reached Eleusis, Aristides crossed from Salamis with Athens's 8,000-man force and 600 Plataean hoplites, linking up with Pausanias. While Themistocles remained back on Salamis to await the outcome of the campaign, the enlarged coalition army, which would grow to close to 40,000 hoplites from twenty-four cities, turned north and marched up into Boetia on the heels of the withdrawing Persians.

It was not until August, however, that they found Mardonius's army encamped on the far side of the River Asopus, northeast of Plataea. The Persians had cut down thousands of trees to build high wooden walls around their vast square camp, running for over a mile in each direction. Occupying high ground on the slopes of Mount Cithaeron to negate the Persian cavalry advantage, Pausanias and the coalition army watched Mardonius's much larger force of between 70,000 and 120,000 men for days.

While camped at the Asopus, Mardonius and his senior commanders attended a banquet thrown for them by the city of Thebes. At that banquet, one Persian officer would confide in tears to a Greek ally that he and many of his colleagues were convinced they were fated to die here on Greek soil, but they had no choice but do their leader's bidding and accept their fate. The loss of so many leading men in the Persian calamity of the Battle of Salamis had sapped the confidence of the Persian commanders, who would have much preferred to have gone home with their king.

Mardonius now threw all of his 10,000 cavalrymen against the coalition army's hillside position. During this battle, 300 Athenian volunteers relieved Megarians holding the most hotly contested part of the coalition line, and these Athenians felled the white Niceaean horse of the Persian cavalry commander, Masistius, second-highest-ranking Persian commander after Mardonius, then slew the man himself with a spear through an eye slit in his golden helmet. Leaderless, the Persian cavalry withdrew, and Masistius's body was paraded around the Greek camp on the back of a cart.

After this, Mardonius used his cavalry to cut off the Greeks' lines of supply, and then, eleven days into the confrontation, to block the spring that watered the coalition army. This forced Pausanias to decide to pull back closer to Plataea to maintain supplies. An organized withdrawal began at night, but one Spartan commander refused to retreat, and his troops became detached from the main army. Mardonius's cavalry began pursuing the withdrawing Greeks, and Mardonius, thinking the coalition army in disarray and engaged in wholesale retreat, impetuously led his native Persian troops across the Asopus to give chase. Greek allies of the Persians joined the rush, but the balance of the Persian army came on at a steady march, led by Artabazus, a noble from Phrygia in Asia who had opposed Mardonius's campaign from the start.

Far from being in disarray, the coalition forces turned and their phalanxes charged the disjointed enemy force. Mardonius and his elite 1,000-man Persian bodyguard were soon hard-pressed by the Spartans, as, all over the battlefield, a series of individual unit-to-unit battles took place. Once frontline Persian shield bearers were cut down, archers behind were exposed and mowed down by Greek heavy infantry. The Athenians fought a tenacious battle with similarly equipped Theban infantry, killing 300 before the Thebans fled. Meanwhile the Theban cavalry killed 600 Corinthians and other coalition troops. Persian leader Mardonius died fighting, felled from his white horse and then finished off by a stone lobbed by a Spartan warrior named Acimnestus. Mardonius's bodyguard died to a man defending his body.

Once the Persian commander in chief was killed, the outcome

of the battle was sealed. Thousands of Persian and allied troops fled back to their walled camp, only to be slaughtered there once pursuing coalition troops broke in. Artabazus turned his Persian units around and made a hasty but orderly retreat. He would lead them all the way back to the Hellespont. Tens of thousands of Persians and their allies were killed at Plataea and some 3,000 fighting men and a host of camp followers taken prisoner. Estimates of coalition dead range from 1,500 to several thousand. Herodotus stated that just fifty-nine Athenians numbered among the coalition dead. One of the Spartans to fall was Aristodemus, the shamed survivor of Thermopylae, who went down fighting, redeeming his reputation.

That same month—some Greek writers would claim that very same day—the coalition fleet destroyed the Persian fleet. They had tracked it to the foot of Mount Mycale on the Ionian coast, where the Persian seamen had beached their ships and built a wooden wall around their hillside camp, linking up with Persian land troop. The coalition admirals landed their marines and fought a battle with the Persians outside the camp walls, defeating them totally. The coalition force then burned every Persian trireme—300 of them.

This Greco-Persian War was over. Persian troops had been driven from Greece, and the Persian fleet had been wiped from the sea. All thanks to Themistocles. And Xerxes knew it, for he now offered a reward of 200 talents to the man who would bring him Themistocles of Athens.

19.
The Bitter End

In the summer of 478 BC, at the Isthmus of Corinth, Themistocles attended a meeting of representatives of the city-states of Greece as Athens's chief representative. The delegates made sacrifices in thanks to the gods. They agreed to jointly fund war memorials such as the monument that would be erected at Thermopylae and the golden tripod at Delphi that would name all the states that had participated in the defeat of the Persians. And Themistocles paid for a banquet celebrating the anniversary of the pivotal Battle of Salamis, which most Greeks agreed was the battle that had saved Greece, and Europe. The victories at Plataea and Mycale would go down in history as mere adjuncts to Salamis. For without the former, the latter could not have been.

Despite being accused by one Athenian critic of being a cheapskate for serving only cold meat at the banquet, Themistocles was here at the height of his international prestige and glowing with the personal happiness that came from recent remarriage and the birth of the first of his five daughters. Respected now as the father of Greece's freedom, his wisdom now proved, he listened unhappily as the delegates discussed the future of their alliance. For now that the victory had been won, unity was being threatened as old Panhellenic rivalries resurfaced. Many cities spoke bitterly of excluding the likes of Thebes, which had fought on both sides during the Persian War, and Argos, which had paid lip service to Xerxes while standing aloof from the fighting.

It took the chief delegate from Athens to change their discordant

225

tune. Themistocles convinced his colleagues to forgive and forget, and to include all Greek city-states in a new Hellenic coalition. Pushed by Athens, that coalition would be formalized at a meeting of members on the island of Delos by the following year. It would become known as the Delian League.

At this same Corinth meeting, Sparta pushed a proposal that those Greek cities whose walls had been reduced by the Persians should not be rebuilt, using the lame excuse that this would prevent these cities from sheltering the Persians should they invade again. This was primarily addressed at Athens, because Sparta now feared Athens's new power and influence. Themistocles agreed to visit Sparta to discuss this proposition. But he had no intention of leaving Athens defenseless, and as soon as he returned home he implemented a crash program in wall construction. As this work was beginning, a leader from Aegina came to Athens. With the Aeginetans ever ready to subvert Themistocles and Athens, the Aeginetan rushed to inform the Spartans.

Themistocles set off for Sparta, but before he left town he gave orders for every Athenian, including women and children, to participate in the wall-building and for any building, public or private, to be demolished to facilitate the construction. He also had a two-man Athenian delegation made up of Aristides and Abronychus appointed to join him but bade them wait at Athens until the wall had been completed to a defensible height. The Spartans likewise sent a delegation to Athens, where they were detained by the Athenians. Meanwhile, at Sparta, Themistocles stalled, claiming to be too unwell to meet with the Spartan leaders, and then saying he had to wait for his fellow ambassadors. When Aristides and Abronychus did arrive, it was with the news that the wall was up. The Spartans were furious. They permitted Themistocles and his fellow ambassadors to leave, but they never forgave Themistocles for blindsiding them.

Archaeologists say that remnants of Themistocles's Athenian wall that stand to this day exhibit how rapidly, and roughly, they were thrown up in those weeks of the summer of 478 BC. But they served the purpose. On his return to Athens, and with the wall-building the talk of the energized city population, Themistocles pressed on with one of his pet projects, dating back fifteen years, the creation of massive defensive walls around Piraeus and its three harbors and lining the route between Piraeus and Athens. At Piraeus alone, the walls would run for more than sixty miles. They were so thick that two carts could pass side by side along the top. These walls were much more carefully and precisely constructed than those at Athens, and this work would continue for some years. According to Thucydides, neither mortar nor rubble fill were used in the construction, but with neatly cut stones held together by iron clamps. As these walls went up, Themistocles encouraged his countrymen to relocate to Piraeus, to provide their skills to Athens's now-large navy and to enjoy the benefits that flowed from his basing the navy at Piraeus.

The Piraeus walls, while impressive, would reach only half the height envisaged by Themistocles. Their construction would be halted by successors, and it would take Pericles to complete the Long Walls between Piraeus and Athens. For Themistocles's tenure as the most powerful man at Athens, and indeed in all Greece, was not long. He was still famous and feted when the Olympic Games of 376 BC came around. As he had in the past, Themistocles attended the games as a spectator, and, according to Plutarch, other spectators from all over the Greek world were more interested in seeing and hearing him than in watching the events. Applauding him, admiring him, they flocked around him wherever he went.

"I'm much gratified," Themistocles remarked to friends on receiving this reception. "I confess that today I've reaped the fruit of all my labors for Greece."

But that fruit soon turned sour. At Athens, some publicly disparaged him. The acerbic poet Timocreon of Rhodes, who had once enjoyed Themistocles's hospitality, branded him a liar, cheat, and traitor, accusing him of being in the pay of the Spartans when he himself was accused of being a Persian sympathizer. The aristocratic political machine was again working hard to bring Themistocles down. Aristides, while not speaking publicly against Themistocles—he did not want to be seen as ungrateful for the 480 BC recall initiated by Themistocles—instead promoted the interests of Cimon. With his political star now on the rise, Cimon again voiced vehement opposition to Themistocles. Behind the scenes, the Spartans, anxious to bring Themistocles down after he'd outsmarted them over the wall issue, secretly supported Cimon with their money, their influence, and their propaganda.

By the second half of the decade, Cimon had initiated a campaign to have Themistocles ostracized. His first attempt failed. But, by 472 BC, at the second attempt, he was able to generate enough votes to ensure that Themistocles was exiled. Plutarch was convinced that ostracism was initiated to humble eminent men, even great men, and this was never more the case than with the banishment of Themistocles. Themistocles chose the city of Argos as his place of exile, and Argos accepted him; he had spoken on their behalf before the coalition council, and his father was said to have lived at Argos for a time. Themistocles's wife, children, and much of his wealth remained at Athens.

Themistocles had spent some seven years of his allotted ten years of exile at Argos—impatiently, according to Plutarch—when a scandal broke over the head of Pausanias, regent of Sparta. It was discovered that Pausanias had been in secret correspondence with Xerxes and had even discussed an alliance with the Persians. This cost Pausanias his life. It also came out that Pausanias had secretly shown this correspondence to Themistocles, asking him to join him in allying with Persia. Themistocles had refused but had kept his word to Pausanias not to speak of the matter. Sparta's magistrates were now outraged that Themistocles had not warned them about Pausanias's treasonous correspondence and demanded his head. At Athens, Themistocles was indicted for treason. In response, he wrote to Athens defending himself.

It was about the spring of 465 BC, when, at Argos, Themistocles received a warning that at the behest of Cimon, armed men were being sent from Athens to arrest him for treason. Knowing his life to be endangered, Themistocles took flight, going west by boat to the island of Corcyra in the Ionian Sea. One generally discredited story had him going on to Sicily from Corcyra, and it is possible he intended heading for Siris, an Italian city he had once advocated as a place of refuge for all Athenians. The rulers of Corcyra, however, worried about offending Athens and Sparta, soon shipped Themistocles to the west coast of Greece. There, in Epirus, he sought refuge with Admetus, King of the Molossi.

Even though Themistocles had once offended Admetus, the king took him in, until Athenian and Spartan agents tracked him down and threatened war on Admetus. Themistocles's wife and children had in the meantime been smuggled out of Athens by one of Themistocles's friends, Epicrates, together with part of his fortune. Themistocles's family joined him in Epirus, but Epicrates was caught, tried, and executed by Cimon. Themistocles was convicted of treason in his absence, with his Athenian property confiscated and auctioned off, bringing as much as 100 talents.

Deciding that he would never be safe in Greece, Themistocles took the monumental decision to seek refuge in Persia with Xerxes, his arch enemy. King Admetus had Themistocles and his family smuggled overland to the east coast of Greece, where, at Pydna in Macedonia and traveling incognito, they took passage on a merchant vessel bound for Asia. But a storm drove this boat to the island of Nasos, where the Athenian navy had begun what would be a two-year siege because Nasos had seceded from the Delian League. The admiral of this fleet was Cimon, and the ships he was using were Themistocles's triremes, which Cimon had remodeled to carry more troops.

Themistocles now revealed his identity to the master of his boat and offered to pay him well if he sped him away from there. When the captain hesitated, Themistocles used one of his old tactics of last resort, threatening that, if he were to fall into the hands of the Athenian forces, Themistocles would tell them that the captain had accepted a bribe to help him escape. The terrified skipper soon had his celebrity passenger on the way to Asia and duly received the large reward promised by Themistocles.

Landing in Ionia, Themistocles learned that Xerxes, the Great King, had recently been assassinated, along with his eldest son and heir—by Xerxes's uncle Artabanus, the same uncle who had opposed his invasion of Greece. Artabanus had in turn been personally killed in a knife fight by Xerxes's younger son Artaxerxes, who was now the new King of Persia. From Sardis, Themistocles wrote to Artaxerxes, cunningly reminding him that twice during the war between Greece and Persia he had secretly sent helpful intelligence to the king's father. He asked to be allowed to spend a year at Sardis, after which he would come to the king and be of great assistance to him. Artaxerxes agreed to the proposal.

While spending the year at Sardis, learning the Persian language and Persian customs, Themistocles visited a temple where he found the same statue he had consecrated at Athens years before, the statue funded by fines he had levied on water thieves. It had been part of the treasure looted from Athens's temples by Xerxes's troops in 480 BC. Themistocles won agreement from the governor of Sardis for the statue to be sent back to Athens, but when the Persian officer appointed by Artaxerxes to keep an eye on Themistocles heard of this, he was furious and threatened to go to the king about it. Themistocles, not wanting to blot his copybook with Artaxerxes at this delicate time, withdrew his request to the governor.

Once the twelve months were up, Themistocles traveled to Susa. Granted an audience by the young king, Themistocles prostrated himself before him and sought his friendship. According to Plutarch, that night King Artaxerxes exclaimed three times in his sleep, "I have Themistocles the Athenian!"

According to Plutarch, too, in a subsequent interview Artaxerxes said that as his father had offered a reward of 200 talents to the man who would bring Themistocles of Athens to Susa, and here Themistocles had brought himself, Artaxerxes was indebted to Themistocles to the amount of 200 talents. He was so impressed with Themistocles that he granted him governorship of the city of Magnesia in Asia. Themistocles and his family moved to Magnesia, where over the next few years he received many noble visitors curious to meet the famous Themistocles who gave him many gifts. Establishing two Athenian-style festivals at Magnesia, Themistocles became popular with the locals. It is likely that his youngest daughter Asia was born there, while another of his daughters—Plutarch indicates it was Mnesiptolema—served as priestess at the city's temple of Artemis, Themistocles's patron goddess.

Yet, he became, understandably, a bitter man. With his fate ironically echoing his father's analogy, years earlier, about Athenians discarding both triremes and politicians when they no longer had use for them, Themistocles told friends: "The Athenians used me like a plane tree, sheltering under me in bad weather, then as soon as it was fine, plucking my leaves and cutting my limbs."

Themistocles died in Magnesia in 469 BC, aged sixty-five. Several authors claimed he took poison rather than answer a summons from King Artaxerxes to serve against his fellow Greeks, who by then were steadily taking all of Greece and Asia Minor from the Persians. Plutarch claimed Themistocles was fearful of being involved in a defeat that shaded his earlier triumphs. But Thucydides expressly denied the poison story, stating that Themistocles died from illness. Themistocles's ashes and bones were initially interred in a sepulchre in the agora of Magnesia, but years later were smuggled back to Attica by his sons, and reinterred in a tomb near Piraeus.

The man principally responsible for his downfall, Cimon, was himself ostracized by the Athenians in 461 BC, after the political faction led by Pericles gained the upper hand. Although, Pericles wasn't doing this to avenge Themistocles; he himself brought in a law stipulating that only a man whose father and mother were citizens could hold Athenian citizenship, an act that would have deprived Themistocles of his citizenship.

So ended the tumultuous career of Themistocles of Athens. A commoner who dragged himself from humble roots to become the most famous Greek of his time; the stubborn visionary whose ambitions for Athens made her the powerhouse of Greece; a brilliant military tactician and fiendishly clever statesman who struggled long and hard with small-minded allies to hold the city-states of Greece together. The Delian League had seemed the culmination of his hopes for a unified Greece, but the league dissolved when Pericles led Athens into the twenty-seven-year Peloponnesian War against Sparta, beginning in 431 BC, which resulted in Athens's surrender to Sparta and fall from power.

Many writers in ancient times, such as Plutarch, would downplay Themistocles's achievements by claiming his chief goal was personal gain, and would deny him his place atop the hierarchy of patriotic heroes because he ended his days a convicted traitor. On the other hand, Thucydides considered Themistocles a man gifted with astonishing intuition and sagacity. More than that, like Aeschylus, Thucydides rated Themistocles nothing less than a genius.

Like so many great men who changed the course of history, Themistocles's star shone briefly. After his fall, the powerful Athenian state he created took just seventy-five years to fall as well.

APPENDIX A.

List of Athenian Tribal Regiments, Fifth Century BC

1. Erechtheis
2. Aigeius
3. Pandionis
4. Leontis
5. Acamantis
6. Oineis
7. Cecropis
8. Hippothontis
9. Aeantis
10. Antiochis

APPENDIX B.
The *Olympias* Project

In 1982, the Trireme Trust was set up in the United Kingdom by historian and academic John Morrison, naval architect John Coates, and writer Frank Welsh with the ambitious plan of rebuilding a fifth-to-fourth–century BC Greek trireme. Their hope was to settle centuries-old questions about the nature and abilities of the trireme, the class of ancient warship developed by the Greeks and still in use by the Romans many hundreds of years later.

The Trust's collaboration resulted in a full-scale trireme reconstruction, the *Olympias*, built by modern Greece's Hellenic Navy, using "old" techniques. Launched in 1987, the *Olympias*, in her sea trials over the next seven years, disproved the widespread academic belief that a three-level arrangement of oars was wholly impractical. With both sail and oar, the *Olympias* showed she could be efficient and fast. Fully decked and equipped with "outriggers," she looked much the same as Themistocles's original triremes would have when later modified by Cimon.

One of the *Olympias*'s volunteer Thalamians on the lowest benches during the 1988 trials was Roz Savage, a woman who in 2006 rowed singlehanded across the Atlantic Ocean between the Canaries and Antigua in the West Indies in a seven-meter boat. As coincidence would have it, the author of this work was at Antigua's Nelson's Dockyard to watch Savage complete that grueling row.

Today, the *Olympias* is housed, out of the water and under cover, at the Hellenic Navy Museum at Neon Faliron near Piraeus. The Trust believes that the practical lessons and extensive technical data that derived from her construction and operation should be used, combined with modern drafting techniques, to construct a second, improved trireme for further research.

That requires significant funding (in the order of U.S.$5 million), and the Trireme Trust would be pleased to hear from commercial sponsors, academic institutions, and private benefactors interested in contributing to a Trireme 2 project. Trireme 2 is sure to add even further to our historical knowledge about naval design and performance, and to add another beautiful example to the small collection of re-created ancient vessels that exist in the world today.

Meanwhile, the Trireme Trust continues to disseminate the volumes of information about the triremes it has collected through the *Olympias* project, to universities, research organizations, scholars, authors, and the general public. It has also advised Hollywood producers making the sequel to the international hit movie *300*. Entitled *300: Rise of an Empire*, it features the Battle of Artemisium. The producers have taken the Trust's advice on a trireme's internal construction for their sets, but, sadly, the entire triremes you see in battle scenes are apparently only computer-generated images (CGI).

For more information about the Trust and its activities, or to inquire about how you might contribute to the Trireme 2 project, visit www.triremetrust.org.uk.

ΠΟΤΕς

CHAPTER 1: THE ROAD TO MARATHON

1. For consistency's sake, names and terms in this work have been confined to the standard Latin-based English form, rather than mixing in Greek spellings as some authors do. To take the Greek form throughout would have meant, for example, spelling Themistocles as Themistokles, Cimon as Kimon, Corcyra as Kerkira, Athens as Athinai, trireme as trieres, etc.

CHAPTER 2: YOUNG THEMISTOCLES

2. Regarding Themistocles's siblings, Plutarch, toward the end of *Themistocles*, in his *Lives*, mentions a nephew, Phrasicles. If Phrasicles's father was Themistocles's brother, we should have heard of him through Themistocles's career. Conversely, like all Greek women, a sister could not participate in politics or military affairs and would go unmentioned.
3. Aristides is also written Aristeides.
4. Plutarch, in *Themistocles* and *Aristides*, details the pair's rivalry.
5. Plutarch, in *Themistocles*, says Themistocles was then worth fewer than three talents.
6. Plutarch mentions the fifteen-talent inheritance in his *Demosthenes*.
7. Thucydides, *The Peloponnesian War*.
8. Herodotus, *History*.
9. Themistocles's direct quotes are all from Plutarch's *Themistocles*, other than the stringed instrument story, which is in Plutarch's *Cimon* and Herodotus's *History*.

CHAPTER 3: TO FIGHT, OR NOT TO FIGHT
10. Details of the Athenian generals' deliberations come from Herodotus.

CHAPTER 4: THE BATTLE OF MARATHON
11. Warry, in *Warfare in the Classical World*, makes the family car analogy.
12. See Billows, *Marathon*, regarding felt skullcaps. Regarding "Come back with this, or on it," see Billows and Warry.
13. Regarding Aeschylus's tombstone quotation, see Billows and also Cookson's introduction to *The Plays of Aeschylus*.
14. Plutarch relates the trophy comment in *Themistocles*, and Caesar's lament in his *Caesar*.

CHAPTER 5: TURNING TO THE SEA
15. See Plutarch, *Themistocles*, for Themistocles's warning.
16. For details on ostraca finds, see Podlecki, *The Life of Themistocles*, chapter 11, "Ostraka."
17. For Plutarch on Aristides, and Aristides's direct quote, see his *Aristides*.

CHAPTER 6: THE PERSIANS ARE COMING
18. Herodotus gives the speeches of Xerxes, Mardonius, and Artabanus verbatim, saying they came from Persian sources.

CHAPTER 7: PREPARING TO FACE XERXES
19. For more on the Oracle of Delphi and the Panhellenic games, see Dando-Collins, *The Great Fire of Rome*.
20. Aristophanes, *The Frogs*.
21. Themistocles's quote about his son is from Plutarch, *Themistocles*.
22. Warry makes the Scythian mercenary suggestion.

CHAPTER 8: THE GREATEST ARMY AND NAVY ON EARTH
23. Herodotus details the marching order of Xerxes's army. Aeschylus describes the crimson curtain on Xerxes's litter.

CHAPTER 9: ATHENS'S FLOATING WALL OF WOOD
24. The vase showing the departing hoplite, a fifth-century BC Athenian red figure *stamnos*, is in the British Museum.

25. See Plutarch's *Cimon* for the Athenian boast.

26. For details of the Themistocles Decree, see Podlecki. For Plutarch's description of the public reaction to the decree, see his *Themistocles*.

27. The Themistocles Decree states that the evacuation of Athens was to commence "beginning tomorrow." The Decree also spells out the process by which the names of captains and crews of Athens's triremes were to be publicly announced, on "the white noticeboards," prior to their being sent to Artemisium. This, as Strauss acknowledges in *Salamis*, makes clear that the evacuation began prior to the Battle of Artemisium and resumed following it. Few authors have commented on the fact that the evacuation clearly stalled after the initial activity and had to be resumed in a rush once the fleet returned from Artemisium. This rush accounts for why some evacuees were now also sent to Aegina, which was closer to Athens than Troizen, and more refugees than old men and slaves were also sent to Salamis, which was even closer to Athens. Herodotus says the Persian fleet waited three days at Aphetae after the coalition fleet left, then took three days to reach Phalerum Bay. If the coalition fleet also took three days to make the same journey, that left just three days for that last, rushed stage of the evacuation before the Persian fleet arrived.

28. Aeschylus's thole pin description is in *The Persians*.

29. For more on trireme construction, see Hale, *Lords of the Sea*, and Morrison, *The Athenian Trireme*.

30. Aristophanes speaks of Aeschylus and also of ablutions from a trireme's stern in *The Frogs*.

CHAPTER 10: THE BATTLE OF THERMOPYLAE, AND THE 300 SPARTANS

31. Dieneces's words are from Herodotus.

CHAPTER 11: CUT AND THRUST AT ARTEMISIUM

32. Aristophanes, *The Frogs*.

33. Adimantus is also written Adeimantus.

34. Themistocles's words to Adimantus and Architeles come from Herodotus and Plutarch.

35. Pausanias, *Descriptions of Greece.*

CHAPTER 12: THE BATTLE OF ARTEMISIUM

36. Aristophanes, *The Frogs.*
37. Themistocles's address to the assembled captains is reported by Herodotus and Plutarch.
38. Abronychus is also identified as Habronychus by some sources.
39. Themistocles's words to Diphilides come from Plutarch's *Themistocles.*

CHAPTER 13: AFTER THERMOPYLAE

40. Both Herodotus and Plutarch report Xerxes's deliberations.

CHAPTER 14: ABANDONING ATHENS

41. Herodotus has Artemisia telling Xerxes that she has heard that the Athenians had not stocked up food on Salamis.
42. Plutarch tells the story of Aristides's dog in *Aristides.*
43. Herodotus reports Mnesiphilus's admonition to Themistocles.
44. Adimantus's and Themistocles's exchanges are in both Herodotus and Plutarch's *Themistocles.* Although Plutarch confuses Adimantus with Eurybiades, I have combined both accounts and attempted to make cohesive sense of them.
45. Plutarch relates the Eritrean ink-fish remark in *Themistocles.*

CHAPTER 15: THE SALAMIS TRAP

46. Sicinnus's message is reported by both Herodotus and Plutarch.
47. Aristides's and Themistocles's exchange is reported by Herodotus, and by Plutarch in *Aristides.*
48. Aeschylus, *The Persians.*

CHAPTER 16: THE BATTLE OF SALAMIS

49. Strauss, in *Salamis,* suggests the date.
50. Herodotus reports the reward offered by the Athenians for Artemisia.
51. Herodotus and Aeschylus speak of the day's westerly breeze and whitecaps. As Strauss points out, this morning westerly is still part of the Salamis Strait's summer weather pattern.
52. Herodotus reports Themistocles's speech to his marines.

53. The battle is described by Herodotus, Plutarch, and Aeschylus.
54. Herodotus reports Xerxes's reaction to the sight of Artemisia ramming another ship.
55. Simonides's description is reproduced in *Greek Lyric*.
56. Themistocles's comment regarding the dead Persian's jewelry is in Plutarch's *Themistocles*.

CHAPTER 17: PURSUING THE PERSIANS

57. See Plutarch's *Themistocles* for Themistocles's comment to Antiphates.

CHAPTER 18: THE BATTLES OF PLATAEA AND MYCALE

58. Herodotus is the chief source for these battles.

CHAPTER 19: THE BITTER END

59. The cold meat story is attributed by Plutarch to Rhodian poet Timocreon.
60. See Podlecki for more on Athens's Themistoclean walls.
61. The latter years of Themistocles's life are detailed in Thucydides, *The Peloponnesian War*.
62. Themistocles's fruit and plane tree comments are in Plutarch's *Themistocles*.

BIBLIOGRAPHY

Aeschylus. *The Plays of Aeschylus*. Translated by G. M. Cookson. Chicago: Encyclopaedia Britannica, 1952.

Aeschylus. *Aeschylus 2*. Translated by D. Grene. Chicago: University of Chicago, 1984.

Aeschylus. *Aeschylus 2*. Translated by D. Slavitt. Philadelphia: University of Pennsylvania Press, 1998.

Aristophanes. *The Plays of Aristophanes*. Translated by B. B. Rogers. Chicago: University of Chicago, 1952.

Billows, R. A. *Marathon: How One Battle Changed Western Civilization*. New York: Overlook Duckworth, 2010.

Boardman, J., J. Griffin, and O. Murray. *The Oxford History of the Classical World*. Oxford: Oxford University Press, 1986.

Burn, A. R. *Persia and the Greeks: The Defense of the West, 546–478 BC*. Stanford: Stanford University Press, 1984.

Dando-Collins, S. *Legions of Rome*. London: Quercus, 2010.

Dando-Collins, S. *The Great Fire of Rome*. Cambridge, MA: Da Capo, 2010.

Euripides. *The Plays of Euripides*. Translated by E. P. Coleridge. Chicago: University of Chicago, 1952.

Green, P. *The Greco-Persian Wars*. Berkeley: University of California Press, 1996.

Green, P. *The Year of Salamis, 480–479 BC*. London: Weidenfeld & Nicolson, 1970.

Hale, J. R. *Lords of the Sea: The Epic Story of the Athenian Navy and the*

Birth of Democracy. New York: Penguin, 2009.

Herodotus. *The Histories of Herodotus.* Translated by H. Carter. New York: Heritage, 1958.

Herodotus. *The Histories of Herodotus.* Translated by W. Shepherd. Cambridge, Eng.: Cambridge University Press, 1982.

Herodotus. *The History of Herodotus.* Translated by G. Rawlinson. Chicago: University of Chicago, 1952.

Herodotus. *The Persian Wars.* Translated by A. Godley. Cambridge, MA: Harvard University Press, 1922.

Homer. *The Iliad of Homer* and *The Odyssey.* Translated by S. Butler. Chicago: Encyclopaedia Britannica, 1952.

Morrison, J. S. *The Athenian Trireme: The History & Reconstruction of an Ancient Greek Warship.* Cambridge, Eng.: Cambridge University Press, 2000.

Pausanius. *Descriptions of Greece.* Translated by W. H. S. Jones. Cambridge, MA: Harvard University Press, 1989.

Plutarch. *Plutarch's Lives.* Translated by B. Perrin. Cambridge, MA: Harvard University Press, 1985.

Plutarch. *Plutarch's Lives.* Translated by F & C. Rivington. London: Mawman, 1810.

Plutarch. *Plutarch's Lives.* Translated by A. Stewart & G. Lung. London: Bell, 1908.

Plutarch. *The Lives of the Noble Grecians and Romans.* Translated by J. Dryden. Chicago: University of Chicago, 1952.

Podlecki, A. J. *The Life of Themistocles: A Critical Survey of the Literary and Archaeological Evidence.* Montreal: McGill-Queen's University Press, 1975.

Simonides, in *Greek Lyric.* Translated and edited by D. A. Campbell. Cambridge, MA: Loeb/Harvard University Press, 1991.

Sophocles. *The Plays of Sophocles.* Translated by R. C. Jebb. Chicago: University of Chicago, 1952.

Starr, C. G. *The Roman Imperial Navy.* Cambridge, MA: Heffer, 1941.

Strabo. *The Geography of Strabo.* Translated by H. L. Jones. Cambridge, MA: Loeb, 1924.

Strauss, B. *The Battle of Salamis.* New York: Simon & Schuster, 2004.

Thucydides. *History of the Peloponnesian War.* Translated by C. F. S. Smith.

Cambridge, MA: Harvard University Press, 1928.

Thucydides. *The History of the Peloponnese War.* Translated by R. Crawley, revised by R. Feetham. Chicago: University of Chicago, 1952.

Timotheus of Miletus. *The Fragments of Timotheus of Miletus.* Edited by J. H. Horden. Oxford: Oxford University Press, 2002.

Vidal, G. *Creation.* New York: Random House, 1981.

Warry, J. *Warfare in the Classical World.* London: Salamander, 1989.

INDEX

Abrocomes (half brother of Xerxes), 116, 118

Abrotonon (also Euterpe, mother of Themistocles), 7; purported suicide of, 14

Abronychus (also called Habronychus), 240 n. 38; Athenian ship captain, 153; Themistocles appoints to oversee Athenian wall construction, 226

Abydos (Mysian port town at Hellespont), 87, 90, 91

Academy (or Lyceum, Athens), 14

Acamantis (fifth regiment), 3, 4, 34, 36, 38, 233

Acarnanians: allies of Athens, 112

Achaemenes (brother of Xerxes), 161

Acimnestus (slayer of Persian commander Mardonius), 222

Acropolis (citadel in Athens), 2, 12, 53, 58, 61; falls to Persians, 177–178; sacrifices to Zeus at, 101; treasurers and priestesses of Athens stay to defend, 100, men and women to defend, 168; Persians try to take, 170, 177; temples on burned, 177–178, 216; wooden wall around, 73, 164. *See also* Sanctuary of Aglaurus

Adimantus (commander of Corinthian squadron), 139, 239 nn. 33, 34, 240 n. 44; accuses Themistocles of having no city, 174; argues against fighting at Salamis, 182, against Themistocles, 171, 174, 184, silenced, 175; wants to take squadron away, 139, 183, leads into battle at Salamis, 191, takes own ship away from, 196–197, told to turn back, 197, returns to battle, 197, claimed share of glory afterward,

208, opposes Themistocles's plan to follow Persians, 213; Themistocles give gift to, 140, Adimantus changes mind, 140

Aeantis (ninth regiment), 34, 36, 233

Aecus (mythological king of island of Aegina), 176, 193

Aegean Sea, 67, 85, 137, 172; islands of, 13, 192

Aegina (Aeginetans), 100, 167; Aeginetans send trireme to save statues, 176, 193; and Aristides, 84, 182, 183, 184; Athenians citizen-sailors captured by, 9, citizens evacuated to, 165, 182, 239, n. 27, remain at, 216, sacred galley *Theoris* captured by, 105, use ships against, 8, 9; and Battle of Artemisium, 146, not trusted, 146, watch ship captured before, 204; at Battle of Salamis, Aeginetans ram Samothrace ship, 201, attack fleeing Persians, 204–205, 206, claim most Persian ships sunk, 205; Persians attack trireme of, 193–194; becomes part of Greek coalition, 84, open to capture if coalition fleet leaves, 173, sends a few triremes to, 134, 135, Persian ships pursue, 136, send a few more triremes, 192; capture Corinthian triremes, 9; emblem of, 107; marines of, 136, 204; old enemy of Athens, 58, 59, 62, 82; Ionians want to be freed from Persians by, 220; submitted to Persia, 59, 79; sea power, 59; and Themistocles, 146, 174, 182, 193, attempt to subvert him by Aeginetans, 226, wants to arm Athens against, 62, worried by Aeginetans, 146, triremes could retreat, 192–193; warships of, 59, 134, 136, 146, 176, at Battle of